NICK

From Short Trousers to Army Fatigues

RUTH E WRIGHT

Copyright © Ruth E Wright, 2024

All Rights Reserved

This book is subject to the condition that no part of this book is to be reproduced, transmitted in any form or means; electronic or mechanical, stored in a retrieval system, photocopied, recorded, scanned, or otherwise. Any of these actions require the proper written permission of the author.

Contents

Introduction 5

Chapter 1 7

Chapter 2 March 1934 18

Chapter 3 1934 (11 years) 29

Chapter 4 Summer 1935 36

Chapter 5 47

Chapter 6 Another War 54

Chapter 7 Christmas 1939 66

Chapter 8 Evacuation from Dunkirk 27th May - 4th June 1940 72

Chapter 9 1940-41 Winter 98

Chapter 10 1941 Scotland 119

Chapter 11 Somerset, 1942 146

Chapter 12 Christmas Day 1942 169

Chapter 13 Norwich Again March 1943 177

Chapter 14 January, 1944 196

Introduction

The story begins with a 7-year-old boy from Walthamstow, London, named Nick Clayton. He had a good family network of parents, grandparents, a younger sister, aunts, uncles and cousins. He is a little scamp, always up to mischief and the bane of his mother's life. He prefers sports, cricket and football to academic studies, which helped him to win head boy status at his school. He grows into a good-looking, charming teenager who is popular with his mates and the girls. On a whim, he passes a recruiting office with a friend and joins up in 1940, aged 16. To his mother's horror, he is sent off to Norfolk the next day to join the Royal Norfolk regiment. After a year with the Royal Norfolk, he gets the opportunity to join the Household Cavalry.

In the summer of 1941, the government formed The Guards Armored Division, which consisted of all the guard regiments: the Grenadiers, Coldstream, Scots, Irish and Welsh guards, along with the Household Cavalry.

The role of the Household Cavalry Regiment was for Reconnaissance. It was formed into 4 Sabre Squadrons A, B, C, and D, each one consisting of 5 troops made up of 2 Daimler armored cars, 2 Daimler scout cars and an AEC Matador mk III armored car. Following behind each squadron was a Support Troop, which consisted of 1 Daimler Scout car and 3 White Scout cars carrying supplies, including medical supplies. Nick was in the B Squadron 5 troop and was trained as a gunner/wireless operator.

The regiment landed on Juno Beach in July 1944. The role of reconnaissance was to find safe and clear ways for the

Guards' division to follow. It was not a fighting regiment but did not avoid some skirmishes. The story I am writing is based on my husband's memoirs which I recorded.

Chapter 1

"Hurry up, Kenny!" yelled Nick. He glanced again at the empty tin can on the ground, and giving it another almighty kick, he sent it smashing against the ancient brick wall of Vestry House.

"And it's a goal!" he whispered to himself, jumping and punching the air.

Kenny emerged from his front door. "Get back here, young man," he called his mother from inside the house.

Kenny's eyes rolled, and Nick sighed, "Dinner is at twelve and then it's Sunday School." Closing the door, she snapped, "And don't be late!"

"Okay, mum," whined Kenny.

Wrestling his arms into his coat, he shoved and grappled Nick's tin. With a running commentary, the two youngsters disappeared along Church Path, jostling each other to get at the clattering can.

"You'd never believe it was Sunday," muttered Mrs. Smith from her doorway, "Get off with you, yer noisy kids!" Nick blew a raspberry in her direction.

Mrs. Smith glowered and clenched a threatening fist at the mischievous boys, "I'll be seein' yer father later."

"Race you to the end of the road, Nick!" challenged Kenny as he set off on a run. "That's not fair," yelled Nick. "You didn't give me a chance."

Grabbing the tail of his friend's coat Nick hung on to hold him back. Kenny struggled to loosen his grip.

"Ger off" he chuckled.

The two friends raced to the end of the road followed by a ragtag tail of yelling children. Nick stopped and grabbed Marie Smith's legs as she swung on the rope that dangled from the lamppost.

"Let go!" yelled Marie, "Let go!" she repeated, "I'm gonna tell me dad!" Little Jessie Webb punched Nick and ran off.

"Ooooo, that really hurt," said Nick clutching his belly in fake pain.

The boys wandered off, down searching for anything that could be rescued from the spoils of the market held the day before. A small group of children played in the middle of the road as the boys entered Hoe Street. They ran on toward the High Street, where they scrambled around, picking up the few bruised apples they found amongst some vegetable leaves and garbage that lay about in the street's gutters. Shop windows busy with customers only the day before were shuttered and fastened securely. The only vehicle that could be seen on the side of the empty street was a dilapidated wooden cart. Harnessed to it was a tired-looking horse resting a rear hoof and, with its nose pointing to the ground, stood patiently waiting for its owner to return. Two or three small family groups wandered along the pavement dressed in their Sunday best.

Just as the two friends came alongside the horse cart, Kenny caught sight of Billy Hawkins rounding the corner of High Street,

"Hey Nick let's go!" he cried.

"I ain't scared of 'im!" Nick declared and walked on. Kenny hid behind the cart watching,

"There's Clayton, let's get 'im!" Billy Hawkins yelled. His little gang of four seven-year-olds charged, yelling and shouting in Nick's direction. Nick belted off across the road, laughing.

"You ain't fast enough to catch me," he called and disappeared up the road as fast as his little legs would carry him.

....

Standing in the church later with a number of other children of all ages, their hands held together for prayer, the minister spoke, "Let us pray." Kenny opened one eye. "He didn't get you, then?" he whispered between his closed hands.

"Nah," whispered Nick and screwing up his eyes he joined in the prayer, "Our Father who 'aint in heaven, Harold be your name…."

Nick spent all day with Kenny and his family; they had grown up together in the close-knit village community of Walthamstow. He was happy to spend time with his mate, totally oblivious of where, with whom or what, his parents were doing but later that day he was to learn that he had a baby sister.

"I got a baby sister!" he called as he opened Kenny's front door on Monday morning, eager to share his news with Mrs. Packham.

"We know!" came the gentle reply.

"Her name's Joyce," added Nick as he waited for Kenny to tie his bootlaces. "I chose her name."

"That's a nice name, Nick," said Mrs. Packham warmly, patting him on the head, "Now get yourselves off to school!" She stood at the door and watched the two friends disappear along Church Path.

Standing between the two coats that lay at each side of him forming the goal posts and with one eye on the ball that was being kicked between the boys, Nick called out to his teacher who was passing through the playground,

"I got a baby sister, Sir!"

The teacher acknowledged Nick with a nod and wink. The moment was gone, as the scrum around the goal diverted the boy's attention.

Suddenly and without any warning Nick's home life changed. For nearly eight years since his birth in 1923, this blonde-haired, brown-eyed skinny boy had been the love of his mother's life. His pale, clear complexion and his mischievous, cheeky face fooled everyone into believing he was an angel, everyone that is except those who knew him well! He had many a walloping from his father for getting into mischief not least the time he set fire to the fringe of newspaper his mother had trimmed and used to decorate the mantelpiece; nor when he once wheeled old Emma home in her bath chair after her usual Sunday trip to church and decided to let go of it. The incident frightened her to death, but she came to no harm when her bath chair went freely down a hill and stopped with a bump against a tree!

"But Dad," said Nick, hoping to stop the thrashing, "she was laughing!"

Old Emma was a "Sitting Tenant" when the family moved into the rented accommodation. The original owner of the tiny two-bedroom premises would not evict her so the new owner was obliged to allow her to stay.

She was crippled with arthritis and dependent on the family for all her needs. Old Emma shared a bedroom with Nick, and though she thought that Nick was the worst child in the world, she still worried about him whenever he developed another chest infection.

The boy grumbled and complained bitterly when his mother would send him to school in winter with an ointment made from the noxious mixture of Ipecacuanha ointment and camphorated oil spread on his chest and covered with a cloth under his Vest.

"They pull faces and say I smell," he yelled. "And I want to punch 'em!" he said angrily, brandishing his fists.

"I hope you don't," his mother retorted. Determined to ensure the cloth was securely in place, she pulled the boy's vest down tightly over it.

Whilst once he had his parents' whole attention, now Nick was having to share them with this little thing that had an odd smell, howled when she was bathed and kept his parents awake at night which often affected his mother's mood the next day!

The solitude he enjoyed with his parents and old Emma in the cozy, two-up, two-down terraced cottage that backed onto Vestry House gardens in Walthamstow was now gone.

Nick liked the child well enough, and as she grew older, her development amused him. But there was no time for him, it seemed, except when he was needed to watch the baby to enable his mother to do the household necessities without any interruptions. At any given opportunity Nick would make a bolt for the door to rake the streets with his friends before his mother had time to pin him down.

"Where are you off to, young man? I need...." The door banged shut before Elsie could finish her sentence and Nick disappeared up Church Path and into the next road as fast as he could go!

As the months went by and warm Spring days replaced the cold, dark winter days, it was not so easy to escape. His baby sister was getting bigger, and during the holidays and weekends, Nick was detailed to take her out in her pram. Even so, it did not deter the lad from leaving the pram in a convenient place in the street or in the park while he joined the local lads for a game of football or cricket. Nick stood by as his schoolmate Ginger Webb struggled to release his grizzling little brother from his trouser leg, "At least she's in a pram," Nick said thankfully.

Ginger sighed and rolled his eyes with exasperation, pushing his sibling away and encouraging him to join the other little ones playing in the street. But to no avail!

Once again, on a Saturday in late summer, Nick was charged with taking his sister out of his mother's steaming kitchen. After initially grumbling and protesting, he went out of the gate, kicking the ground with frustration while Joyce smiled and gurgled in her pram. The day was bright and warm as the miserable boy dressed in knee-length, thick, worsted trousers and braces over a grey short-sleeved shirt, he pushed the pram along. His socks hung at different heights as he scuffed his way through the few autumn leaves that had recently gathered in Church Path. He passed Mrs. Smith on her doorstep, her large shape wrapped in a faded pinafore with her hair hidden underneath a scarf and knotted at the top of her head. She was gossiping to her equally dressed neighbor holding two bottles of milk she had picked up from her doorstep. They both gave Nick a knowing look as he passed by and smiled sweetly at his sister. The boy went on his way.

"'E looks 'appy," said Mrs. Smith with a smirk. Her neighbor nodded in agreement and disappeared indoors.

Nick gave them a cursory glance and, finding only small children playing in the street, wandered grudgingly towards the railway station hoping he might find some amusing distraction on the way. He passed a stationary coal lorry by the side of the road and stopped to let the leather-apron-clad coalman pass by. Carrying his heavy sack of coal on his back he smiled at Nick and went through the garden gate to one of the cottages. Nick pushed through a group of women gossiping by the milk cart waiting their turn to pay their weekly bills to the milkman. St Mary Road was busy with people doing their usual Saturday morning business. He crossed over the busy Hoe Street wending his way idly forward unnoticed by the crowds of shoppers. Nearing the railway station, he heard the familiar sounds of hissing steam and the intermittent clunk of doors as they banged shut announcing the arrival of a train that had just pulled into the station. He noticed a small child holding an open hand to the few people spilling out of the station in pursuit of their destination. Just one person recognized the child's need and, as he continued hurriedly on his way, rummaged in his coat pocket for a few coins. Slowing down, Nick watched him turn and hand what small change he found into the child's outstretched hand, never stopping between the process. Holding on to his hat, the man went on his way while the child bent his head to count the coins.

Nick had an idea! He waited for the next train to arrive then, looking cautiously around, leaned forward into the pram. A cry of pain ensued from within. People were very generous, especially Bishop Barker, when they saw the child in the pram crying,

"She's 'ungry mister," said Nick sadly.

Nick went off happily with his illicit earnings and the red mark on the little girl's arm remained a mystery to her mother!

Life was good for Nick. He lived in a close village community in Church Path where doors were never locked, and neighborly helping hands were ready when needed. Church Path ran between the white, wicket-fenced gardens of a terrace of old cottages. On the other side of the Path was a wall. A gate in the wall gave access to another row of six cottages that stood parallel to the rear of the back garden of Vestry House; one of which was Nick's home.

Living in a secure and safe neighborhood, Nick was also blessed with kind and loving parents. Dick and Elsie Clayton and a wonderful extended family of Aunts, Uncles and Grandparents who lived within the vicinity of less than a mile or two of his home. Nick could always find a comforting family member to escape to if he was in trouble with his parents or from whom he could scrounge a penny or two for sweets. Weekdays were spent in school, and Saturday was a busy day filled with household chores and cooking. Sundays were restful.

The afternoon for Nick was spent in Sunday School at the local church where sixty or seventy other youngsters gathered for hymns and prayers. This was not a favorite pastime for a lively, mischievous boy, but he knew that if he didn't attend, then he missed out on the Friday evening activities that included woodwork and metalwork and the annual trip to Southend in the summer. While the boy was at Sunday School his parents took a rest, after which the family visited one of the many relatives' homes for tea. On these visits' cousins entertained each other while the adults remained at the tea table to catch up with news and gossip.

The families often gathered in dozens at their Grandparent's homes to celebrate an anniversary or birthday in style. Christmas Day swelled the little front room of Nick's Grandparent's home to bursting! No excuse for not attending was acceptable! Arriving for tea one Sunday Nick strolled in holding his sister's hand.

"Where's yer mother and father?" demanded his grandmother. "They're 'aving a row," replied young Nick.

"What they rowing about?" Nick looked away, screwed up his face and shrugged his shoulders. After more pressure from his grandmother, he answered, "I dunno. Somat about Mrs. Porter's garden. Dad went and done some work for her, and mum said her fancy man should do it, and she just started shoutin'".

"Right! Well!" huffed gran, "Bill," she snapped. "Get the car out!"

Elsie's overweight frame appeared sheepishly at the door shortly after, followed by Dick's rather small frame and

Grandad, "What did you tell Gran that for?" hissed Elsie. Nick ducked as she lifted her hand to clip the boy's ear!

Family gatherings were wonderful events for Nick and Christmas 1933 was one such occasion when family members turned up laden with Christmas fare. If there was no room at the table, they ate wherever there was a space to do so, albeit perched on benches around the flowery papered walls, sitting on the stairs, or on the narrow terracotta-tiled hall floor where colored rays of light filtered through the stained glass window of the front door. Entertainment was tantamount to food! Nick's dad and his brothers were great entertainers dressing up from whatever could be found in the old suitcase Dick owned.

"As soon as we clear away we can get started," grumbled Granny. Charlie called to his brother Bill, "'ere giv'us a hand with this table."

"Where do you want it?" came the willing reply.

The two men heaved the heavy, wooden dining table to the side of the wall while the women busied themselves in the small kitchen. "I'm getting out," cried Auntie Winnie, "before one of us suffocates!"

"Don't blame you," retorted Auntie Ada, adding "There's too many in here. For goodness sake, get out from under my feet, Billy!" She flipped her nephew with the tea cloth. The situation lightened as the sound of Elsie's nimble fingers on the piano drifted into the busy kitchen and set their feet tapping. Humming the song to herself, Auntie Ada and her daughter Eileen picked up the song, and together they began to sing gustily, "Button up your overcoat when the wind is free, take good care of yourself. You belong to me." Their laughter filtered into the sitting room where the rest of the family gathered on seats around the room. Nick and Joyce sat together on the floor at their mother's feet watching intently as their father and uncle Sid were deciding about the contents of a small suitcase. Then, when Sid began to pull a collection of ladies' wear out of it, Nick whispered to his mum, who was chatting to her sister, "Is Dad going to dress up again?"

"Er, Yes!" she said impatiently. Nick rolled his eyes as the two men began to don a dress complete with a hat and handbag. Joyce clapped her hands with delight. Elsie overheard Nick groaning, "Just sit still and behave yourself, my Lad, or you will be sitting at my feet under the piano for the rest of the evening," Elsie threatened.

Once the women from the kitchen were settled the fun began. They laughed and joked their way through the evening with songs, poems and sketches. "Do I 'ave too?" whined Nick.

"It's your turn," urged Elsie. Nick reddened as his melodious little voice began, "In Dublin's fair city where girls are so pretty...." He smiled and felt more comfortable when everyone joined in to sing, "Alive, alive O, alive alive O...."

The hour was late when the children and women left for their homes. Those who stayed retired to bed sleeping anywhere they could find that was comfortable, while the men played cards until dawn.

Chapter 2
March 1934

It was a bitterly cold morning when Nick and Kenny peeped furtively around the corner of the junction between Hoe Street and St Mary Road to watch the hearse pass by. Nick remembered how members of his family had wrestled with his grandfather only a few weeks earlier.

Disturbed by the noise of frantic voices coming from the vicinity of his grandparent's garden one Sunday, Nick had ventured out to see what was happening. Crammed in the doorway of the wooden hut that served as an outside toilet near the vegetable patch, his dad and his brothers Uncle Harry and Uncle Sid appeared to be fighting. Cries from within sent shivers down the boy's back as he drew closer to the scene. His mother and her sister Winnie stood together on the garden path comforting his distraught Grandmother. Elbowing his way between the women, his mother frantically grabbed him by the arm, "Get back indoors. Now!" she shouted. Turning to free himself he noticed tears streaming down his aunt's face.

"No!" the boy yelled defiantly. He wriggled out of his mother's grasp but she caught him firmly and yanked him behind her back. The bewildered boy turned back up the garden path toward the house. The struggling and yelling continued as he stood just inside the scullery door anxiously straining to see what was happening next. He watched his uncle turn and hurry towards the women with something in his hand.

They stood for a moment in deep discussion about the past few weeks that Granddad had been complaining of discomfort and pain in his bowel. There was no respite, and in the last few days, the pain had become so acute that he felt he could no longer stand it.

"The doctor gave him some medicine but it didn't do any good," said Winnie tearfully.

"Can't imagine what it must have been like to make 'im want to……." Elsie broke off and they turned to walk towards the door within earshot of Nick.

"Charlie's gone for the doctor," Elsie said tearfully.

"What's happening?" enquired Nick

"You clear off and mind your own business. Go and find something to do!" snapped Uncle Harry. Nick crept out of sight but within hearing distance.

"Thank Gawd we got the gun off him," he heard his mother say. "Huh!" replied Uncle Harry, "I can understand him wanting to do himself in!"

Hearing the conversation between his mother and her brother, Nick began to put two and two together. The conclusion was disturbing and he felt alone and isolated; he needed an explanation. The next hour was fraught with anxiety as Nick watched and listened. He saw his grandfather being helped through the house by his uncle followed by the doctor. They put Grandad in the car, and Uncle Sid drove to the hospital.

"It doesn't look good," said the doctor, "If he's in so much pain then there may be a blockage in his bowel." Gran broke down sobbing.

"So, what does that mean?" asked Elsie.

"Try not to worry." The doctor said. "I'll let you know more when we find out what's wrong." Picking up his bag and hat he walked out of the door.

A breeze filtered through the tall black plume feathers adorning the heads of the magnificent gleaming black horses as they walked slowly past Nick and Kenny. People removed their hats respectfully, stopping on the pavement to watch the hearse pass by. The grinding of the wheels and the heavy, slow clink of the horseshoes on the road broke the reverent silence as the two youngsters stood open-mouthed, watching the black-robed figures of the family follow the hearse carrying Nick's Grandfather in the direction of the cemetery.

"Cor! What a sight!" exclaimed Nick in a loud whisper, "Yeah, they look huge in the stables," commented Kenny. "But when they're dressed up.... phew," he whistled.

Nick had not been allowed to go to the funeral so the boys continued to watch from the corner of the street. They slipped behind the procession as it went on dodging between the people on the pavement but keeping well behind. Stopping for a moment at the cemetery gate in idle thought Nick sniffed and wiped his nose on the sleeve of his jumper, "I better go round me gran's house. See ya later Kenny."

He started to walk off, "Yeh! well I'll come with ya!" called Kenny.

Running to catch up with his friend Kenny flung a sympathetic arm around his friend's shoulder.

Closing the back door of his home, Dick walked in, announcing, "Well, that's sorted," Unbuttoning his coat, he slipped it off and hung it on the coat hook along with his cap.

"How did you get on with yer brothers then?" called Elsie from the stairs. "I'll be down in a minute," she added.

Elsie appeared in the room. "Just had to take old Emma's tea up, she ain't too well today."

"We've all agreed to give mum a shilling a week." replied Dick, "We worked out, her pension is seven bob a week, so with all five brothers giving a bob each she'll get twelve bob,"

"That's good," commented Elsie, "she'd never have managed otherwise. She'd end up in the work'ouse!" Dick glanced sharply at his wife.

"I doubt that love," he said firmly, "There are no workhouses now!"

"You know what I mean, one o' them institutes." Dick sighed with frustration at his wife's silly ideas.

....

The meal was finished and cleared away as always on a Saturday evening. Nick was excited, he was going to a show at the Palace Music Hall. Little Joyce was happy to spend the evening with a neighbor, Mrs. Green and her daughter Margaret who was the same age. Nick was ready to go. He watched patiently while his mother put on her coat and hat. "Stop fiddling with that hat, you look very nice," Dick snapped, "Hurry up, or we'll be late!"

Unable to contain his excitement, Nick danced about as they walked to the Music Hall in the High Street. Waiting for the doors to open under the warmly lit, filigree, wrought iron shelter, he looked down the long, crowded queue that formed noisily alongside the huge, elegant red-brick building. In doing so, he blocked the pavement.

"Nick, mind out there's people trying to get by," scolded Elsie. She pulled him back into the queue. Nick was too excited to care and spent the rest of the time mesmerized by the gaily colored posters.

"Are we gonna see them acrobats Mum?" he questioned, pointing to a poster. Elsie was talking to another waiting person, "Yes Son," said his father. Nick gasped, "Cor!" he breathed. Dick smiled down at him.

The lights dimmed in the auditorium, and the organ, rising slowly out of the ground, started to bellow out its dramatic musical chords. Once again, Nick was not disappointed. The acrobats and other glittering musical entertainers added glamour and sophistication to the evening and Nick's world. When everyone laughed at the comedian, he laughed too, though he wasn't always sure why! Nick warmed to the sound when he and the whole auditorium joined in to sing the chorus of 'The Man Who Broke the Bank of Monte Carlo.' The magic was over too soon and the family came out into the warm night air lit up by the neon lights from the Music Hall Theatre.

"Can I go with you on the milk round tomorrow, Dad?" asked the sleepy boy. "No, you can't," snapped Elsie.

"Not tomorrow, but maybe next Saturday," his dad gently added.

A watery sun began to rise with the promise of another hot day when, on the following Saturday. Dick and his son set off at 5 am to start the delivery round of milk. Sitting alongside his father with only the echo of the horse's feet and the gentle clinking of the bottles on the cart to accompany them, they passed down the streets between the terraced houses in the still-sleeping suburb of London.

Placing the milk bottles on doorstep after doorstep he was aware of his own footsteps and the occasional clunk of a gate latch as it closed behind him.

These trips became more regular, but as the year went by, the mornings got colder, and on one very cold Saturday, his dad advised him not to go.

"Stay home today, son, it's too cold and dark to go out today." But the boy was not going to be put off. He climbed up on the cart beside his father. They hadn't gone far when a pathetic little voice said, "Dad, I'm cold." His dad looked at him, "I thought you would be," he said, and, with a slight jerk of his head, he said, "Run along home then."

....

Nick and Kenny had been friends ever since they could remember. Kenny had an older brother called Joe and a younger sister called Cissie. He had met up with Kenny in Church Path every morning on their way to school. Meeting up with other friends on the way, they bundled noisily through the school gate and onto the playground, jostling each other in good humor until the bell rang for lessons.

One day one of the Marsdon brothers yelled across the playground at the top of his voice, "Bollocks!"

Nick and his friends laughed. "Whatzat mean?" he asked, and they put their heads together, whispering and giggling.

Puffing and panting from running, a breathless Nick opened the kitchen door to his home and looked into the cozy room where everything happened, from meals to socializing and listening to the radio. All was quiet and serene; in the corner, by the window, his father sat reading the paper. His mother was taking the iron off the range and gossiping quietly to her neighbor Mrs. Green. He watched as his mother spat on the iron and heard the hiss that followed.

"Is that you Son?" called his mother. Getting ready to run, the boy yelled "Bollocks!"

He fled round the table and opened the door to the stairs. Mrs. Green threw up her hands and cried in horror; his mother gasped. Holding the iron with one hand she steadied herself with the other.

"What!" cried his dad. Throwing the paper aside in a crumpled heap he leaped from his chair. He chased after the boy and up the stairs. In haste, Elsie put down the iron and followed, yelling, "Dick, Dick stop, he doesn't know what he's saying."

As they listened to the yelling that followed Elsie shook her head in despair. "I don't know what's going to become of him," she said to Mrs. Green. She picked up the hot iron again. "He'll be the death of us!"

Mrs. Green shook her head in disapproval. "Well, there's not much I can say; he really is a little terror! Where did he hear that word?" she said. "You 'eard about the fire he nearly caused when 'e lit the paper over the mantelpiece? And poor old Emma when 'e let go of her bath-chair and nearly put 'er in 'ospital?"

Getting into deep conversation Elsie decided to put the iron back on the hot black range.

"Well that's not all you know," she continued, "Dick caught him smoking!"

"Really?" enquired Mrs. Green relishing the gossip. Resting her hand on her hip and turning to look at Mrs. Green, Elsie continued: "Well," she began, "Dick was in the garden digging last week, and he saw smoke coming out of the gap at the top of the wooden door of the toilet down the garden!'

Absent-mindedly she picked up the iron again. "Tell you what it didn' 'alf give him a fright!" she said. Spitting on the hot iron, she continued, "Dick opened the door, and he was sitting there, trousers down to the floor, puffing away on a fag end."

Mrs. Green sniggered and covered her mouth. As she was speaking, Dick appeared again in the doorway "That'll teach 'im!" he said.

"Aw Dick don't be so 'ard on 'im!"

Dick fired a look of obstinance at his wife, sat down in the chair, picked up his newspaper, gave it a shake and resumed reading.

"Anyway," said Mrs. Green eager to know what happened next, "What did he do then?" she said, trying not to laugh, "Dick whacked him good and 'ard right across his bare bum!" Elsie began to fold up the garment she had just ironed but creased it again as they both curled up with laughter.

"Still, he is a wild one, Nicholas," Elsie said. She returned the iron to the stove and, putting her hands on her waist, she stretched her back and yawned. You'd think he'd learn with all the whacks he gets, but he's just as bad at school, you know. He's always in trouble!"

Nick was well-liked by his teachers, but his cheeky humor got him into trouble more than once.

"Was that Sweeney Todd?" He called out, to the teacher's comment about the Barber of Seville.

"I'll give you Sweeny Todd" came the slow reply as he dragged Nick out of his seat by the ear and sent him off for the stick and book.

The stick and book were kept in the headmaster's office and brought out when needed as punishment; With two cracks of the stick on each of the boy's hands the teacher entered Nick's name in the book and sent him to put them back.

On another occasion, he dared to cross a young, inexperienced teacher who was unprepared to accept Nick's behavior. "I'll see you at playtime," said the teacher, his eyes flashing with anger. The lesson ended, and Nick stayed behind as the other children noisily left the room. "Get the stick and book," the teacher curtly ordered, rubbing the chalk off the blackboard. Nick did as he was told and returned later with the dreaded tools.

"Put your hand out," demanded the teacher. Nick turned up the palm of his right hand to take the punishment. Screwing up his face, he turned his head, awaiting the sting that would inevitably come. He heard the swish of the stick and felt the pain on his hand which he immediately began to rub.

"Put it up again," spat the teacher, tapping his right hand with the stick. Nick prepared his left hand. "No, the same one," snapped the teacher. "No!" said a worried Nick. We don't have the same hand twice."

"Well, you do now!" came the sharp reply. "Open your hand" he demanded.

"No!" cried Nick and he ran for the door. Before the boy could open the door, the stick came hard down across his back. Nick let out a yell of pain. Turning around, he saw the savage look in the eyes of the angry teacher wielding the stick, ready for another thrashing. It struck! A frantic Nick yelled out again as he struggled to open the door. He ran out of the classroom. He didn't stop running. He ran through the school and onto the playground tears streaming down his face and yelling for his dad. He opened the school gate and ran across the road to a building site where he knew his dad was working.

The school gate opened and an angry father came striding through the playground, his son trotting miserably behind. Watched by a crowd of curious children they went into the main entrance of the school building, "Where is he?" demanded Dick.

Nick led the way to the classroom and opened the door. A surprised and still irate, disheveled teacher stood up towering over the small, neat frame of the man that faced him. With clenched fists, Dick squared up to the shocked teacher. "I've got a bunch of fives here," he said, "and you can have 'em all."

Down the corridor, hurried footsteps could be heard coming in the direction of the classroom, and a flustered head teacher, Mr Bubber, entered the room. "Mr Clayton, Mr Clayton," he hissed. " Um," he stuttered, "We can sort this out, we can sort this out!"

The situation calmed, "Come," said the headmaster. With a hand gesture, he beckoned them all to his room. After a long and bitter discussion, the matter was sorted, and Dick returned to his job.

Shortly after the teacher resigned and left the school. Some months later he was reported as having rescued a colleague on a mountain climbing expedition.

Chapter 3
1934 (11 years)

The monotony of school work was lightened in the playground and on the sports field where Nick excelled. His love of sports and his bright, friendly disposition made him popular with students and teachers alike, but when his enthusiasm spilled out onto the street, other boys were reluctant to let him join in with their game of cricket.

After some persuasion came the remark, "Okay, you and Kenny can play if you don't bowl mad!" However, the mischievous, winning streak in Nick couldn't help but make a few heads duck under the ball that bounced and whizzed at great speed past their ears!

"That's it," came a loud voice, "you ain't playin' no more!" the ball was held back. Pleading and promises were of no use, so both Nick and Kenny sidled off to find another occupation! It was not long before the boys came across another group of friends.

"You going up the 'Oller Pond?" called Kenny to Stan and his little brother Sidney.

"Yeh, why, you comin'?" replied Stan. The boys went off at a jog to catch up with Stan and Sidney. Jumping, skipping and running like playful young animals they went on their way.

The Hollow Pond at Leighton Flats was a favorite place for kids to gather to swim and play on warm summer days; or to paddle across to the island in the middle. This was one such day, and little Sidney followed the boys over to the island and back, but when Sidney was only halfway back, Nick and Kenny called out,

"Leeches, Sid, leeches," whereupon the poor, frightened little boy turned back to the island and the boys curled up with laughter.

"'E's going back to the middle again,' they jeered. Why don't 'e just come back here? He's only got to cross again," chuckled Nick. He ruffled Kenny's hair, and they ran off.

Winter days were no different; Nick was always out playing in the nearby streets close to home, often idle and looking for mischief. It had snowed hard the night before and all the local children had been out playing, stirring up the pure white snow blanket that greeted them through their windows in the morning into flattened grey areas and icy glass sliding tracks. Here and there various sizes of snowmen stood awkwardly wearing old woolen hats, a row of stones for a smile and two more positioned for eyes. By dusk, most of the children had returned to the warmth and comfort of their homes. Two were still out loitering by St Mary's Church, "Look, Kenny, there's ol' PC Burns," whispered Nick.

They followed the policeman round to Vestry House Museum where they stopped on the corner. With his balaclava helmet slightly askew, Nick bent to pick up some snow and molded it into a ball.

"You wouldn't dare," gasped Kenny. "I dare you!" Nick challenged. Finding the right opportunity, the boys hurled their snowballs at the policeman, hitting him square in the back of his heavy black cloak. They took off at a run, racing along Vinegar Alley and into the graveyard, where they hid until they thought the coast was clear.

"Do you think he saw us, Nick?" said Kenny, jogging backward down Church Lane. "Nah! He was facing the other way, he didn't see us."

They wandered casually into Church Path, separating as they neared their homes. Nick turned the handle of the scullery door and closed it behind him. He hung his coat on top of his dad's at the back of the door, adding his hat, which dropped immediately to the floor. As he bent to pick it up, a voice called for him.

"Hello Son," called his dad. Nick came out of his reverie and turned to look in through the open door to the living room. On the table was PC Burns' helmet and sitting beside it was PC Burns!

"Wash yer feet!" His mother snapped, "You're going away!" Nick was speechless! PC Burns looked grave, "Did you and Kenny Packham throw those snowballs?" he asked knowingly.

"It weren't me! "urged Nick.

"Don't try wriggling out of this one son," Elsie said, "The policeman saw you!" Nick looked at the floor. "So, what have you got to say for yourself young man?" his mother remarked.

Nick looked at his mother, "Don't look at me," she said with an air of surprise, "you need to say sorry to PC Burns,"

"Sorry," Nick said sheepishly.

"And what do you not do again?" asked Nick's dad. "Not throw snowballs at PC Burns," Nick replied. Frowning, he added quickly, "Are you going to see Kenny too?"

"I certainly am," said the policeman. "And you two had better behave yourselves or you're going to be in serious trouble before long."

With a jerk of his head Dick said to his son, "You'd better take yourself off to bed!"

"I haven't had me tea yet," Nick grizzled.

"And you ain't gettin' any," retorted Elsie.

Muffled sobs could be heard as the boy climbed the stairs. Turning to the policeman Dick asked;

"Now that you're here would you like a little glass of whisky?" PC Burns smacked one hand on his knees and straightened up. "Don't mind if I do!" he said, pushing his helmet aside to make room for the glass.

The snowball incident and the threat by PC Burns didn't deter the youngster's mischievous and daring exploits. Later in the year he and Kenny decided to walk the railway bridge wall! A great throng of children came running out of school one day jostling each other and chanting, "Kenny and Nick are gonna walk the wall! Kenny and Nick are gonna walk the wall!" More children joined the throng following their heroes along the road. They turned into the next street toward the railway bridge on Orford Road. This was an exciting occasion that rarely happened. Arriving at the bridge, the boys prepared to climb onto the bridge wall, which was at least twenty feet high above the railway line and twelve feet long.

"We'll tell yer dad Nick Clayton," yelled Billy Hawkins.

Undeterred, they looked around for any adults who might be watching. Then, satisfied there were none, the boys climbed onto the bridge wall to the delight of the squealing young onlookers. They balanced their way cautiously along the dangerous, foot-wide edge to the end, whereupon they jumped triumphantly to the ground. They didn't wait long before careering off back around Vinegar Alley, chasing Billy Hawkins.

Billy, or Bully, as he was well known, was always fighting with someone. He had his own following of friends who went around in a gang intimidating others, and Nick was no exception. This time he was not going to get away with it. Careering up with Billy, he slammed him up against a wall and rolled his hand into a fist, aiming it at Billy's face. Nick caught him a good one on the nose, but when the second blow was coming, Billy moved his head. Nick let out a howl as his fist hit the wall behind him. Billy went off laughing but holding his bruised nose while Nick clutched his skinned, bleeding and painful hand. He returned home angry and annoyed.

, "Well serves you right for fighting," Elsie said as she washed the dry blood off her son's knuckles. The boy winced as Elsie washed the blood off her son's knuckles. "Well serves you right for fighting" remarked Elsie. But he won't bully me again thought Nick

On a warm sunny day during the school summer holidays of 1935, Nick opened the back door to go out and called to his mother, "I'm off up the park with Kenny, mum."

His mother called him back. "I need you to take Dad his lunch,' she said, handing him the prepared sandwiches and a bottle of warm tea wrapped in a towel.

"Aw, mum," protested Nick. Do I have to?"

"Yes!"

"Why can't Joyce take it?"

"Don't be daft; she's too young, and anyway, how can she? She's in bed with chicken pox! Anyway, it's on your way to the park. Now get along with you." Elsie pushed the boy out of the door and closed it.

Grumbling and reluctant Nick wandered off. Swinging the package carelessly he went through the bollards at the top of the Path. He took a deep intake of air as the bag hit a bollard, the bottle smashed and the sandwiches were drenched. He had no option but to return home with the contents of the towel dripping out onto the ground. Fear of his mother's wrath turned to sorrow, sadness and guilt when in despair she slumped into a chair and put her head in her hands.

"I have no more to give your dad," she said tearfully. "That was the last of the bread and milk."

Nick knew that the family was struggling financially. His dad had been out of permanent work for more than a month. The Great Depression that began in 1929, though nearly five years on, continued to leave many unemployed people destitute and without food or basic necessities. For some the only option left to them was the Workhouse. The government ordered such places to close in 1930 but they were still in use under the name of Public Assistance Institutions. They continued to operate with relatively little change and were still regarded as workhouses by those who feared them. The unemployment benefit system paid out according to need and was subject to a strict means test. Dick had refused to subject his family to the humiliation of the means test that would have meant selling the radio and the precious piano. He found work anywhere he could. His brother, Charlie, was able to give him a week's work occasionally, and the few flowers he had in his garden he cut and sold for pennies outside the cemetery. Now he had some temporary work with the undertaker in Orford Road.

Nick was mortified. He left the house and ran to Kenny's home. He knocked and pushed open the door, "Is Kenny in Mrs. Packham?"

Wiping her hands on her overall, Mrs. Packham looked at Nick. His face was screwed up ready to cry.

"No dear, he's not," she replied, "Whatever is the matter?" Tears began to fill Nick's eyes, "I smashed the bottle of tea, and it messed up the sandwiches Mum made for Dad, and there's no more food left for him," he grizzled, "Mum's crying, and I don't know what to do."

"O dear!" said Mrs. Packham. "Well now perhaps I can find a way to help." She rummaged in her larder and brought half a loaf of bread and a tin of luncheon meat. Nick watched as she prepared the sandwiches and wrapped them in newspaper. "Go and take them straight to your dad, then go and tell your mum so she won't worry." With a gentle push on his back, Mrs. Packham sent Nick off.

"Thank you, Mrs. Packham," Nick called back gratefully.

Chapter 4
Summer 1935

At last, a few weeks before his twelfth birthday, Nick was given a chance to deliver newspapers from Mr. William's newsagent shop. He knew Kenny's brother Joe would be leaving school in July and would leave to look for a proper job. To get a paper round, he bothered Mr. Williams and helped Joe deliver his round. It worked! Joe left, and Nick got the paper round! There was just one small problem: Nick needed a bicycle!

"Mr. Williams said I could do the paper round, but I need a bike," Nick told his dad.

His dad went with him to the cycle shop, which displayed bicycles of all shapes and sizes lining the pavement outside. They stepped inside, and Dick nudged the boy forward to ask the question.

"How much does it cost for a bike?" asked Nick sheepishly.

"Depends what you want, Son," said the shopkeeper.

"Wot I like is a 'Hercules' like my friend's got,"

The shopkeeper looked at him and sighed, "Well, it'll cost you three pounds, nineteen shillings and sixpence, but you can pay two bob a week on the never-never!" Nick looked at his dad.

"Can I earn that with my paper round, Dad?"

"I reckon so. Let's go outside and talk about it."

Outside the shop, Nick's dad said, "Now, Son, you do know that you can't stop the paper round 'till you've paid for the bike?"

Nick nodded, "Yeah!"

"Alright then!" said Nick's father, "I'll lend you the first instalment; after that, it will be your responsibility."

Nick proudly wheeled his new bike out into the street.

All was well in the summer months, but as winter approached, Nick started to get bored with his paper round, and he soon grew to hate the cold, dark early mornings.

"Nick," yelled his mother, "I'm not going to tell you again. It's time you got up."

Nick dragged himself out of bed in a bad mood every morning. He rushed to the newsagents in time to begin sorting the papers before going out to deliver. It didn't take long to manipulate someone into helping him out.

"Go on, give us a hand with me paper round," he repeated once again to the beleaguered Ginger Webb.

"Okay then, but only if I swap you for your cigarette cards," bargained Ginger.

"Aw, that's not fair!" moaned Nick. He thought for a moment, "Tell you what, I'll let you have some, but not me, Tommy Meads, nor Les Howe, 'cause they're my heroes; they play for Spurs." Nick reluctantly forfeited a few of his treasured collection of cards for Ginger's help, but as far as he was concerned, he had got what he wanted!

Soon after, Nick was selected to play goal for the school team. Training began early on Saturday, but the paper round was a priority.

"Tell Mr. Watson, he might be able to give you different hours," Dick advised his son.

"It worked, Dad," Nick called out from the scullery, "He seemed pleased that I'm playing for the school team, and I'm helping now in the evening, sorting and loading piles of newspapers onto a van and delivering them to the shops."

He entered the room, rubbing his hands together with glee. "I just have to drop bundles of newspapers outside the shops instead of going from door to door!"

1936/37 13/14 years

As he grew older, Nick's skills and his love of sports developed and before long, he became the school sports hero. His bowling and batting averages earned him the privilege of opening the bowling for the school cricket team in the summer of 1936. Nick gloried in the applause he got at the succession of runs he accumulated off his bat, and as he bowled, one by one, wickets fell. When the cricket season was over, he kept goal for the football team where he heroically saved ball after ball from going into the net, once again glorying in the applause of the spectators. In his last year at Monoux School, his name was put forward for head boy, and he was selected not because of his academic ability but because of his personality and sports skills.

Now, in his fourteenth year, he loved the new attention he was getting from the girls and the new sensations he felt when they were around him. At the end of the day, he and Kenny gathered with friends to hang around at the school gate, flirting with the girls. They learned where the girls hung out, mostly at the Hollow Pond at Leighton Flats and sometimes at the local park near the High Street. Lolling on the grass one evening, waiting hopefully for the girls to arrive at the Hollow Pond.

Kenny was gazing up at the sky, "Cor hasn't Susan Parker got the biggest tits!" he murmured dreamily.

Cupping his hands under his chest, Nick chuckled, "No, she hasn't. Pauline Noble has. She's got huge knockers!"

The boys fell about laughing. Sitting up and leaning on his elbow, Kenny winked and said, "Here they come, Nick."

The girls, equally interested in the boys, pretended to ignore them but hung around at a distance in a small group. "Come and join us, Noble, and bring yer friends," teased one of the boys. The girls giggled flirtatiously.

Nick got up and started kicking a football about. Soon, the boys joined him, and a competition began in earnest. The girls sat down to watch. Before long, the ball came flying through the air, landing in their midst. Susan Parker scrambled to her feet and grabbed the ball before Kenny could get it. She passed it to Pauline and dropped to her knees with her friends.

"Give us the ball, Noble," yelled Kenny.

"Me names Pauline, Kenny." she retorted haughtily.

Kenny looked around at the sniggering collection of watching boys and sighed.

"Give us the ball, Pauline," he said, emphasizing her name. She lobbed the ball over his head and into the air, and the girls giggled.

"I'll get you, Noble," he called back with a grimace as he ran for the ball.

Nick deliberately kicked the ball back into the midst of the girls, "Whatcha do that for Nick?" exclaimed Kenny.

"I dunno," replied Nick, shrugging his shoulders.

"Don't let them have it back this time," Pauline whispered. She got up and ran with the ball, passing it backwards and forwards to her friends.

"You can get it this time," grumbled Kenny to Nick.

Nick thought for a moment before setting off at a run, "Come on, then let's get it off her,"

The girls scrambled away from the pond and ran under the shade of the trees. They dodged between the trees, passing the ball nimbly between them, giggling and tripping. The boys held back, unsure what to do and how to get the ball without touching the girls. Nick knew exactly what to do! He grabbed hold of Pauline just as she was about to throw the ball and wrestled it from her. She giggled and shrieked with delight and turned to run after him. The game was on! The boys versus the girls.

The energy was spent, and they sat for a while. One by one, the girls left to go home. Pauline and Susan stayed longer. They followed the boys at a distance when they left, giggling, flirting and calling out to them on their way. The boys stopped by a lamppost, whispering and nudging, and the girls caught them up.

"Grab them," called one of the boys.

Quick as a flash, they grabbed Pauline, but Susan managed to run off. The poor girl struggled and whimpered as they tied her to the lamppost. They ran off, leaving the humiliated girl alone under the lamp's light.

Shortly after, there was a knock at the door, and Nick's mother opened it. Mr. Noble stood on the doorstep, "Where's yer boy?" he demanded.

"Why? What's he done now?" she sighed.

"'e's 'umiliated my daughter that's what! 'e's a bully, and you need to lock 'im up!"

"Nick, come 'ere!" yelled his mother. "Nick, now!" she repeated angrily. "Mr. Noble wants to see you."

With that, Mr. Noble barged past Mrs. Clayton and entered the scullery, "Where is'e? let me get me 'ands on 'im!" Nick appeared from the backyard with his dad marching behind him.

"What's all this about Mr Noble?" Dick calmly asked.

"E!" said Mr Noble, pointing a dirty finger at Nick" tied my girl to a lamppost and left 'er there, the little bugger. Susan Parker found 'er, and you need to see to 'im!"

Nick's mum gasped in horror, and he flinched in response to the hard clip around the ear from his dad.

"It wer'n't just me," the lad fretted, holding his throbbing ear.

Mr Noble turned and left the house, muttering, "I'll get the police onto you before long I will."

Nick's interest in girls didn't waver; if anything, it grew. He was charming and funny, and the girls liked him, and he liked them! Even Pauline forgave him and followed him around adoringly with the other girls. He took a liking to Mary, who lived in one of the big houses where he once delivered newspapers. Taking her home one night, he dared to kiss her just a few yards from her home. They were disturbed by the click of a key turning in the door at the top of the steps. A crack of light appeared from within, followed by a muffled conversation. Nick snatched another kiss from Mary before starting off at a trot as her father's silhouette appeared in the glow of the open door.

Shaking his clenched fist in the air, he yelled, "I know your sort, Clayton! You keep away from my daughter!"

Blowing a defiant kiss from her hand Mary slipped past her Father and in the open door.

May 1937

Red, white and blue bunting hung from lamp posts and windows at the top of St Mary Road, leading into Church Path one bright and sunny day in May 1937. Neighbours were bustling about arranging tables and chairs. Mr Smith fro number Six and his son Dan were hauling a large table down the narrow Church Path.

"'Scuse me," said Mr Smith, "out the way," he yelled impatiently to the girls playing there. The children tripped over themselves to move and ran down the Path straight into Mrs Cohen carrying a pile of plates.

"Nearly dropped them," she said brightly. "Go and see Jessie's mum," she said, directing them with a nod of her head, "in number four, she needs some help with the sandwiches in the kitchen."

The excited girls went off in the direction of Jessie Webb's home. "Here comes the van," yelled Nick, running in through his garden gate. "The van's arrived, Dad," he repeated.

Dick called from the front room of the house, "Right, Nick, go and get Kenny and anyone else you can find, and we'll get the piano out." Nick met Kenny coming up the congested Church Path and told him to hurry up. Dick and his son pulled the piano away from the wall that concealed the front door.

He turned the key in the door and unbolted it, "Right, you go to that end with Kenny, and I'll direct it from this end, ready?"

"Yep," replied Nick. Between them they got the piano out of the house and wheeled it up the Path followed by another stream of idle children.

"I've got the planks," said another neighbour. He put his cigarette in his mouth and strategically placed the planks in the open doors at the back of the van.

"O my gawd," said Elsie, "Wot a lot of trouble to go to. I'm not looking," she added, turning away as the men prepared to guide the piano onto the van.

"Well, it ain't every week we get to celebrate a coronation, love," puffed Dick as he steered the front wheels of the piano onto the planks.

Between them, they pushed, pulled and heaved the piano into the van. Elsie added the piano stool and sat down, "Reckon, that'll do nicely," She said. Clapping the dust of her hands, she tinkled over the keys.

"You are my sunshine, my only sunshine," sang out the girls in the street.

Linking arms, they wiggled and giggled. "Get off, Clayton. I'll tell me mam," giggled Cissie Packham as she turned to peel Nick's hands off her waist.

Holding up the palms of his hands in a gesture of innocence, he said, "I'm only dancing with yah Cissie,"

His cheeky grin made Cissie laugh, "You are a one Nick Clayton," she said.

"Think I felt a drop of rain," said Mrs Smith clattering the tea cups onto the saucers.

"I hope not," replied Mrs Webb, "that'd be a shame. though it wouldn't surprise me if we get some, that sky don't look too good!"

The shower and the rush to cover everything up came and went, and by two o'clock, all was ready. The street party was soon in full swing. The children settled on each side of the long row of cloth-covered tables in their best patriotic clothes and hats in anticipation of winning the prize for the best effort. Their mothers stood around still in their aprons, watching their adorable charges, occasionally leaning across to help themselves from the plates that held the sandwiches and cakes. Gathered together in a cloud of cigarette smoke, the men answered any call to help keep everything going well. "Think we need some more lemonade down this end, Mrs Packham, if there's any left," called Jessie's mother, Mrs Webb.

"There's some here," someone called from the other end of the table, "I'll bring it up."

Dick and Elsie were standing together, surveying the scene. Tea was finishing, and the children were beginning to show restless signs, "Give us a tune on the joanna now, love," whispered Dick.

Elsie climbed into the van and started to play just as the first drop of rain fell. "It won't be much," a confident voice was heard to say.

There was a scramble and shouting to get out of the pouring rain. The older children steered their siblings home as quickly as they could. Everyone else grabbed what they could carry and scattered in all directions out of the rain to their homes. Dick grabbed Joyce, and they climbed into the van with Elsie.

The street was empty except for a few pieces of crockery that lay abandoned on the tablecloths, which were now soaking wet and clinging to the legs of the tables. Chairs stood randomly where they had been vacated; soggy paper hats lay in the road, and the bunting hung heavy from the lampposts underneath a dark sky. The only cheerful sounds came from inside the van. Dick turned an orange box on its side. He sat down, making himself comfortable.

"This is all right, love," he said, rubbing his hands together. Elsie moved to make room for her young daughter to perch on the edge of her stool. Dick put his arm around his wife's waist, "So what shall we sing then? No use sitting here doing nothing, eh?" he said, glancing round to Joyce.

"Won't hear much with that lot coming down on the roof!" Elsie replied.

"Go on, mum, play Nick's song 'Molly Malone,'" Joyce persuaded, and her sweet little voice began to sing: "Alive, alive, O, O."

All three joined in, making a cheerful sound echoing into the drenched empty street.

The early evening was damp, but the sky was bright when the neighbours spilled into the street again. Wet tablecloths and crockery were soon cleared away to begin all over again. Around a table sat some of the men with their fags and a couple of jugs of beer and pint glasses brought out of the Nag's Head in Orford Road; others joined hands to jig and clap to the hokey-cokey. Once the team games, fancy dress parade, and prize giving were over, Elsie resumed playing the piano. Cissie put her hands on her friend's waist, and they started the Conga. Others joined as they threaded their way carelessly high-kicking around the tables. It began to rain again, but nobody cared as they wobbled their way down the street like centipedes, aprons waving in the breeze and girls giggling. Grizzling and quarrelsome children signalled bedtime, and gradually, they dispersed to their various homes with their parents. Nick, Kenny and the young people stayed late in the warm, damp night, flirting and joking together until a window opened, and a voice echoed into the still night, "Ain't you got 'omes to go to? Some of us needs to sleep and get up for work tomorra."

Chapter 5

When Nick left school in the summer of 1937, he was tall and lean. His once fair hair now turned chestnut brown, was parted at the side and plastered down with Brylcreem, and his brown eyes still shone with mischief.

Schoolwork for Nick had not come easy. He reached a reasonable grade in mathematics, but he struggled with English. He failed miserably at spelling and could never get the words in the right order! However, now, just three months before his fifteenth birthday, he needed to find a job. It wasn't long before he found work as a delivery boy at a local butcher's shop. For a few months, he delivered meat to all the big houses six days a week before hearing about a job in the City of London close to where Kenny worked.

Kenny, who had passed his eleven-plus exam and had gone to the local Grammar school, had been working in the City of London since he left school. He encouraged Nick to try for a job as a clerk that was advertised at *'The Religious Tract Society of London'*.

"It's in Queen Victoria Street, Nick and we could travel together," Kenny told his friend.

Dressed in his best shirt and tie, Nick went to the interview. Later in the day, he saw Kenny, "I got the job, Kenny, thanks! And it's fifteen bob a week, great, eh?" Nick said, giving him an elbow dig.

The day began early for the two friends. They travelled by train from Walthamstow Station to Liverpool Street and then went by underground to Bank Station. Together, they walked to

Mansion House, where they separated, each to walk to their place of work.

"See you at lunchtime, Nick?" called Kenny as he turned into Cannon Street.

"Okay, where?"

"Meet you here on the corner of Mansion House at twelve," said Kenny, and he set off quickly, leaving Nick to finish his journey.

Nick's first introduction to another employee was not the warmest. After the initial introduction to the work that Nick was assigned to, the belligerent clerk haughtily demanded that Nick should refer to him as Mister Thomas, adding with a flick of his hand, "So start sorting through all this correspondence before you break for lunch."

Nick shrugged his shoulders and glanced at the pile of letters. With a quizzical expression, the clerk bent his head to look into Nick's eyes, "yes, Mr Thomas!" he snapped.

Nick repeated the requested words and began sorting the mail.

Nick and Kenny met every day for lunch to eat their sandwiches on a bench in St. Paul's churchyard if it was fine. Woolworths was an excellent place to spend their lunchtime and to keep warm and dry in inclement weather.

"Interesting, some of those gravestones," said Nick as he strolled around the churchyard. "One of them has got the names of a whole family, and they died within a few weeks of each other. Wonder what happened there?" he said, finishing the last bite of his sandwich.

"Probably had a disease like typhoid or something," said Kenny, getting up to have a look. He turned to pick up his bag and said, "Anyway, best get back! See you later."

Summoned to the manager's office one day, Nick was asked why he was doing all the mail.

"Mr Thomas told me to," the lad replied.

"Mister Thomas?" enquired the manager.

"Mr Thomas, sir," Nick repeated nervously.

"Since when has he been called mister?" retorted the manager.

"Since I came sir."

"Well, you can stop calling him Mister Thomas; he's just Thomas, and he is to share the mail sorting with you in future."

Nick left the office and returned to his job.

"So what did he want then," enquired a scornful Thomas.

"He told me to call you Thomas, and you are to help with the mail," Nick boldly replied. Gloating, he pushed half the pile of envelopes across the desk.

Later that day, Nick opened the door of his home, blurting out, "I 'ate that bloke I work with!" He threw off his coat and, pulling out a chair, slumped into it with a sigh.

'It don't get any better then, Son?' his dad questioned, looking up over the top of his newspaper. "Well, he did kind of get his comeuppance today,"

"Oh? Howsat?"

Nick took a sip of his mother's tea on the table and recounted what had happened.

"Good!" spat Elsie from the kitchen, adding, "Well, I've got a nice dinner of corned beef hash ready for you!"

"As if that's going to make everything better, Mother!" murmured Dick putting his paper aside and joining the two at the dinner table.

A few weeks passed when Kenny suggested they cycle to work. "It'll save us the train fare!"

"I suppose, but it's ten miles," Nick said reluctantly. "No, it 'aint. It's eight, maybe nine miles," retorted Kenny.

Nick got tired of the journey after a few short weeks of cycling to the city every day. The atmosphere with Thomas failed to improve, so when he saw a job at the local Co-op, he applied for it. Nick soon settled into the job, learning the trade of a butcher. He was pleased to tell Kenny his earnings had gone up by two bob!

Spring 1939 (16 years)

For ten years after the end of the First World War, Britain struggled to get back to some kind of normality before the Great Depression in 1929, which brought it to its knees again and caused massive unemployment and poverty that continued for another ten years. In 1939, the country was again facing the threat of a major war.

The British government had been arguing for nearly five years about the question of disarmament, and now, with this new threat, politicians were still in conflict about re-armament. Some were sure that it was a necessary evil for the future safety of the country against Hitler's rising power in Germany.

In September 1938, the German Fuhrer's threat to take the German-speaking part of Czechoslovakia, Sudetenland, by force was deterred by Britain and France. Determined to avoid war at all costs, negotiations were held between Germany, Britain, France, and Italy when the British government made a Policy of Appeasement, allowing Hitler to invade and take Sudetenland. The Czechoslovakian leaders were not included in the negotiations and later cried out that they were abandoned.

"Peace for our time," said the Prime Minister outside Number Ten Downing Street, waving a document signed by Herr Hitler. That same year, in November, soon after the Policy of Appeasement was made, the horrors of Kristallnacht finally convinced politicians that Hitler was a formidable opponent.

The world learned that on that night, violence had broken out against the Jews in Germany when two hundred and fifty synagogues were torched; thousands of Jewish businesses all over Germany were trashed and looted, along with the burning and looting of hospitals, schools and homes and the defiling of Jewish cemeteries. Worse still, thirty thousand Jews were imprisoned, and ninety-one Jews were brutally killed while the authorities, the police and fire brigades stood by and let it happen.

One Sunday afternoon in the Spring of 1939, the family were gathered in the living room at Dick's brother's home; Nick listened to the conversation.

"That appeasement policy that Chamberlain made with Herr Hitler is rubbish." said his Father.

"I agree," said his brother Bill. "We've given him the Sudetenland and that without firing a shot! Betrayal, that's what I call it, Betrayal! What was it the man said?' Bill frowned thoughtfully. 'Somat about an agreement with Hitler promising not to invade Britain, 'Peace for our time?'" He sneered, "I don't believe it!"

"Yeh, and now I see 'e wants to take Poland," retorted Dick. Frustrated, he whipped over to the next page of his newspaper.

Bill tapped a cigarette out of the Woodbine packet and placed it in the corner of his mouth. He struck a match and lit it. Taking a drag and shaking the match, he said: "Have you sorted out the air-raid shelter yet, Dick?"

"Not finished yet," said Dick glancing up from his paper.

"We've just got to get the bunk beds in, haven't we, Dad?" said Nick,

"Yeh, well," he said, raising his eyebrows, "We'd have had that done if you'd been around to help yesterday instead of gallivanting uptown spending yer money on a new hat and coat. Look at you! Who do yer think you are, George Raft?"

Bill sniggered; he took another drag from his cigarette and blew out the smoke with satisfaction. "They're calling for conscription now," he said, glancing at the end of his cigarette.

Elsie sighed and pursed her lips angrily, "Oh, for goodness sake haven't you got anything else to talk about, you two? Stop talking about war, and don't you dare start talking about conscription Dick Clayton," she said tearfully, "It's worrying enough as it is, and anyway it may never happen. Me nerves won't take it, so shut up about war!"

"Come on, Elsie, don't let on so," said Bill's wife, Ada. Wrapping an arm around her sister-in-law's shoulder, she added, "I know how you feel pet, but keep your chin up. Would you like another cuppa?"

"Well, it's frightening! All that talk about evacuating the kids out of London, too". Elsie fretted as she went into the kitchen with Ada. "I aint sending Joyce, and that's that! Dick don't want her to go neither." She added. "If we're gonna go, we'll all go together!"

Chapter 6
Another War

At eleven o'clock on a warm September day, the sun shone into the comfortable little room in the cottage. Newspapers littered the red velour cloth on the table that filled the centre of the room. Empty tea cups lay abandoned next to a pretty teapot and matching milk jug and sugar bowl. Nick sat at the table, waiting patiently by the wireless to hear the Prime Minister's speech. In one corner of the room next to the window, Dick sat in his high-backed wooden armchair. Breaking the almost reverent silence, the resounding chimes of Big Ben struck eleven o'clock, penetrating the walnut wireless set. Dick lay down his newspaper to listen to the distinctive, refined voice of the Prime Minister. Elsie entered from the scullery, wiping her hands on her apron. She perched anxiously on the edge of a chair to listen to the last sentence of the speech, '.......for it is evil things that we shall be fighting against - brute force, bad faith, injustice, oppression and persecution - and against them I am certain that right will prevail.' Neville Chamberlain's message to the nation confirmed that a state of war existed between Britain and Germany.

"Turn it off, Dick, I've heard enough!" said Elsie.

Dick turned off the wireless. The tick of the clock on the mantelpiece was deafening in the silence that followed. The family sat together, trying to make sense of what they had just heard. Nick looked from his father to his mother. There was an atmosphere that he had never felt before, one he didn't quite understand. His parents had always been in control, but now he saw them helpless, so helpless that it unnerved him.

Elsie's voice broke the silence, "I just 'ope it will be over before they get a chance to call you up, Son," she said. She got up and began busily clearing the table. Her voice trembled, "I couldn't bear it if you went to war, not after what happened to those poor young men in the last one."

"Don't fret, Mother." interjected Dick, "It'll be over by Christmas."

Nick wished he felt convinced by his father's last comment. The mood changed as the kitchen latch clicked open, and Joyce entered brightly with her friend Margaret.

"What?" enquired Joyce, sensing the tension.

"Nothing, dear," said her mother. "I, um, I was just on my way round to see your mother, Margaret, so I'll see you later. I'll be back soon, Dick, to get the dinner on."

Picking up her bag, she headed for the door. She turned to go, then stopped. "O, just a minute, Nick, run down to Sainsbury's and get me half a pound of butter, will you?"

Opening her purse, she took out a few coins, which she placed on the tablecloth. Nick left soon after his mother. He wandered down the short length of the front garden where his dad's beloved dahlias grew. He hadn't really noticed them before; he studied them briefly as he passed through the gate. He paused to look down the row of cottages that faced him. No one was around, so he turned left, down the narrow Church Path towards Hoe Street and Sainsbury. He waited absentmindedly while the shop assistant patted the butter into shape with wooden butter paddles. He counted out eleven pennies and placed the money in her hand; taking the brown paper package, he slipped past the queue and out of the door.

In the weeks that followed, three boys from the cottages in Church Path, Kenny's Brother Joe Packham, Bobby Marsdon and Danny Smith, were called up. Children as young as two years old were sent off to the country's safety.

Half the town turned out to watch the crowd of local children carrying cardboard boxes strung over their shoulders and around their necks, walking with their parents in a long line down Church Hill Road. Crossing Hoe Street, they arrived at the Station. Some carried a favourite toy, others seemed confused and worried about what was happening, and others seemed to be enjoying the adventure.

Elsie walked down St Mary Street alongside Mrs Webb and her small children, "You've still got time to change your mind, love," she said.

Anxiously squeezing the hands of her children, Sam and Peter Mrs Webb replied, "I don't know what to do. I wish I had your confidence that we won't be bombed 'ere." Turning to Jessie, her 14-year-old daughter, she said, "I'm glad you're not going, but I wish you were 'cause you could look after them."

"I wish I were going too, but you know I can't!"

"I know you've got your job now."

"Mum, they'll be fine. Stop worrying." Elsie and Jessie stood by Mrs Webb as the great steam train roared its way out of the station with her children on board, drowning out the muted sobs of the parents who disconsolately waved the train out of sight. Walking with the crowd of other parents and grandparents, the two mothers finally left the station. Elsie felt helpless, but putting a sympathetic arm around her friend's shoulder, she managed to draw some consolation at the thought that the two refugee youngsters would enjoy a holiday in Cornwall and the hope that the war would end by Christmas.

Apart from the sudden reduction of children playing in Church Path and those lads conscripted into the forces, nothing much changed in Walthamstow. The imminent expectation of bombing and fighting didn't happen, so people were calling it a Phoney War. The only indication that the war had begun was news of sea battles that dominated the headlines. Soon after the announcement of war with Germany, Britain and France agreed to block valuable shipping supplies of metals, minerals, food and textiles in an attempt to stop Germany's progress. Germany replied with a counter-blockade that began the 'Battle of the Atlantic'. The British liner Athena was sunk within hours of the blockade. Dick scoured the paper daily for news of local lads on board the ships at sea.

"I see Jerry is facing France over their concrete wall," muttered Dick one morning from behind his newspaper.

Elsie rolled her eyes in despair and handed him a cup of tea from across the table, "Is there any good news?" she asked cynically.

Unaware of Elsie's comment, Dick reached for the cup, "Thanks love," he said. He took a sip of the tea, placed the cup on the table, and resumed reading. "It's just a matter of time before one of 'em takes a pot-shot!" he added.

Ignoring Dick's remark, Elsie carried on fixing the top button of her daughter's coat. "You going to the match, Nick?" she asked, opening the door for her daughter. She pulled her cardigan tightly around her body as she watched Joyce wander up the Path. "Cold morning," she called to her neighbour and quickly returned indoors.

"Yep," replied Nick in answer to his mother's question. More interested in his father's conversation, he added, "What do you mean, Dad, what concrete walls?"

"Well," replied Dick. He closed his newspaper and drank from his cup. "Have you heard of the Maginot Line?"

"No."

Making an imaginary line on the table with his finger, Dick went on, "After the last war and to stop Germany invading France again, the French built this great long concrete defensive line between it and Germany to stop another invasion from Jerry. Right?' Dick paused.

Nick nodded for him to continue.

Dick went on to explain the meaning of the Maginot Line.

After the First World War, France built a huge wall, a defence against any other war with Germany. They named it the Maginot Line after the French minister of war at the time. It was a line of concrete fortifications, obstacles and weapon installations to prevent enemy invasion from Germany. At the time, the wall was considered an engineering military genius. It included air conditioning, mess rooms and comfortable sleeping quarters for the army. An underground railway gained access to other areas of the wall and could be used as a backup. However, the southern part of the wall was built stronger than the north, based on the understanding that the south of France was the most vulnerable to attack. At about the same time, Germany decided to build their wall - the Siegfried Line, which ran parallel to the Maginot. It was a system of pill boxes and strongholds, bunkers, tunnels and tank traps that stretched the length of the German Western Front.

The conversation between father and son continued; various items of crocks and condiment pots were placed strategically around the table where Dick tried to explain the two defence walls.

"But," added Dick, "there is a weakness in the northern part of the French wall where the German army could get to France through Belgium,"

"Don't suppose that would be difficult," said Nick, turning up his collar. "See you later!" The door closed behind him.

"Heaven help us if they do!" said Dick to himself. He folded his paper, pushed his chair back and said, "Better be off too, Love." He kissed his wife on the cheek and left the house.

Nick stepped out into the chilly November air and walked the short distance to Kenny's home. He knocked, opened the door and entered the scullery. "Morning, Mrs P," he called.

"Morning, Nick," replied Mrs Packham. She wiped her hands on her apron and called up the stairs, "Nick's here, Kenneth." With a jerk of her head, she added, "Go on up, Nick. I think he's decent!" Nick ran up the stairs two at a time. "Who're they playing today then?" Mrs Packham called after him.

Nick turned at the top of the stairs, "Blackburn Rovers."

"Ooh!" remarked Mrs Packham, "That's gonna be a tough game,"

"Spurs'll thrash 'em!" Jeered Nick.

On their way to White Hart Lane, the boys passed the local hall. They noticed a poster advertising a tribunal amongst the morale-boosting posters that clung to the brick wall of the building. The main door was wide open. Curious, they slipped into the back of the hall to listen.

Drawing his head close to Kenny, Nick whispered, "Hey, there's old Mother Mellor sitting up there."

"What's going on then?" enquired his friend. With his mouth open and straining to comprehend, Nick replied, "I dunno. Somat about er …..um,"

"Sh! Listen!" interjected Kenny. Glancing at Nick, he hissed, "That's Gordon Fuller standing over there from Wood Street; they're talking about him."

Nick strained his neck to see between the heads in front of him and nodded to Kenny in agreement. "He's….he's... not gonna join - I think!" said Nick, glancing again at Kenny. "Somat about a farm…….Yeh! I think they're going to send him to a farm."

"He's a conscie!" Kenny hissed. Nick screwed up his face, "Whassat?" "A conscie - conscientious objector, you know!"

"O, he don't want to be a soldier and fight!"

There were twenty-five thousand conscientious objectors during the Second World War, mostly protesting based on their religious beliefs. Some were put to farm labouring while others did military service in non-combatant roles, such as the medics in the Army who didn't carry guns. There were also those who objected to serving in the military and were deployed to serve in the Home Guard or the fire-fighting service. Some worked in mental hospitals or were sent to conservation areas to work on projects in rural areas. There were six thousand who refused any employment for the war effort and were jailed.

The tribunal ended, and Mrs Mellor came down between the chairs. She caught sight of the boys as they shuffled with the crowd out of the building. "Huh, what are you two nosing around here for? Seen enough?" she snapped. "Go on, run 'ome and tell yer mothers will yer," she added brusquely.

"Course we will," said Nick under his breath as they stepped out into the street. With a mischievous grin, he pointed to the bill post, "Keep calm and carry on missus," he sang to Mrs Mellor. Leaving her glaring, Nick and his mate swaggered carelessly off to the football match.

Nick continued working at the Co-op. Christmas was the busiest time when the boys stayed up until two in the morning, plucking turkeys and preparing T-bone steaks. They slept on the premises and awoke early at dawn on Christmas Day to deliver the meat in large carriers on the front of bicycles.

The highlight of Nick's year had been an invitation to join Essex Colts Cricket Club. Dick was the proudest dad in the world when Nick arrived home with the news that he was given the invitation. He began training with the Colts in the spring of 1939 and, for the rest of the season, went on to play a few winning matches proudly watched by his father. Earlier in the year, Nick had signed up to play goalkeeper for Walthamstow Avenue Amateur Football Club reserves. Dick had always encouraged his son's interest in sports. Unable to afford a pair of football boots when the boy was younger, he nailed strips of wood on the soles of a pair of old shoes. When he was twelve, Nick's Uncle Sid gave him his first proper pair of football boots.

They came from Sid's employer and were a size too large, but he wore them with pride at every match.

Cricket was Nick's greatest love, and playing in goal for Walthamstow Avenue Football Club in the winter months added to the young man's joy in sports. Dick was there on the terraces at every match, watching and cheering along with other spectators. Sadly, the 1939/40 football season ended after only a few matches when the government agreed that for the sake of public safety, all sports where crowds gathered should be cancelled.

Nothing, however, was going to interrupt Nick's social life! Interested as ever, he met up at Whipps Cross Lido or the Hollow Pond with the girls and boys from work or canoodled with a girlfriend in the double seats at the cinema. Trips to 'Walthamstow Dogs' with his dad added occasional highlights to his social calendar of events, along with the popular 'pie and mash' with Kenny at 'Menzies' in High Street.

At the age of sixteen, Nick considered himself to be a young man. He decided that he was past taking baths in the old tin bath that hung on the six-inch nail on the outside wall of the house when not in use. He had taken a bath in the tub in the kitchen for as long as he could remember. Friday evenings were spent heating water so each family member could take a bath. The water never changed; it was only topped up with hotter water as each one took its turn.

Wiping the water from his face after a swim in the local indoor pool with Kenny and Ginger Webb, Nick asked, "What do you know about the slipper baths next door, Ging? Do You have to wear slippers?"

"No! I heard they're called 'slipper baths' because they're shaped like slippers." "What d'you mean," said Nick poking the towel in his ear.

"I dunno. I think they have a bit that comes up the back that looks like the back of your slipper." Ginger Webb sat down to put on his socks, "So why do you want to know? Are you thinking of going?"

"I might," said Nick, "What about you, Kenny?" he added.

Kenny screwed up his face and shrugged, "I dunno," he said.

The first bath and washhouses were established for public use in 1828. By 1842 they had developed from salt water to warm fresh-water. They combined aspects of public bathing and self-service laundry facilities.

In due course, Nick informed his mother that in future he would not be taking a bath in the kitchen on Friday. "Me and Ging are going to the slipper bath on Saturday."

"That's nice! Save me a bit of work, but it'll cost you money," she said. "Dad won't be interested in such luxury. He's happy to take a bath in the tub as always."

"I might!" muttered Dick from behind his newspaper, "Let us know how you get on, son."

"Hmph," grunted Elsie, "wonder what the next newfangled idea will be."

The two friends walked to High Street, where the indoor pool and slipper bath were situated. They joined the short queue where various people, including two women carrying bundles of clothing, stood waiting in the street. Shuffling nervously, they wondered what had happened once you went inside. Nick spotted another old school friend in the queue, "Hey Cliffy," he called past the others waiting in the queue, "what do we do when we get inside?"

"This your first time then?"

"Yeh! Me and Ging thought we would try it,"

"They gives yer a towel and soap and shows yer to a bath."

"Is it private then?" asked Ging, frowning.

"'Course it is! There's separate cubicles and locks on the doors."

"And don't forget to ask for more hot water if you need it," interjected a friendly voice. Nick nudged Ging with his elbow and said, "Cor, this is gonna be good,"

The two friends paid their fourpence and were given a small piece of soap and an equally small thin towel. Conversations, off-key singing and splashing resounded behind various doors as they followed the attendant along the dimly lit, blue-tiled corridor that smelled carbolic.

"That's yours," said the middle-aged attendant, "And that one along there is yours," he said to Ginger, pointing along the corridor where a door stood open. "Make sure you clean it after you've finished. There's some cleaning powder on the floor! " he added, his voice disappearing down the corridor.

Nick soaked in the hot bath for as long as he could, observing the tiled surroundings. His eyes followed the line of the pipes from the ceiling to the curious contraption at the end of the bath. He could hear indistinct conversations between two men and the occasional call from the attendant telling a customer time was up. Before long, his turn came, and he lifted himself out of the bath. He stood on the duckboard, towelling himself dry, watching the bath water empty, circling lustily, the last dregs of the grimy water sucked into the plug hole. Once dressed, he looked at the cleaning powder on the floor, wondering what to do with it! He shook it into the bath, wiped it around and left it.

"I guess that was the grittiness I felt at the bottom of the bath," he complained to Ging later.

"Blimey, it was a bit hot; I came out looking like a boiled lobster!" said his friend.

"You gonna do it again then?" enquired Nick, wrapping one arm around his mate's shoulder.

"Yeh" replied Ginger. The lads crossed the road and sauntered home feeling very pleased with themselves.

Chapter 7
Christmas 1939

Family members were silent as they sat around the dinner table, listening intently to the King's Christmas speech. Stripped of meat, the turkey carcass lay bare in the centre of the dining table; cutlery littered the gravy-stained plates nestled between screwed-up serviettes. The sombre, slow and careful speech delivered by King George VI offered a message of reassurance to the people. Someone turned the radio off, and raising his beer glass, Uncle Charlie repeated the last sentence of the King's speech: "May the Almighty Hand uphold us all." Chairs scraped the floor as the family stood up, and glasses clinked together, "The King," they said in chorus.

Christmas Day 1915

"I was adrift on a raft in the Atlantic Ocean," Dick's voice cut into the sombre mood.

"O no, not that one again!" remarked his wife. A ripple of laughter followed.

"Go on, tell us again, Dick, just to annoy Elsie," chuckled Bill.

"Me ship had sunk in the Irish Sea," continued Dick.

"What, the Engadine?" interrupted Charlie.

"No, she was a nice little ship," he said thoughtfully, "I was on her at Jutland in 1916 and later in the Med. No, this time, I can't remember the ship I was on," Dick added thoughtfully, "It'll come to me later!" Dick paused, "Hm, yeh," he went on, "I managed to get on this raft with an officer. It was bloody cold, and he was in a bit of a state, so I started singing Roll out the Barrel, but 'e didn't appreciate it and told me to shut up!"

"I woulda done an' all!" remarked Charlie, adding, "An' what about the time you had that dead man's leg in yer 'ands?"

"O yeh! He was blown to bits, and I was curious as to how the leg joint moved, so I picked up what was left of it and bent it to see," said Dick making a movement with his hands to demonstrate.

"O shuddup," came Elsie's angry voice, "You've got a morbid sense of humour Dick Clayton."

"She's off again," said Charlie, laughing. "What was it that attracted you to him then, Elsie?" asked Sid,

"Huh you may well ask," Elsie retorted. Then she gave a wicked smile, "The deep dimple in his chin," she chuckled.

The rest of Christmas Day continued with the old songs, sketches and cards routine until dawn.

Severe weather hit Britain in the New Year. All activities that involved a crowd gathering, including football and rugby matches, were cancelled, adding to the already miserable prospect of 1940. The rationing of basic foodstuffs began in January. The ongoing Battle of the Atlantic and the depressing news of Hitler's plans to invade Denmark and Norway gave no relief to the prospect of hope for the country.

Nick wrapped his coat tightly around him and turned his collar up around his woollen balaclava. Bending his head against the biting cold wind that stung like knives in his face, he walked the short distance through the cleared area of snow to Mrs Green's home. He knocked before opening the door, closing it quickly behind him, "Hello, Mrs Green, is Margaret ready?" he called.

"Almost," came the reply, "Get her indoors quickly, Nick, it's so cold," said Mrs Green, handing a small parcel to her daughter. With a protective arm around the girl Nick walked her back to his own home. Joyce met them at the door with a large white ribbon in her hair and dressed in a pretty frock and a soft white Angora bolero, clapped her hands with delight.

"For goodness sake, let them in, out of the cold, Joyce, and shut the door!" Elsie said with an exaggerated shiver.

They were greeted by a low, warm fire flickering in the grate. The large square table dominated the centre of the room, and small bowls of jelly and blancmange and a decorated birthday cake were arranged on a pretty tablecloth.

Joyce celebrated her ninth birthday on one of the coldest days in living memory. Heavy snow had fallen, and during the days that followed, eight miles of the River Thames froze over. People were skating on the Serpentine, where ice formed six inches deep. Snow and ice storms lasting up to forty-eight hours caused damage to telegraph wires, and roads became impassable. The severe weather did not abate until the middle of February. There was very little work for Dick and very little money to go around.

Later in the month, Elsie prepared a frugal meal of parsnip soup and dumplings. Adding a slice of bread for each family member, she sniffed, "That's all I could get," she said.

"The weather'll break soon, Love. It can't go on forever," said Dick to his wife, "Don't forget next week I'm going next door with Arthur Webb to help clear out some rubbish and break up some of the old furniture that's been lying about in Vestry House Museum, that'll give us a bit of money."

"Perhaps we can 'ave some of it for the fire," muttered Elsie.

Vestry House Museum was situated at the east end of Church Path in Vestry Road. It was built in 1730 as a Workhouse. Thankfully, it was no longer in use as such; it had since been a Police Station and a private home, and in 1931, because of its history, it opened as a museum for the local people. There was still a lot of rubbish that had been stored in the hope it could be used at some stage. Now ten years after the museum opened, a decision was made to remove the rubbish, and Dick was given some work.

....

The long cold winter passed as Dick predicted, and Blossom was about to burst on the tree outside the pub where three brothers, Dick, Charlie and Sid, sat together on a bench in the corner of the Nag's Head.

"Morning, Jack," called out Dick, signalling for his friend to join them.

"Can't stay long," puffed Jack,

"What do you want to drink?" asked Dick getting up from the bench.

"Only allowed 'alf an hour, so I'll have 'alf a brown ale with you," Jack replied.

"Right, mate!" said Dick.

Jack pulled out a seat and, dipping into his pocket, drew out a packet of tobacco and a pipe. Laying them both on the table, he sat down and said, "The missus has gone over to her sister. She's sick with worry about her son. He's landed with his troops somewhere in Norway."

"Tough! Sorry to hear that." murmured Dick returning with the glass of ale.

"I read yesterday that Jerry bombed Norway," commented Sid.

"Yeh well. It's enough to worry any mother." Jack replied.

"I hear Jimmy Webb's been called up and another of the Marsdon brothers," added Sid.

"Now there's a woman who should be worried, Mrs Marsdon; her son's 'avin' a tough time at sea," said Charlie from behind his newspaper, "It says here that Denmark's surrendered and another destroyer's gone down - the 'Gurkha, yesterday, off the coast of Stavanger."

"That's in Norway, isn't it?" enquired Sid.

"Bloody 'ell!" exclaimed Charlie. He closed his newspaper and took a swig from his beer glass. Swallowing hard, he added, "How many ships is that now?"

"Gawd knows," said Dick. "There was about three 'undred gone at the end of last year, I think."

"You're right, Dick," said Charlie thoughtfully.

Nothing was said for a while, then Dick spoke, "Elsie's talking about taking Joyce and going down to Chichester for a few weeks with her sister. They 'ave a brother lives there,"

"Sounds like a safe option," said Charlie.

"Right," said Jack, sucking back the last dregs of his beer, "Gotta go," he added, wiping his mouth on the back of his hand.

"You got a nice roast dinner to go to then?" chuckled Sid.

"Not bloomin' likely!' retorted Jack, heading for the door. "Be lucky if we get anything. The missus gave half of the ration coupons to the young'un to feed the kids!" Jack closed the door behind him.

A week later, Elsie packed a suitcase with enough clothes for Joyce and her to last for a few weeks.

"Now, Love," said Dick firmly to his wife. If this don't work out, you will come 'ome, won't yer?"

"This 'as got to be the better of the two evils. Either we stay and get bombed and killed, or I take a chance with me sister, and one of us kills the other!"

"I'll miss yer both; look after yourselves. You know how difficult Winnie can be, and mind you, Joyce doesn't get into any trouble with that son of hers!"

"Well, don't go on so Dick, I can't stay 'ere, and that's that!" spat Elsie.

Elsie met her sister at the station, and they travelled to Chichester safely.

Chapter 8
Evacuation from Dunkirk
27th May - 4th June 1940

Gathered outside Walthamstow Station, a crowd of people waited. Nick and his friends stood together, listening to the conversations between them.

"Jack told me that over three hundred thousand were rescued so far," murmured one woman.

"Thank God, Frank's safe and on his way home!" said another.

"Yeh well, we've said it all before. Mr. and Mrs. Jones are blimmin' lucky," said Mrs. Marsdon, "not like poor Mr. and Mrs. Cohan not sure where Eli is or if 'e's alive or dead."

"Nor young Danny Smith," said another, "His parents must be devastated."

"Ow shuddup," hissed Elsie under her breath.

Frank Jones was a regular in the army when war broke out. He was in one of the regiments that formed the British Expeditionary Force and was sent to France to assist the French and Belgian armies against a German invasion. Still, the German army, ignoring the Maginot Line, advanced to Northern Germany and invaded the Netherlands. They broke through the Ardennes, ploughing through the French and Belgian armies in their advance to the coast in an attempt to capture the ports and trap the British and French armies before they could evacuate to Britain. Trapped on the beaches of Dunkirk, the British soldiers needed rescuing. A call from the government for as many ships and boats of any size or shape to cross the Channel to lift the stranded soldiers off Dunkirk Beach inspired an extraordinary response. The British Admiralty sent out cruisers, destroyers and various other craft. Hundreds more sailors from the coast of Scotland down to Hastings and along the coast to Cornwall followed in speedboats and ferry boats. Included in the armada were three hundred and forty-five tug boats and smaller sailing crafts that went to the rescue of thousands from the clutches of their German enemy.

Children moved between the women's skirts on the station platform, laughing and teasing.

"Stop it, will you? If you can't stand still, you can go home." said a mother, grabbing her child by the arm.

The girls looked at each other and giggled quietly. Conversations continued between the crowd gathered on the station platform.

"Loads of little ships went out from the ports and rivers," said one man to another, "Brave, that's what I call it."

"Did you hear what Churchill said?"

"No, me wireless is on the blink!"

Overhearing the conversation, Dick said, "Here, read it."

He unfolded his newspaper and handed it to Mr Green, who read it aloud: 'We shall defend our Island whatever the cost may be. We shall fight on the beaches; we shall fight on the landing grounds; we shall fight in the fields and the streets; we shall fight in the hills. We shall never surrender.'

Mrs Green blew her nose, and Elsie put a comforting hand on her shoulder. "I'm glad you're back," she said to Elsie, "I missed you, and Margaret missed Joyce too,"

"Should've known better than to go and live with me, sister; we never did get on," said Elsie. Frowning with thoughts of the time she spent in Chichester, she added, "It was an awful house anyway. I swear I heard mice scuttling about the place. My sister made sure she had all the best things - the best bedroom, chair, and everything- and she was rude about my cooking, too! And as for that brat of a boy! 'E's downright spoiled an' 'e needs a good 'iding if you ask me!"

"You didn't stay with your brother then?"

"No, no, we rented a small cottage, and a month was enough, thank you very much! Anyway, we're 'ome now, and we'll just 'ave to take our chances altogether."

A sudden outburst jolted the women from their reverie: "'ere it comes, I can see it," yelled a young lad watching from the top of a wall.

Soon after the train steamed into the station, faces appeared one by one out of the carriage door windows, scouring the platform in anticipation. Above the noise, Frank yelled and waved when he saw his family. Hardly had the train drawn to a halt; the carriage doors flew open and mingled with the passengers. Half a dozen uniformed men jumped to the platform with their belongings. Family members milled about peering above and around heads searching, while others, seeing a familiar face, pushed through the locals and ran along the platform. Frank came into sight, his gaiter straps flapping over his boots. Approaching his family, his heavy great coat hung open, revealing a tin helmet strapped to his belt. He buried his head in his mother's neck, visibly exhausted. They held each other lost in the noise of the billowing steam exhaling from the train engine as if in sympathy for its recent passengers. It had been a long and hard few weeks for the young men returning from France.

June 1940

On one of the warmest days of the year, Ginger Webb was waiting for Nick at the end of Church Path. Nick pushed his rolled-up towel under his arm and jogged down the Path to join him. "Me mum's on the warpath," he said, "Me pillows covered in Brylcreem again!" Ginger slapped him on the back and said, "You're gonna have to wear her bath cap in bed," Nick chuckled and gave his mate a playful thump. They went on their way to walk the distance to the swimming baths in the High Street. Turning out of Folkstone Road and into Church Hill Road, the boys passed the Drill Hall. Nick stopped to look at the display of posters pasted on the wall advertising various ways to help the war effort, from *'Grow A Garden - Plant Today'* to *'Volunteers Wanted.'*

"What you doin' Nick?" Ginger asked. He followed Nick into the hall's entrance, which was heaving with young men waiting to join up. Ushers milled around, directing them to one or other of the six trestle tables where personnel waited to take their details. Groups of two or three strolled out of the building, scrutinising the information on the ticket handed to them. "What you doin' Nick?" Ginger repeated.

Nick had a look in his eye that spelt mischief, "I'm gonna join. You coming?"

Ginger balked, "We're not old enough," he said.

"Ow, old are you?" said a stern voice behind them.

"Seventeen!" said Nick indignantly,

"No you're……." Nick stopped Ginger with a stab of his elbow.

Inside the hall, the boys were separated and sent to different tables.

"How old are you?" asked the man behind the table.

"Seventeen," said Nick.

"Birth date?"

"Twenty-second of July nineteen twen'y two," Nick replied.

A medical examination proved he was in good health. "'Appy birthday,' said the medical officer as he handed the lad a train ticket to Norwich.

"We're off to Norwich then, Ging!" exclaimed Nick, clutching his train ticket. "Not me, I'm joining the East Surrey Regiment."

'What!' Exclaimed Nick, "Bloody hell, I thought we would stay together." "Dunno about staying together. Wait 'till I tell me, Dad!"

"Me too!"

Nick arrived home and ventured into the Kitchen, "You're back early," commented his dad from behind his newspaper.

"I'm off to Norwich," said Nick.

Dick lowered his newspaper and peered over the top, "What do you mean, you're off to Norwich?"

"I've joined up."

"You've what?" exclaimed his mum,

"I've joined the army, and I'm off to Norwich, 'ere's me train ticket!"

"You're going nowhere, my lad. You're underage," said Elsie firmly.

Nick shrugged.

"Dick, Dick don't just sit there, do something," she yelled.

"You're a bloody fool!" said Dick, but you've made yer bed, so you're gonna have to lie in it. Should've joined the Royal Navy like I did!" He shook out his newspaper and continued to read.

Elsie burst into tears and grew hysterical. "Dick, he can't go, I won't let him!" she cried.

Norwich

Baby-faced lads clutching small brown suitcases milled around Liverpool Street Station when Nick and his father arrived. "Gawd blimey," muttered Dick, "they don't look much older than twelve,"

"What did yer say Dad?" Nick asked, "Nothin' Lad!"

The train approached, steaming and hissing its arrival throughout the vast station. Standing with his dad and Joyce, Nick looked smart in grey flannel trousers and a blue sports coat. Laying a hand on Nick's shoulder, Dick said, "Good luck Son,"

"Thanks Dad."

Clinging to his hand, his ten-year-old sister looked up into his face, "I don't want you to go."

"I know," said Nick tenderly, "You look after Mum and Dad for me."

"He'll be home again soon." said Dick hoping to avert any tears that Joyce was holding back, "I still think you're a bloody fool. Make me proud of you," he whispered to Nick.

"I'll do my best Dad."

The two of them watched as Nick was fed through the carriage door along with the crowd of young men, suitcases and bags to begin the first leg of his journey bound for Great Yarmouth. "Don't forget to send them clothes home like your mother said," Dick called through the noise and confusion. Nick nodded and gestured with his thumb from the carriage door before disappearing into a compartment. Dick and Joyce watched the train burst into motion, labouring away from the station and along the line. They left the station with other parents and family members in a sombre mood.

....

Filled with young men, the train carriage soon buzzed with talk of the war and the excitement of joining up. Each one gave an encounter of how they came to be going to Norfolk.

Nick shared his story, "Me mum didn't 'alf let off. She's gonna write to my uncle to see if he can stop me."

"Is he important?" asked another lad.

"He's the Deputy Chief Constable in Chichester."

"I had no choice. I got called up," said another.

The subject changed quickly when an excited voice yelled, "Buffalo!"

The boys crammed to look out of the window.

"They ain't buffalo stupid; they're cows!" said another boy, falling carelessly back into his seat. Laughter rippled through the carriage.

"Never seen a cow before," said the embarrassed young man.

Carelessly, Nick began to hum a tune, "We're gonna hang out the washing on the Siegfried Line,"

"'ave you any dirty washing, mother dear?" joined the others. Soon, the carriage filled with voices gustily continuing:

'We're gonna hang out the washing on the Siegfried line 'cause the washing day is here. Whether the weather may be wet or fine, we'll just rub along without a care. We're going to hang out the washing on the Siegfried Line If the Siegfried Line's still there.'

As the train continued its journey, Nick soon became familiar with some of the young men he would be living with for the next couple of years. He learned that thick-set, dark-haired Wilf Grant from Clapham was married with a daughter. He had a maturity beyond his years that Nick warmed to. He was quiet and observant, while Alfie Fletcher from Dulwich was short and stocky with a round, red face that seemed ready for a laugh. Wearing a pin-striped suit, Jim Brown looked like a spiv! He was tall and thin, and his fair hair showed signs of thinning that belied his good looks and pale blue eyes. He smoked heavily and gave off an odour of nicotine. Baby-faced Bob Howe from Chingford is married and has three children. He seemed friendly and outgoing enough. If Nick had any doubts about joining up when he did, he now felt content and smug at his decision.

Nick arrived in Great Yarmouth with his new friends and was directed to the drill hall on York Road, where he was issued a tin plate, mug, and cutlery. Standing to attention with the other recruits, Nick is shown a large sack and a pile of straw.

"That there is your paillasse," yelled the sergeant. "Fill it with straw, and you will use it as your bed from now on!"

Bemused, Nick looked furtively around at the other lads, who immediately set to work filling the sacks. Nick followed suit. A few days later, they were issued uniforms. Nick screwed up his face, "Don't mind the boots and shirts, nor the rough trousers but cellular draws?" he said.

"What's that?" yelled a voice.

Nick looked up and flushed with embarrassment. "You got a problem with draws, boy?" bellowed the sergeant,

"No," Nick answered meekly.

"No sir!" barked the sergeant, "And stand to attention when you speak to me!"

Nick quickly straightened up, "No sir!" he shouted.

"Just as well," said the sergeant. With his face close to Nick's, he added, "cos you ain't got yer mother 'ere now to mollycoddle you!"

A month later, they were taken to more comfortable billets in a requisitioned holiday camp in Gorleston.

1940 July - September

The new recruits spent the next six weeks training hard, learning everything from basic cleaning boots and obeying orders instantly to bayonet fighting and round marches.

Early mornings, with no time to wake up slowly, came hard to Nick, "I can hear me mother waking me for me newspaper round all over again!" he grumbled.

Uniforms were donned correctly before entering a makeshift parade ground for drill practice.

"Qui-ick march," the Corporal Major bellowed. "Left, left, left right left, aboouut turn, sloooow march."

At the command, a cacophony of heavy boots on tarmac came noisily to a halt. "Nah then, you 'orrible lot, you're a disgrace to the army, and rigorous square-bashing will continue until you get it right!" His voice screeched to a crescendo as he finished.

The Norfolk climate and Army discipline came even harder for Nick. He hated the cold north-easterly wind that blew across from the Broads, even in mid-summer, as he charged with his bayonet again and again at stuffed sack images. His knuckles bled from hand-to-hand fighting, and blisters formed on his feet while he marched on the thirty-mile-long round. Hours were spent crawling on his belly through mud and barbed wire. If they were not out on a round march, they would have spent even longer hours on the square in the camp. Even so, with the discipline and round marches, Nick noticed how fit he was getting, adding to his already large ego.

Silently, the NCO strolled between the lines of soldiers. He stopped between two lines, his eyes darting up and down the line before resting on Nick. Tucking his chin into his chest, he confronted the lad, "Ello," he said, "What 'ave we 'ere?"

Uneasily, Nick stared ahead, "Dunno sir,"

"You don't know what that is in your hat?" he snapped.

"No sir, er yes sir!" Nick replied nervously.

"I'll show you what it is," said the NCO, and he flicked the beret off Nick's head with his baton. It fell to the ground. "Pick it up, lad," demanded Nick's superior. Inside the cap's peak was a broken piece of a toothbrush handle, "And what do you suppose this is for?" he asked.

Nick reddened, "To support the peak, sir," he answered.

"I'll show you what I think of your peak support," retorted the NCO, and he dropped it back on the ground. Lifting his foot, he promptly stamped hard on the beret, breaking the offending support.

No one saw the grimace on Nick's face as he bent to pick up the beret.

"Bad luck, mate," said Wilf Grant, "Guess a few of the others will be removing theirs now,"

Nick shrugged, "I'll stick another one in," he said defiantly, "Just make sure he don't find it again!"

The Recruit Company, as they were called, was split up. Nick and Wilf, Bob, Jim Brown, and Alfie Fletcher were posted to the 4th Battalion near Great Yarmouth. Guard duty was included in the ongoing training and round marches, which entailed manning six-inch guns situated at various points along the coast both night and day. To prevent an enemy invasion, mines and Dragon's Teeth were laid along with scaffolding. Roadblocks were manned, and traffic was stopped for identification purposes.

The night had been long and uneventful when Nick and Wilf finished their guard duty one night. It was pleasant enough. The only sounds in their lonely gun emplacement came from the beach below, where the waves rolled onto the sand, blending with their muted voices.

"Where are you from then?" Nick asked Wilf.

"I was born in Aldershot. My dad was in the army there, but when he was discharged, we moved back to me mum's home in Clapham. I've got two sisters," Wilf rummaged in his breast pocket, pulling out his wallet. He opened it and drew out a photo of his family to show the lads who murmured all the right sentiments. "And that's my wife and little girl," he said proudly, showing off another small, glossy, black-and-white photograph.

"What about you then?" He asked Nick.

"Me? Born in Walthamstow! Got a sister Joyce, she's ten years old. Not much else to tell yer."

"Have you got a girlfriend?"

"Had lots of girlfriends. I love 'em! But not going steady with one."

Their conversations carried in the air under the vastness of the Universe where the evening star shone brightly, and a crescent moon hung in the clear sky. A cool breeze gently stirred the gorse as the soldiers on duty watched and waited, at the ready for the arrival of enemy aircraft.

"It's a quiet night," murmured Nick.

"Just as well," said one of the ARP wardens,

"We don't want another lot like we've 'ad for the last couple of weeks,"

"Hmm," muttered Nick in agreement, "Yeh! The clearing up we 'ad to do was enough. And we saw some pretty gruesome sights an'all! Some dead!"

Earlier in the month, enemy planes had dropped bombs in the area, destroying a factory and nearby houses, killing ten people and injuring sixty-eight others. The recruits were ordered to help rescue those who may be buried under rubble, clear the debris, and make it safe. Arriving in the area, Nick and Wilf approached a woman clearly traumatised, standing in the rubble of her home holding a baby while her other children clung to her skirts. Between them, the lads did what they could to comfort the woman and her children.

"Dad's still in there!" exclaimed one of the children.

As the lads stood wondering what to do for the family, a woman, followed by a young girl, came rushing along the road.

She approached the woman and explained to Nick and Wilf that she was the woman's sister.

"We're family", she said.

Taking control of the situation, the woman who had just arrived joined the recruits to find the father. They found the father later, badly injured from a blow to the head and buried under rubble.

"Reckon, he's only just alive!" whispered Wilf. They carried the body into the street, where they left him with his family and the local services. It took another two days to clear the area and make it safe before returning to the gun emplacement.

Dawn broke, bringing with it another group of soldiers, releasing the lads from guard duty. Leaving the gun emplacement, Nick and his fellow soldiers walked to a clearing where two soldiers were waiting. "No canteen arrived yet, then?" said Wilf, removing his rifle and letting it drop gently to the ground.

"Nah, not yet," Alf said, coming out from under a canvas tent.

"It gets bloody cold standing around doing nothing and I'm starving," added Wilf.

"Just spotted it coming up the hill," called Nick from a distance.

"Where've you been?" asked Wilf.

Nick laughed, "Got caught short and had to stop for a pee, if you must know." he said.

"There wasn't a girl there, I suppose?" Alf asked.

"I wish!" Nick chuckled.

The canteen lorry ground to a halt, and then the boys enjoyed a welcome meal of sausages, fried bread, and baked beans, swallowed down with a hot cup of tea. The driver hung around while finishing a cigarette, then climbed back into the lorry, "Better be off then," he chirped. "Oh!" he said, throwing a newspaper to Nick, "you owe me a penny!" and climbing into the lorry, he banged the door and drove off, disappearing noisily back down the road in a cloud of dust.

In idle thought, Nick said, "Clapham don't 'ave a football team, do they, Wilf?"

"What are you on about now?" Alf added, "Football! 'aven't you got anything else to talk about?"

Nick ignored him, "What football team do you support then, Wilf?"

"Don't follow football," murmured his friend.

Nick got up from his seat and stamped the ground in an attempt to warm up. "I was playing for Walthamstow Boys before the war. Would've gone on to be a professional but for this bloody war!"

"Hm, Interesting," interjected Alf, "I was going to start an apprenticeship at the garage near where I live," he added. The boys continued in idle conversation for another half hour before returning to the gun emplacement

1940 Late September

'At ease,' yelled the sergeant.

The sound of the young men exhaling was audible. The day had been long and hard, and they were exhausted. "You lucky lot!" The sergeant drawled, "You have forty-eight hours leave. Spend it wisely. Be sure not to wear yourselves out because you will be back on parade at five a.m. on Monday for more rigorous training! Dismissed."

Nick lay on his bed in the Nissan hut that served as a barrack room, his hands behind his head. He mentally counted the lengths of thin metal tubing that hung down at intervals from the ceiling, at the end of which was a dirty white plastic lampshade over a dimly lit light bulb. Deep in thought, he recalled a letter he received from his mother the day before.

He pulled the letter out from under his pillow, opened the pages and began to read again:

Dear Nick

I hope you are okay. It's not good here; there's not much good news. We've been in the air-raid shelter every night for a week since the Germans started bombing London. Dad has made it as comfy as he can, and it's okay, but I could do with a night in my own bed. A house was demolished at the top of the High Street, thank God no one was killed, and another bomb but it didn't go off and the people were evacuated. My nerves are bad, and I hate the noise of the sirens and the bombing. Dad and Mr Green and Mr Cohen are in the Home Guard now, and Johnny Webb found a piece of shrapnel in Hoe Street. His mum let off at him for picking it up. Kenny gone and done the same as you and joined up; he's gone in the RAF. Broke his mum's heart; it did. You boys don't know how hard it is for us mothers. It's harder for her, with two boys already in the services. Thank you for the seven bob. I worry about you, as always. I hope you feel more settled and got used to the army life. Old Emm has had to go in a home, what with the bombing and all, she couldn't cope. Just as well, really it's nice to have the house for ourselves. Anyway, that's all for now. Don't forget to write soon.

Your loving mum x

The barrack room was quiet compared with the noisy canteen where Nick had eaten earlier. Some of the boys had already left to go into town. A few stayed playing a game of cards; Jim lay on his bed reading.

"Are you coming or not?" Bob asked.

Nick lifted his head off the pillow, "Yeh," he said, adding, "You got any money, Alfie?"

Alf's head appeared from inside his locker, "Enough!" he said, "Why?"

"I dunno! I could do with a bit more," said Nick. "I don't mind the army sending seven bob 'ome, but I can't think how they can charge us two bob a week for breakages we don't break!" He grumbled.

"I had a bloody sight more than five bob a week left over when I was working at the Co-op three months ago!"

Jim looked up from his book, "You've still got your civvy clothes," he said, "If you're hard up, there's a shop down the road who'll buy 'em off you,"

"Might do that," Nick said thoughtfully. He got up and glanced sideways at the piece of broken mirror on the wall.

"Come on, Clayton, stop admiring yourself and let's go, ya big girl!" said Alf.

Nick pushed a stray hair into place and walked over to the boys waiting at the door.

"They love me!" he said with a coy pose. "What's it gonna be then, the cinema?" he added, rubbing his hands together.

"I heard there was a dance at the local hall, so we could go there," suggested Alf.

"Use yer 'ead; that's not 'till seven," said Nick.

The young soldiers were driven as far as Great Yarmouth.

"So where's Gorleston from here?" Bob asked the driver. Pointing in the direction of the town, the driver said, "Three miles that way. It'll take you less than an hour to walk it!"

"Bloody hell!" declared Nick. "It's a bloody Route march!"

"Aw, stop moaning," said Wilf, "we've got all afternoon!"

....

The four lads headed off in the direction of Gorleston dance hall.

"Look at that!" cried Wilf, and a chorus of whistles from the boys echoed across the street to the delight of a group of giggling girls.

Arriving in the town, they passed the cinema, "Hey, there's a John Wayne film on," Nick said, trotting backward in front of his friends in an attempt to stop them, "My hero!" he whined.

"Too late, mate, it's already started!" Pushing him out of the way, they continued walking.

Ribbons of Union Jack bunting hung from the ceiling in the well-lit dance hall, and a few couples were dancing around the floor to the sound of a small band playing, '*Moonlight Serenade.*' Girls sat together on chairs placed against the walls, some in uniform, others in neat frocks and court shoes. Lads in both civies and uniforms leaned against the bar, holding drinks. Nick peered over the heads of his friends and glanced around the room.

Bob removed his hat, "There's not much happening here," he said. "Shall we stay or go?"

Nick had already caught the eye of a pretty girl sitting against the wall. "Stay!" He said dreamily, "I'm going over to her!"

"Who?" enquired Alf.

With a jerk of his head toward the girl, Nick said, "That girl in the blue dress, she looks very nice! The girl next to her don't look bad neither."

The boys watched as Nick took off across the floor in the direction of the girls, who fidgeted and giggled as he came closer. Boldly, he held out a hand to the girl in the blue dress. She looked him in the eye and confidently put her hand into his. He swept her towards him. Holding her in his arms, he looked over her shoulder and winked at the boys standing with their mouths open in astonishment.

"I'm Nick," he whispered, "I'm Moira,"

Nick's charm and charisma were far better than his dancing skills, and soon, leaving his friends behind, the two of them were seen walking out of the door and into the cool air of a September evening, "It's a nice evening isn't it?" said Moira quietly.

"Yeh!" replied Nick, "You don't look old enough to be allowed out to a dance alone at night," "I'm eighteen, I'll have you know. You don't look old enough to be in the army!"

'What are you talking about? I'm eighteen, too!' Nick lied, putting his arm around the girl's waist.

"Steady on," exclaimed Moira, removing Nick's arm, "I'm not that sort of girl!"

"Okay, let's take a walk." They spent the rest of the evening strolling along the promenade, chatting and joking.

Returning to the dance hall from their walk, Moira said, "You're funny. I like you."

"I like you," said Nick. Can I see you again?'

They arranged to meet again a week later.

The following weekend, Nick was getting ready to meet Moira when Alf blurted out, "There's a John Wayne film on this afternoon, Nick, we're going. Do you fancy it?"

"Bugger off, you know I've got a date you, sod," replied Nick, "Cancel it, she'll get over it!"

"Nope! Just for once, I'll forfeit J.W. for the arms of a beautiful maiden," he said, wrapping his arms about himself and circling the floor dreamily.

Nick arrived at their rendezvous just in time to see Moira approaching him from the opposite direction, "Watcha," said Nick casually. He removed his cap, releasing a lock of hair. He pushed it back before replacing his hat jauntily to the side of his head. "Hello," replied Moira sheepishly,

"That's good timing," said Nick, "What do you want to do?"

'Don't mind,' replied Moira, fiddling with her headscarf.

Bemused, Nick asked, "It's a nice day. Do want to go to the seafront - or we could go to the pictures,"

"Don't mind," Moira repeated, looking down at the ground.

"You okay?" asked Nick, bending his head to look into her face.

"Yeh, 'course I am. It's just a bit er, you know,"

"You ain't shy, are you?"

"No!" said Moira indignantly, pulling away from Nick's gaze, "Just - I don't know," She stammered. Summoning some energy, she added, "Oh come on let's go for a walk."

She smiled at Nick and started at a trot toward the seafront. As she ran, she took off her scarf, releasing a shock of dark curls caught up in a fashionable net at the nape of her neck the last time Nick saw her. He was astonished and ran to catch up with her. Grabbing her waist, he stopped her in her tracks,

"Okay, let go," she cried, "Keep your hands to yourself!"

Nick turned her around to face him, "You are shy!" he said, grasping her hand in his.

Moira giggled, "Just don't want you to think I'm easy, 'cause I'm not!"

The couple strolled playfully along the promenade, where families gathered in little groups, making the most of the last few warm days of the season. Children played beneath the danger signs, warning people not to go onto the beach where there was a conglomerate of barbed wire, tank traps, and other dangerous objects, which were visible reminders that a war was on.

Nick gazed at Moira's profile, "I love your beautiful hair," he said.

"You wouldn't if you had to look after it!" Moira retorted, "I might get it cut in that new short fashion,' she added, ruffling it with her hand.

"That would be a shame," said Nick.

"Why?" quizzed Moira,

"Well, it's part of what makes you attractive."

"Really? Do you think I'm attractive then?"

"Yeh! 'Course I do."

Moira sighed, "It's nice here," she said thoughtfully, "I wish there wasn't a war on. My brother's in the Air Force."

"So's my best mate,"

"He flies in the Spitfire planes. Is that what your friend is doing?"

"What, Kenny, flying a Spitfire? Nah, I think he's training to be a gunner on the Wellington planes." Nick gave Moira a quizzical frown,

"So, you tellin' me your brother was on those sorties over Dover with the German planes?"

"Yes,"

"Blimey! And he's okay?"

"Not really. Some of his friends got shot down, and he's pretty cut up about it all. He's home on leave at the moment and he's very depressed. My parents are really worried about him. That's why I was a bit off when we met. I nearly didn't keep our date."

The couple walked silently along the promenade for a while before Nick spoke, "Mr. Churchill reckons that the last air battle finished off the German Air Force."

Moira remained silent. She walked closer to Nick, who squeezed her hand, "Let's not talk about it anymore," she murmured.

"Do you fancy a boat ride on the lake?" Nick asked.

Moira frowned, "Not really, let's just walk to the bandstand."

"We could turn back and go the pictures if you like."

"No, it's too nice here."

Nick grimaced, "The wind's gettin' up, and I'm really enjoying looking at all that barbed wire and stuff!"

Moira sniggered, "All right, but let's just stay here for a while longer."

They climbed a few steps up into the bandstand. Moira was pensive as she looked around, "My mum and Dad come here often. They used to come and listen to Pete before he joined the Air Force,"

She turned to look out at the sea. Nick pushed her hair aside and touched the nape of her neck. Moira leaned her head sideways to enjoy the touch.

"Did he play an instrument then?" Nick murmured.

"Yes, he plays the trombone," she whispered.

Nick baulked and turned to face Moira, "What like Glen Miller?"

"Yes."

Leaning on the bandstand rail, Nick looked out to the sea thoughtfully, "I wish I'd learned to play the piano. My mum could play, and she taught my sister. Me mum couldn't pin me down to learn; she reckoned I was too busy raking the street! Huh!" He thought for a moment, then said, "I really like Glen Miller's music."

"So do I," murmured Moira, "Touch my neck again. It was nice."

Nick lifted her hair and gently brushed his lips against her slender neck. Moira turned to face him, and a solitary tear rolled down her cheek.

"Don't be sad," said Nick.

Touching her chin, he asked, "Can I kiss you?"

Moira lifted her chin, pursed her lips and closed her eyes. Nick clasped her shoulders in both hands. Moira opened her eyes suddenly at the unexpected firmness of Nick's grasp. His lips met hers, soft and warm against her taut lips. Moira shuddered and gasped. She drew back, touching her lips with her fingers, then, regaining her composure, she grabbed the lapels of Nick's army jacket with both hands and pressed her lips against his again. Nick drew her into his arms, pressing his body against hers. Everything inside the girl warmed. She had never felt so out of control of her own body. She took an intake of air.

"Nick, let go, she cried, pushing him away. Nick let go of her, looked into her eyes and smiled, "Come on then," he said, grabbing her hand, "Let's walk back. The weather's changing, and we may be in time for the second showing of the film."

The wind whipped around Nick's neck; he pulled up his jacket collar as they walked. People were beginning to pack up and leave the seafront.

"Where do you work then?" Nick asked, glancing up at the threatening sky.

"At the Civil Defence Headquarters in Trafalgar Road," replied Moira. She let go of Nick's hand and walked ahead of him. Turning to walk backward into the wind, she wrapped her headscarf around her hair and tied it under her chin, "But my best friend has joined the W.A.A.F, so I'm a bit restless now, I suppose."

She drew level with Nick and slipped her hand into his again. "So when I saw a notice outside the Civic Office saying that women wanted to work in the emergency services, I applied. I'm hoping to get a job driving."

"Well, I hope you don't go off just yet," Nick said, swinging her around to steal another kiss.

Moira pulled away, "Stop it, Nick, people are looking,"

"So, what? I don't care," shrugged Nick. Swinging their joined hands in the air, he began to sing,

"Don't sit under the apple tree with anyone else but me, anyone else but me, anyone else but me, no, no, no, don't sit under the apple tree with anyone else but me 'till I come marching home." Laughing and giggling with not a care in the world, they ran along the promenade, singing at the top of their voices.

Chapter 9
1940-41 Winter

Sometime later, the Regiment spent a short time at Langley Park, Lodden, before being stationed in Cambridge. The days grew shorter, and by late November, the autumn gold and red avenues of trees overhanging the lanes and byways were stripped bare.

Hours of rigorous training and exercise continued for the soldiers in all weathers, moulding them from young boys into young men. Football games and intervals of a few hours' leave allowed Nick time for fun and relaxation. Moira, the girl in the blue dress, eventually joined the WAAFS and was stationed in Norfolk at Marl Pit Lower Bodham. Air battles between Britain and Germany raged along the East Coast since July. After losing the Battle of Britain in the air, Germany began its terror tactics on London. The Blitz started in September and by November had all but raised London.

Entering the barrack, an orderly dropped a mail sack on the floor, "Mail lads," he snapped.

Letters and cards spilled out of the bag and onto the floor in front of the eager soldiers.

"Okay, get back and wait yer turn," he yelled.

Picking up the letters, the orderly began sorting through them. One by one, he called a name and gave them out.

Nick recognised his mother's writing, "There's one for me there," he said, making a grab for the letter.

"Ah said, wait yer turn," snapped the orderly.

Nick dropped his shoulders, turned and punched the mattress of the nearest bunk. The orderly finally left with his empty sack, and Nick lay on his bunk reading.

My dear son

I got your letter. We are all safe, and the bombing has stopped. If it starts again, I'll go mad. It's been terrible in London, killed thousands of people and bombed hundreds of houses. There is not much damage here, but one house got hit on the High Street. There's lots of people homeless too. We are really lucky, but my nerves are shot to pieces. Dad said that Bobby Marsdon's ship had gone down somewhere in the North Sea. Mr and Mrs Marsdon are devastated. We're managing to get by with the rationing. Christmas won't be much, though, not that I care, just as long as we all stay safe. Joyce and dad are okay. They send their love. The allotment should be ready for planting in the spring. Good job, too. It will save us some money. All the family ask how you are, and they send their love. I'm glad you're not posted in London. It's still not safe, but it's nice to hear you're making friends. Write again soon.

Mum

"One of me old mate's gone and bought it," Nick murmured, "His ships gone down in the North Sea."

Wilf glanced up at Nick, but no one commented, each one reading their own letters from home.

It was Jim who broke the silence. "It's funny how they write and tell us their news. Our lives are so different from theirs with the mundane things they do. Didn't appreciate it when I was home. Makes me homesick."

"My sister's had her baby," broke in another voice.

"That's nice, what did she 'ave," said Wilf.

"A boy. But it ain't nice. She got put up the chute by a soldier she met, and 'e's cleared off somewhere! Me mum and dad are furious."

Bob was waving a photo. "Well, my lovely wife sent me a photo of her and the children. Now, what do you think of that?"

Nick jumped off his bunk to take a look, "You got three kids then? Cor, she's a nice looker. What does she see in you?"

"Get lost, Clayton; you ain't good enough to tread in her shadow!"

"My wife's pregnant again," murmured Harry.

"Ha, we know what you got up to on your last leave," chuckled Nick.

A ripple of laughter followed.

"Not sure it's a good thing. She suffers from nerves and finds it hard to cope with one child."

"The bastards have started on Coventry now," said Nick one evening.

"Let's have a look," said Harry, "That's where my family and my wife live." Nick handed him the newspaper, and he read aloud, "Last night, the centre of Coventry was destroyed by five hundred German Luftwaffe bombers," He shook his head in despair and carried on; "It says that one hundred and fifty thousand incendiary devices, five hundred and three tons of high explosives….. unbelievable!" Harry's voice wavered, "They've bombed the whole city! Hundreds are dead, and my dad works near the Cathedral. The boys stopped what they were doing; another sat up from his bed and leaned on his elbow.

"He'll be alright," chirped Nick cheerfully. "No point in worrying about somat that may not've happened. I'd be in me grave by now if I'd worried about my family while Hitler was bombing the shit out of London."

"You've got no heart, Clayton," said Harry.

Nick frowned, "Yes, I do. You know what I mean!" Nick shrugged and gave Harry a friendly pat on the shoulder,

"And my Jane will be going mad with fear, especially now she's pregnant again," added Harry,

"Sorry about that. My mum suffers from her nerves too," said Nick, "Not that she's pregnant!" he added quickly.

"Oh shuddup Clayton," Yelled Bob, "You aint helping!"

By the middle of December 1940, Britain had endured three months of heavy nightly bombing by German aircraft. In November, Birmingham, Southampton and Bristol were hit, and Sheffield and Liverpool in December. Thousands were killed or injured in the wake of enemy reprisals. Germany was determined to break the British people into submission.

………………………………

Christmas 1940

The powerful couplings on the great steam train began to turn as it pulled slowly out of the station on one bright, cold December day. Nick and the boys were in a relaxed mood on their way home. Villages and green fields flew by as the train sped along the track. Tape crisscrossed over windows and sandbags offering defence were the only sign that the country villages were aware of a war, in contrast to the devastation seen as they passed through the towns and cities.

Soldiers and civilians alike were milling around as Nick stepped off the train at Liverpool Street Station, with the last sentence of information resounding from the echoing tanoi. Nick dropped his kitbag onto the dirty tarmac platform; he fiddled with his uniform jacket and straightened his cap. Hoisting his heavy bag onto his left shoulder, he took the train to Walthamstow.

It was dark by the time he arrived at Walthamstow Station. No one was there to meet him. He looked around fondly at the familiar station and smiled. Pushing open the door, he stepped into the street.

As he approached Church Path, he caught up with Old Mother Smith and Mrs Green, who were walking together. "Hello, Mrs Smith, nice evening!" he called.

It's "im back!" scowled Mrs. Smith to her neighbour, "Ow are you Love?" she said brightly as Nick drew level with her!

"Fine, and you two?" chirped Nick.

"You 'ome for Christmas then?' asked Mrs Green.

"Yep! You're out late," replied Nick.

"We've been to the pictures."

"What did you see?"

"Gone With the Wind," remarked Mrs Smith.

"Oh. I've seen that. It's a long film! No wonder you're so late home!"

"Proper soldier, aren't you?" called Mrs Green. "Did you pass the flattened 'ouses at the top of the High Street?"

"I didn't," Nick replied. "But, don't worry, me and the lads will sort Jerry out for you," he added with a wink. He walked on past the two women.

"Does your mum know you're home?" called Mrs Smith.

"Nope," replied Nick, "thought I'd surprise her!"

Elsie heard the gate close; she pulled aside the blackout curtain covering the window. Nick saw her shadow and smiled. A muffled cry came from within, becoming more distinct as Elsie flew into the garden to meet her son with Joyce in hot pursuit. Joyce was too excited to say anything. "Run and get Dad Joyce quick!" she said. The ten-year-old got as far as the gate, "Get your coat on, it's freezing." bawled her mother. Joyce nearly fell over herself as she turned to run back into the house. She emerged two minutes later with her coat unbuttoned, pulling a hat over her shock of fair, curly hair.

"Are you done, Mother?" Nick laughed.

"O Nick, yer back safe," said Elsie with a sigh. "Come on in Love, you must be 'ungry, and they'll be yellin' at me for leaving the door open."

"Who will?"

"The A.R.P!" retorted Elsie, adding, "Why didn't you let me know you was comin'?" Her voice drifted off into the house as she closed the door.

The cosy little room was a welcome sight to Nick. Christmas decorations hung from the ceiling, and the Christmas tree was adorned with trimmings. Remains of a recent tea were evident on the blue and white embroidered tablecloth square covering the familiar red velour cloth. The click of the latch door sounded, and Dick entered with Joyce.

"It's good to see yer Son, 'ow long you 'ome for then?" he said, hanging his coat on the hook behind the door. "Ten days, Dad, then the regiment is off to Scotland."

"Scotland!" exclaimed his mother. She put down the tea pot, rolled her eyes and shook her head in despair. Much news passed between the family. Sitting with her chin in her hands, Joyce was the only listener, glancing with interest from one to the other as each conversation changed. Elsie pushed her chair back and said, "You carry on talking while I get you something to eat, Nick,"

"Good, you've got a permanent job at Leadenhall Market, Dad. Do you remember the time you were working at 'The Bell'? Those men…"

"Huh, do I!" interjected Dick. "Tell us again, Dad, what happened?"

"I told you, they were taking the mickey out of me because I was picking up glasses at the pub," Elsie entered with some cutlery and laying it on the table," she remarked, "That's right, and you had a fight with them."

"Who's telling this story?" Dick said, frowning. After a moment, he continued, "We 'ad no money, see, so I had to get work somewhere. Old Sam Smith at The Bell wanted a potman, so I asked him if I could get the job. Didn't like it, but we needed some money."

"Me dad helped us out a couple of times with food and that… " interrupted Elsie.

"Yeh, I know that Love, but we couldn't keep relyin' on your dad. Anyway!" Dick tutted and gave his wife a sideways glance, "These blokes came in, not much older than you, Nick, and they started taking the mickey. Well, I weren't 'avin' that, so I put me fists up at 'em. But I wasn't expecting them to take me on!" Dick chuckled. "The next thing I knew, I was battling with all four of them! There was a hell-of-a-ruckus! Chairs and tables fell over, and fists flew everywhere like somink out of an MGM film."

"Yeh but……" Nick blurted out.

"I know! I know!" said Dick impatiently, "I didn't get the sack. Sam Smith reckoned it was the best fight he'd seen in ages."

"That's a great story, Dad. You said your brothers were gonna sort them out. Did they ever get 'em?" asked Nick,

"No!" snapped Elsie from the scullery. Appearing in the doorway, she added, "They didn't! Nothing more 'appened, thank gawd!"

Early the next day, there was a knock on the door, and Mrs Packham put her head around it. "Heard you were home, Nick," she said warmly. "Morning, Elsie; sorry it's so early, but I thought Nick might like to see Kenny before he returns."

"He's home?" asked Nick, standing and pushing his chair back. "Came 'ome yesterday but only for seven days."

"What about Joe?"

"He was 'ome last week. Been really good to see them both in a short time."

"And Cissie?"

"She's home. She's working as an usherette at the Granada. That reminds me," she added, "Cissie said she would like to write to you, Nick. What shall I tell 'er?"

Nick shrugged, "If she wants to I s'pose," replied Nick casually, adding, "I ain't much of a letter writer though!"

"And don't I know it!" remarked Elsie. "Be lucky if I get one every 6 months!"

Nick smiled sheepishly.

"Did you know, Nick," enquired Mrs. Packham "They're talking about calling up single girls aged twenty or more to work on the land and in the factories?"

"She's only fifteen!" remarked Elsie. "The war will be over before she's twenty."

"I hope you're right!" remarked Mrs Green.

"Is she still dating that Alan whatsisname?" asked Elsie.

"A couple of months now!" replied Mrs Green.

"Is she?" enquired Nick.

Mrs Packham nodded and raised her eyebrows in the direction of Elsie. They exchanged glances for a moment, then on impulse, Mrs Packham said, "Oh, did you hear about Bobby Marsdon…..?"

"Yes, Mum wrote me. That's too bad," said Nick thoughtfully, adding, "What ship was he on?"

"Don't know," replied Elsie.

Mrs Green shook her head, "Your dad might know."

"Know what?" said Dick poking the fire.

"What ship was Bobby Marsdon on?"

"Yeh! The destroyer HMS Ivanhoe, I think. Struck a mine in the North sea. Tragic." Nick and his dad withdrew into quiet conversation.

Elsie rose from her chair, "Do you want a cup of tea then?" She asked Mrs. Green.

"Don't mind if I do, thanks," she said, pulling out a chair.

Christmas Day came in the usual way, a welcome distraction for the family from the war that continued fiercely in Europe, although it was never long before one or the other started to discuss the war's progress.

"Did you see Italy has surrendered in Libya," said Dick to his brother.

"I thought we had agreed there would be no talk of the war today!" snapped Elsie, "Ain't you got something better to talk about?"

Embarrassed, Dick and Charlie exchanged glances. "Guess it's time for a bit of entertainment," chuckled Charlie.

Dick nodded in agreement and opened the battered suitcase that held the props for a sing-song.

……………………

Sunday 29th Dec when the boys went to town

"You off out then, Nick?" commented his mother.

Nick buttoned up his uniform jacket, "Yeh, Kenny and I are going up the Smoke!"

"No!" Elsie gasped, "You can't go to London. It's a pile of rubble!"

"So what!"

"It's dangerous. Don't go,"

"What you worried about? They ain't gonna drop any bombs now!"

"'Ow do you know?" whimpered Elsie.

"Stop worrying, Mother, and help me with this heavy coat."

Elsie held one side of Nick's thick khaki coat while he put his arm into the sleeve. It's huge collar covered his ears.

"That reminds me," said Elsie, "Have you brought those other clothes back with you?"

"What other clothes you talking about?"

"The ones you went to Norwich in."

"Oh, them!"

'I told you to send them home, remember?' Elsie put her head through the loop of her apron.

"Did yer mother?" Nick said with a wry smile. He opened the back door, "I sold 'em!"

Elsie followed him, tying her apron strings, "'Ow much did yer get for them?"

"Five bob!" The door closed shut behind Nick. The comments from within were inaudible until the door flew open, and his mother repeated what she had said.

"Nick Clayton, you're a fool!" The door banged shut again, and Nick swaggered off to meet his old friend.

Passing through various underground stations before arriving at Oxford Circus, the boys gazed open-mouthed at the pots and pans, makeshift beds and piles of blankets that were heaped up against the walls of every station. Women and young children were sitting around chatting and playing.

"They've made their 'omes there," said an elderly woman passenger in response to the lad's curiosity. "Government don't like it, but they 'aven't much choice. The people are scared." She continued. "It was bad at first, people peeing up against the wall and worse! The places began to stink, so the government put proper toilets in. They can stay as long as they like now."

Surprised, Nick said "Don't they go 'ome then?"

"Nope! Some of them don't 'ave 'omes to go to!" The men still go to work, and the kids go to school when they can."

"Those women we saw are looking after their belongings, I suppose," said Kenny.

"Someone 'as to," retorted the passenger.

Oxford Circus underground station was as smelly as the woman on the train described, and Nick was grateful for the clean, fresh air when he got to the top of the steps and into the street.

Signs of the Blitz in London were everywhere, but morale was high. Oxford Street was cleared of debris, and the broken store windows covered with paper and cardboard advertised business as usual. A street vendor dressed warmly in a long raincoat, flat cap and thick scarf stood on the corner selling newspapers. Nick rummaged in his pocket for some change to buy one.

He shook the paper out to read, "Don't know why I bother getting a newspaper; there's no good news and no bloody sports. It's all about the North African Campaign, and we're under pressure there now that Rommel is in charge."

The boys strolled along the road, Nick's head buried in the newspaper.

He was distracted by Kenny, who said, "look at all this, you gotta give 'em credit!"

Nick rolled up his newspaper and whacked Kenny on the arm with it before tucking it under his arm.

"Looking up at the building, Struth!" he uttered. One huge department store was covered in advertising, while another was covered with painted murals on their blocked-up windows. A furniture shop had a message stating: 'They can smash our windows, but they can't beat our furnishing values.' A snack bar covered in paper advertising said: 'We are carrying on Hitler will not beat us!'

"Yep, when the chips are down, the British are at their best!" Nick remarked.

"Let's go on to Waterloo and see what's going on there," suggested Kenny

"Okay," said Nick, "But Piccadilly ain't far."

"We can go there later," Kenny replied.

The pungent smell of grease mixed with carbon, oil, grime and smoke from the steam trains filled the air at Waterloo's vast Station as the lads reached the top of the escalator. Noise and bustle greeted them as people went about their business; queues formed at the ticket office and the platform gates; two or three anxious children hung onto the clothes of a woman pushing a pram through the crowds Next to stacks of newspapers tied up with string awaiting collection, two idle men stood smoking. Under the great four-faced clock that hung from the iron rafters was a sad-looking woman anxiously searching the station. A row of black taxis were lined up against the pavement; a continual flow drove in and out of the station, and pigeons flew and foraged everywhere.

The lads passed a small mobile tea-trolley surrounded by uniformed soldiers flirting and laughing with the girls serving them. Nick looked at the tea trolley, "Fancy a sausage roll and a cuppa, Kenny?"

"Yeh, why not," said Kenny.

Nick opened his coat and felt in his pocket for some change.

"Out the way, you lot," he said to the young soldiers, "Give another fella a chance!"

"You got no chance, mate," said one, "she likes blue eyes!"

The girl giggled coyly, "I declared no such thing," she retorted.

An icy wind caught the faces of the two friends as they walked out of the station into the street. Like Oxford Street, evidence of bomb damage was everywhere. The exit into Waterloo Road was blocked by a huge barricaded hole in the ground and a warning notice. They found another exit and went on in the direction of Westminster Bridge. Crossing the bridge, they turned up Whitehall, silent observers, passing damaged buildings close to Horse Guards Parade. Bricks and debris still lay piled up on the side of the road. Scaffolding supported the front of the buildings, and traffic was diverted around a gaping hole in the road. An empty bench seat, seemingly missed by the bombing, remained undisturbed nearby.

By the middle of the afternoon, Nick and Kenny reached Piccadilly Circus, where a huge covering was placed over the place where Eros once was.

"Strange not seeing Eros there," remarked Nick,

"Yeh! It's good they took it away for safekeeping."

They hung around Piccadilly for a while before Kenny decided to move on. "How about we take the underground to the City?" he said.

Nick glanced across the road where a group of girls were flirting with some soldiers.

Kenny raised his eyebrows, "Don't even think about it. I heard the Yanks call them girls "Piccadilly Commandos,"

"Yeh well, so what!" said Nick. He turned, and the two of them walked on.

He pushed Kenny in the back, "Bet they can teach you a thing or two!" he chuckled.

"Yeh, all right. Come on, you sex-crazed lunatic," quipped Kenny, "let's go to the City and a trip down memory lane," he suggested.

"Sex crazed!" retorted Nick, "I just like the girls. They're soft and warm-like."

Nick and Kenny arrived at Queen Victoria Street. Along the street, office blocks stood open to the elements with empty window casements "looking as though their eyes had been plucked out," thought Nick.

At one end of the street, buildings had been reduced to piles of bricks and rubble. The road was cleared of metal and iron that still lay twisted and broken in considerable piles to clear footpaths for pedestrians. The boys walked on towards St Paul's Cathedral. Woolworths was closed; the windows that were not blocked up were crisscrossed with tape. The warm glow through the taped-up windows of a pub and the smell of hops beckoned them in. They joined a group of other young soldiers in a cheerful mood, drinking, laughing and singing.

It was dark when the lads and soldiers spilled out of the pub. Some traffic, with headlights dipped and fitted with compulsory slotted blackout covers, continued cautiously through the cleared roads. Out of the darkness came a voice: "Careful where you're treading, lads; there's danger everywhere."

"Fang you," slurred one of the soldiers. The effects of too much alcohol made his attempts to stand to attention and salute the warden impossible.

Nick and Kenny chuckled as he went off into the darkness held up between two of his fellow soldiers.

The warden went to leave, "Were you here when this happened?" asked Kenny.

"Was I!" exclaimed the warden, "You never seen - nor 'eard anything like it! 'Apocalyptic,' someone said, whatever that means! Somink to do with the end of the world!"

"Huh, you must have thought it was," said Kenny. "It were the underground stations that saved a lot of lives; in the end, they stayed down in 'em and didn't come out. Where 'ave you been?"

"Norfolk and Cambridge. We had some bombing but nothing like this," said Nick.

The low wail of a siren began to rise, "Hang on, whatsat?" said the warden in panic. "Gawd, it sounds like another attack. You two had better find somewhere safe," came his urgent call as he ran off to meet up with a fellow Warden along the street.

The siren continued its eerie wail, rising and falling like a wave echoing around the City. People seemed confused; others didn't stop to think and went running for cover; buses stopped and expelled their frantic load into the street.

"Can't be another attack?" questioned Nick.

The lads stood rooted to the ground.

Someone barged past them, "Don't just stand there. Get off the street," he called back.

Realising the friends were not sure where to go for safety, the man stopped and beckoned to them. "This way," he called.

The boys followed.

"I can hear 'em coming," said Nick, gazing at the sky.

With panic, Kenny said, "Sounds like hundreds of em too."

"Cor, me mum'll be worried now!" said Nick.

"Come on, Nick, better get going," said his friend.

They took off towards Mansion House Underground Station just as the first bomb hit the ground close by. The ground shook.

"Crikey mate, give us a chance!" jeered Nick as they reached the station.

Kenny entered, but Nick stopped to look. Another resounding blast, and another, followed immediately. In the distance, he could hear the muffled thud of other bombs hitting the ground, and he felt the vibration under his feet.

"This is another blitz on London," he thought with a mixture of horror and excitement.

There was no sign of Kenny when Nick entered the underground station; he took shelter inside. His curiosity would not allow him to go any further, so he stayed for a long time watching and listening. The noise was deafening, the clanging of fire engines mixed with crumps, thuds and explosions. The ground shook, and the night sky lit up as bombs hit close by.

Nick stepped warily out into the street. He walked to the corner of Queen Victoria Street and Cannon Street. The bombing and the drone of enemy planes ceased, but the roar of flames drew his attention further down the street, where he watched them whipping out of gaping holes in the walls; the whole street was alight; flames roared out of every crevice. At the end of the street, a building front crumpled to the ground amidst a cloud of dust and debris. He glimpsed the silhouettes of firemen struggling in the rubble to douse the flames. Cars and buses stood abandoned and damaged in the otherwise empty street. He continued to watch, mesmerised by the sights and sounds that rent the night. Silhouetted against the firelight, the remains of buildings damaged by previous air-raids stood out like unfinished jigsaw puzzles.

Further along the street, another building shuddered and gave way, crumbling like building blocks; smoke and dust billowed into the air dangerously close to St Paul's cathedral. Nick jumped as a surge of water suddenly shot out of the ground six feet high, flooding the area nearby and settling the dust.

"Are you mad?" screamed a Warden. "Get off the street, you idiot!"

Returning to the underground station Nick ran down the escalator, keen to share his experience with his mate and vanished into the labyrinth of passages. Every space was tightly packed with people polluting the air with body odour. Smiling faces advertising sunny family holidays on yellow sands gazed down on them from the walls. A few strains of singing were coming from somewhere further down, but there was no sign of Kenny. Arriving on the platform, he could distinguish individual family groups that had taken up residence from those who were there just for the night. Most had a cheerful countenance, sharing and friendly. But others wore worried, anxious faces. Nick looked along the platform, searching for Kenny. Someone was edging along with a pot of tea.

He turned to go when he heard Kenny call, "Nick!"

He scrambled to his feet and climbed over the people who had bedded down for the night.

"You had me worried," complained Kenny.

"You've never seen anything like it," breathed Nick excitedly,

"No, an' I don't want to," grumbled Kenny, "I've gotta be back in less than twenty-four hours."

"Well, we ain't goin' nowhere right now, so we may as well make ourselves comfortable." They lay still and quiet for a while before Nick added sleepily, "I think they've got St Paul's. It looks like it was going up in smoke."

It was still dark when the two friends surfaced from the underground station. The cold early morning air blasted in their faces as the crowd, directed at the exit by Air Raid Wardens, poured out into the street. The last strains of the siren sounding the 'all clear' dwindled away, mixed with the subdued voices of those who went on their way. No public transport was available to get the boys home, so they walked in the debris of the smoking streets.

"Bastards!" said Kenny bitterly.

Nick sighed, for once unable to speak. They walked on in silence, climbing over bricks, rubble and broken furniture; they passed exhausted firemen sitting on piles of debris with their heads in their hands while their colleagues continued to fight the blazing buildings. Coming down Cannon Street the magnificent dome of St Paul's could be seen through the smoke billowing up around it.

Nick found his voice, "Cor, what a sight! I didn't expect to see that again!"

It was late morning when Nick opened the garden gate to his home. His mother was relieved at seeing him, "I told you not to go," she snapped in angry despair. "You got no idea how worried we were and Kenny's mum….. well!" She shook her head, "I just thank God you're home."

"There wouldn't have been any room for me in the shelter anyway," Nick quipped, lifting his mother's chin and smiling.

Chapter 10
1941 Scotland

Arriving at the beginning of January in bitterly cold weather, the regiment transferred to Stobs Camp 5 miles from Hawick on the southern border of Scotland. Training was harder than ever in the frozen terrain surrounding it, and Nick longed for the comfort of Norwich and Cambridge.

Worn out from yet another long route march, Nick struggled to remove his boots, "I bloody hate this place!" He complained bitterly.

"Stop moaning," said Alfie.

Ignoring Alfie, Nick resumed moaning, "I thought Norwich was cold and boring, but this place……"

Nick's boot flew off, hitting the ground with a thump. "Now I suppose I've got to clean them things before inspection," he added. "We're in the middle of bloody nowhere, with no chance of having it off. The ground's too hard to play football, and there's no point in living!"

" 'Course there is," a voice chirped. "Look at the beautiful countryside, see the sunrise, listen to the birdsong………" at this point, a pillow from a neighbouring bed whacked the speaker in the face. He was soon buried under other pillows that came hurtling through the air in his direction. The atmosphere of the barrack room lightened.

A weekend leave brought a brief respite to the gruelling training the young soldiers had experienced over the last month.

"It's your lucky day," came the sergeant's sharp announcement, "There's a 'Passion Waggon' laid on to take you to town!"

Harry gave Nick a quizzical look, "Passion Waggon?" he mouthed.

Nick smiled and winked, "Think about it, Harry! Passion....?"

Harry raised his eyebrows and said, "O, You'll be alright there then!"

There were many journeys into town on the 'Passion Waggon.' Over the next few weeks, the boys got to know the places where plenty of local girls were willing to make their time exciting and enjoyable.

A stir was always caused when, on the rare occasion, letters arrived. There was no letter from Nick's mother this time, but his interest was aroused by one he received from Cissie.

Dear Nick

I was pleased when mum told me I could write to you. I hope you don't mind. I like writing letters, and it's nice to think this one is going somewhere different. Your mum said you are now in Scotland. That's nice. Have you seen any men in kilts? Ha ha. I guess you are still marching and training, and I know you don't like it very much. I hope you or Kenny don't have to go to war. Our mums are very worried about you. Anyway, I thought you would like to know about the films I've seen recently. Last Saturday I went to see 'Gone With the Wind' for the second time. It's my favourite but such a long film you have to see it more than once to understand it. And I went to see the

'Wizard of Oz'. It was good. I missed it the last time it was at the cinema. I'm still working at the Granada cinema, but it's not much money, and my boyfriend Alan doesn't like me working in the evening or at the weekend so I'm looking for another job.

Kenny is doing well in the Air Force. I hope you are okay and that it is not too cold up there in Scotland, and I hope you will write back. Mum and dad send their love.

Love from Cissie

Nick sighed and held the letter in his hands for a while.

By April, the regiment was on the move again, this time to Blackburn and by June, training and exercise ended with a two-day endurance test. Nick and his fellow soldiers were exhausted.

"At ease," boomed the Corporal Major. The men relaxed in unison. "You will be pleased to know that your efforts were not in vain. You passed the endurance test with flying colours. You will not be so pleased to know that you will return to Scotland very soon to learn new skills to prepare for posting abroad. Audible groans sounded, and shoulders dropped!

"Na then, na then, none of that, you 'orrible lot!" growled the Corporal Major, "You ain't considered to be men yet!"

Nick kept up with the news as often as possible, buying newspapers to read at any opportunity. The battle of the Atlantic continued, and the quest to sink the largest German battleship fascinated him. He was astounded at the news of the sinking of HMS Hood by the Bismark, and later, he read the news to his fellow soldiers. "As a result of a relentless pursuit by the Royal

Navy involving dozens of battleships, the Bismark was sunk three days later." The barrack room erupted with cheers as he finished the last words.

July 1941

The summer of 1941 continued with hard training that included both day and night landing craft operations. In the barracks, the lads discussed the demanding and exhausting week.

Jim fell on his bed and opened a book to read. Sighing deeply, he searched for his page, "If I'd known we were going to have anything to do with boats, I'd have joined the bloody navy!" he muttered.

"It's not the boats I mind. It's that bastard corporal pushing us around," said Wilf. Raising his voice to a higher decibel, he mimicked: "Stop pussy-footing around and get yourselves into that bloody craft at the double, you lazy lot!" His listeners laughed. He began rigorously shuffling a pack of cards, "and 'is bloody irritating clicking fingers!" he muttered. "You playing Nick?"

"Nah!" came the reply from Nick, "Restin'" after crawling under barbed wire, through mud and shit." He paused deeply, thinking, "It would be nice to get into a hot bath! Wish there was a Mrs Chapman around."

"Who's Mrs Chapman," questioned Wilf, dishing out the cards to those who chose to play. "She's the mother of one of the girls I met in Cambridge. They had a white china bath..."

"Ceramic, don't you mean," corrected Jim. "Yeh, well! She let me take a hot bath more than once!"

"Did she wash yer back?" laughed Archie.

Nick raised his eyebrows about to speak when Wilf interrupted, "Before we get into Nick's hot, sordid personal life, I reckon things are hotting up here?" He laid down a playing card and replaced it with another.

Harry looked up from his book, "Yep, it won't be long now," he said, "and we'll be off."

Jim scrutinised his hand, "Where do you reckon it will be then?" he said.

"Egypt!" echoed a voice from the other end of the barrack room.

"You seem very sure," said Nick, straining to look at the speaker,

"It don't take a brain to work that out, " Archie interjected. "That was the plan before it was cancelled in April last year, remember?"

"May get to see some elephants and monkeys!" chuckled Nick

"Yeh! You may get to meet some of your relatives at that rate!"

Annoyed, Nick jumped off his bed to confront Archie, but Harry stops him. "Come on, mate, have a fag and calm down!"

"Aw, shuddup you lot," Wilf snapped. The mood changed, and the boys quietly continued their game of cards apart from the odd outburst from a winning hand.

Nick lay back on his bed, looking at the ceiling. He thought about the parcel and letter he had received yesterday. Reaching over the side of his bunk, he pulled a navy sweater and woollen knitted socks out of his locker. The letter dropped to the floor. He reached to pick it up and re-read the letter from his mother:

Dear Nick

Thank you for your letter. Nice, you got a letter from Cissie. She's hoping you will reply to her. You should. I think she likes you. I told her you're not good at writing letters. Sorry, you're so tired of training. It's your own fault! I told you not to join up. Dad said to tell you that Preston North End won the FA Cup v Arsenal 2-1. Did you know?

(Silly woman muttered Nick, it's the 'Football War Cup')

Joyce goes up to the Joseph Barret school in September after the holidays. I can't believe she's eleven. She's still the apple of Dad's eye. I heard that Hitler's thugs are in Russia now, and they can stay there. I just want you to stay safe in this country. Don't ever tell me you're going abroad, or I'll die. There's still no word of Eli. Poor Mrs Cohan is so depressed. Mr Cohan said he fears for her sanity. I hope you like the socks and the jumper I knitted for you. Let me know if you got them.

Love Mum

Nick picked up the sweater and socks his mother had sent, admiring them with approval.

"What do you think of these then?" he asked his roommates.

Bob laughed and quipped, "O, I'm so jealous! That's my favourite colour!"

Nick sniggered, "Huh! You won't get another one like it anywhere, so grieve on me, old son!" He chucked the sweater to the end of his bed, laid down, and closed his eyes. He found himself thinking of Cissie.

The months passed, and spring flowers and new growth began to appear. Jim closed his book and shook his pillow, "You playing this weekend, Nick?"

"What?" muttered Nick. He sat up and threw his legs over the side of the bunk, "O yeh! Lucky! I managed to swap me guard duty thanks to the Corp." Nick lowered his voice to mimic his superior, "Can't 'ave that lad. A cricket game without you won't do!"

Jim chuckled, yawned and stretched, "I'm turnin' in," he said, 'so keep the noise down.'

By the middle of April, the cricket season had begun well for the company. Nick loved keeping goal in the football season but was in his glory opening the bowling on the cricket field. The latest match had finished, and the team was changing after a good result.

"Another good win, well done, lads!" said the team captain.

"Yeh, but their opening batsmen were doing well at a hundred and two for none," interjected Harry.

"That catch by Brett put a stop to that, and then they collapsed," said Jim. He picked up the scorebook, navigated the page with his finger and said, "What was it? A hundred and two; hundred and four; then a hundred and twenty, all out for a hundred and forty-seven. Nick got the lot!" They were right pissed off!"

"You're a canny bowler!" said Harry.

Nick gave him a sideways wink.

In September, the cricket season ended, but no football matches began. Training and exercise were a priority, and the lads were issued with tropical gear at the end of the month.

"Do you think the girls will like me in these," said Nick, parading in his tropical shorts.

Jim glanced at him; with a jerk of his chin, he rolled his eyes and said, "Be lucky if you get to see any, where we're going."

"Not gonna be much fun in the desert then?" Nick said, stepping out of the shorts.

"Nope!" said Harry.

No one said another word, and a distinct air of foreboding hung in the air.

The lads learned soon after that orders were given for the Regiment to leave for Liverpool Port, where they were ready to embark and sail. In October, the Regiment sailed to Halifax, Nova Scotia. Nick and three others were not on board.

....

While Nick was training with the Royal Norfolks, an Armoured Car Regiment was being formed. Permission was granted by the King and the Colonels of the various regiments involved to bring all the armoured divisions together. In September 1941, The Guards Armoured Division was officially formed. The new Division comprises The Grenadier Guards, Coldstream Guards, Welsh Guards, Irish Guards and the Scots Guards.

At the beginning of the war, the Royal Horse Guards at Windsor and the Life Guards in London came together to form a composite regiment, which was renamed the 2nd Household Cavalry Regiment. The 1st Household Cavalry mobilised in 1939 to fight the war in Egypt and Palestine. The plan for the Second Household Cavalry was to form a Reconnaissance Division for the Guards Armoured Division. Trained soldier recruits from all the infantry regiments were enlisted.

When the opportunity arose, Nick was amongst ten soldiers from the 4th Battalion Royal Norfolk Regiment who volunteered to join the 2nd Household Cavalry Regiment at Windsor barracks. Nick was one of four to be accepted, along with Wilf Grant, Bob Howe and Harry Parks.

The young soldiers were given ten days' leave for Christmas 1941 when Nick was able to tell his parents the news. The main news at the time was the bombing of Japan's Pearl Harbour just two weeks earlier, on the seventh of December. A great discussion occurred between family members over the Christmas celebrations, much to Elsie's annoyance!

"Stop worrying Mother! The war will end much sooner now that the Americans have come in," reassured Dick.

Returning to Norfolk after Christmas, the four soldiers spent the next few months manning roadblocks and gun emplacements along the Norfolk coast. The long hours of boredom in bitterly cold winds were relieved intermittently by pretty girls passing by or sightings of enemy planes and the action that ensued.

Nick enquired after Moira at Lower Bodham and met her for the first time in a year while on a weekend leave. He sat waiting for her in a tea room, watching heavy rain hit the window, distorting the view outside where people bent under umbrellas, hurried along the street, disappeared into shops, and went out of sight. Nick was shaken from his reverie when the doorbell tinkled. Moira stepped through the door, dripping wet but looking as pretty as ever. She smiled a greeting to Nick and hovered by the door to take off her wet coat. Nick watched her as she hung her coat and cap on a coat stand; she had matured, Nick thought. Her smart uniform made her even more desirable.

He stood up, kissed her cheek and pulled out a chair for her. "It's nice to see you," he said.

Moira smiled, "It's nice to see you too," she said.

They ordered tea from a young girl dressed in a white pinny and cap,

"You look very nice in your uniform Moira," said Nick.

"Thank you," she said sweetly, "And before you go any further, I have to tell you that I'm dating a nice young man who wants to marry me,"

"Damn!" exclaimed Nick, "I was going to ask you to marry me."

Moira laughed. "I really like you, Nick, but you're not ready for marriage," she said, "Anyway, what have you been doing for the last year? There must have been a few more girls on your arm since I last saw you!"

"What?" chirped Nick, "Never! My heart belongs to you," he said, clutching his hands to his heart. "Anyway, I've been too busy training to have time for girls."

"I don't believe you!" laughed Moira, shaking her head. The waitress placed the tea service on the crisp white tablecloth.

"Thank you," said Moira politely, "Talk about training," she added. "I think I know enough about aircraft maintenance now to build one on my own."

Nick chuckled.

The two friends whiled away the next hour, chatting about the past year's events before saying goodbye.

"I guess I won't get a chance to see you again, especially since you're going down south," Moira said, adding, "Good luck with the new regiment."

"Thanks," said Nick, "It'll be good going back down south, and me mum's pleased I'm closer to home."

"Just stay safe," said Moira, "We don't know what the future holds."

"You too," said Nick.

He helped Moira with her coat, kissed her, and they left the tea room together. He then walked Moira to the bus stop, where they said goodbye.

………………………………...

January 1942

Four young soldiers arrived together on a freezing cold day in January 1942.

Entering the gates of Combermere Barracks, Nick whispered mischievously, "Do you reckon I'll get a black stallion?"

"Don't start all that again," said Wilf, slightly irritated, "We're not here to train for the 'Charge of the Light Brigade so shuddup!"

Nick chuckled and gave him a friendly shove.

An inspection by the sentry guard allowed the boys through the gates. Then, as they were about to pass an open doorway in the next building, a voice boomed from within, "And where do you lot think you're going?" Regimental Corporal Major Johnson stepped through the door. Taken by surprise, the four new recruits stumbled to a standstill; standing to attention, they saluted.

"Not sure, sir," said Harry.

The Corporal Major tucked his chin into his chest and circled the group, eyeing them curiously. "Not sure?" he bellowed. "You more of them new recruits then?"

"Yes, sir," they replied in unison.

"Get yourselves round to the orderly room at the double!"

"Which way, sir?" asked Nick.

He pointed his baton toward the orderly room and roared, "At the double. Now!"

With the weight of their kit-bags on their shoulders, they went off at a trot. "And get yer 'air cut, you're an a-b-s-o-l-u-t-e dis-grace!" he screamed.

Their first week at Windsor held an event that none of the new recruits expected. Jumping to attention, the soldiers stopped what they were doing when Corporal-of-Horse Noyce entered the barrack room.

"At ease," said the Corporal, "You will be pleased to hear that their Royal Highnesses, the Princesses Elizabeth and Margaret, are performing in a pantomime at the Waterloo Chambers in Windsor Castle, and you have been invited," He waved a sheet of paper, "All the information is on this poster, which will be pinned on the notice board in the messroom."

"If this is what we're in for the rest of the war, then I'm happy," Nick hissed to Wilf.

The young soldiers duly attended the pantomime. Finding their seats, the Lt called for order, "You will enjoy the show," he demanded, "And respond accordingly. When I laugh, you laugh. When I clap, you clap! Understood?"

"Yes sir," replied the collection of various voices.

The next five months were disappointedly less entertaining. Classroom training in communication skills began in earnest using a wireless set and Morse code. Though grateful that the dreaded long route marches he experienced in the North were no more, Nick endured daily exhausting drills on the parade ground.

Standing on the edge of the parade ground an observer would have seen the neatly arranged company on the square and heard the rapid bellowing orders of the Lt echoing in the confined space of outer buildings, "By the leeeeeft, quick march! Left, left, left, right, left!' Boots crunched the ground in unison and in precise formation. Like a shoal of fish wheeling and darting left then right, the young soldiers marched for what seemed like hours until they were brought to a halt and dismissed.

Staggering into the barrack room, Nick fell on his bed, "Take me boots of Wilf me, ol' mate!"

Wilf turned his head to look toward Nick, "Huh!" he said, "Get lost! And you know what you've gotta do next,"

"Clean 'em!" cried Bob with glee.

Cleaning his kit was something that continued to be a labour that Nick did not enjoy.

He found it a tedious job, one that didn't come easy for him. Webbing had to be whitened with blanco, brass buttons and boots highly polished.

Nick was puzzled the first time he was handed the tin of Blanco.

"What's this for?" he enquired at the store room.

The orderly leaned across the storeroom counter that divided them. He took the tin and held it reverently between his forefinger and thumb, "This, my lad, is a tin of Blanco. You take this," he added, whipping a small sponge out of Nick's hand, and you wet it, see? Then, making a circle over the sealed tin, the orderly continued, "You wipe it over the Blanco block see and stir it up to a nice paste. Got it?"

"Sir," said Nick stiffly.

"And then you spread the paste on your webbing, see," he added, waving his hand to and fro in the air. "Got it?" he snapped.

Nick's chin drew back into his chest to leave space between him and the orderly! "Sir," he replied.

Corporal Noyce had rejected more than one inspection, and Nick dreaded the next one. He thought it was worth trying his old trick of bribing someone to Blanco for his webbing.

"The Corp hates me!" Nick whined. "Anyone willin' to clean my kit?" he enquired of his fellow soldiers. "You can have my butter ration. I hate the stuff!"

"Get lost, Clayton." came the replies.

All his efforts failed miserably; he was again doomed to meet the Corporal's wrath on kit inspection day.

Kits were laid out in perfect order on the bed of every trooper in the room, at the end of which a trooper stood to attention. With an air of superiority, Corporal Noyce walked stiffly between the rows of beds. Eyes darted and rolled as he passed by each nervous and relieved Trooper.

The corporal stopped, "And what do you call this?" he snapped at Trooper Vic Jenkins.

"Not sure, sir," came the rapid response.

"I'm very sure this is a loose button." said the corporal, pulling the kit apart, "Get it fixed!" he snapped.

"Yessir!"

Coming alongside Nick, Corporal Noyce bellowed, "And what do you call this mess?"

Standing stiffly to attention, a worried Nick stared straight ahead, "My kit, sir!" he snapped.

The Corporal sniffed and looked toward the sash window. Picking up the kit, he said, "This is what I think of your kit." Nick's eyes darted toward the window as Noyce threw the whole kit out through the open window.

Picking up his muddy, rain-soaked kit, angry and humiliated, Nick spat. "Bloody Noyce! Bloody Blanco!"

Wilf and Vic bent to help, "You're gonna have to learn to like it 'cause it ain't gonna get any better." said Wilf.

Vic Jenkins, Basil Shaw, Charlie Smith, Benny Osbourne and Archie Golding were among other young soldiers who volunteered to join the Household Cavalry.

Vic was tall and dapper, witty and intelligent. He smoked a pipe and looked for all the world suited to another rank or profession. But he had fitted in well with his fellow soldiers and complimented the squadron with his sensible attitude and bright sense of humour.

Archie sported a head of thick, dark, curly hair. He proved to be moody, bad-tempered and argumentative. He had arrived with Charlie Smith and Basil Shaw. Unlike Basil Shaw, who spoke good, well-pronounced English, Charlie proudly owned to being a London Cockney with a variable cockney slang vocabulary. Basil came from a wealthy family in the Cotswolds and sported a sandy moustache that matched his head of hair. He carried a hunting horn that hung at his belt when allowed.

He irritated Archie, who sneered at Basil and was determined to ignore him.

Nick took to Benny Osbourne as soon as they met up. His swarthy dark skin denoted his employment before the war on the building sites around London. He was born in Poplar, one of a brood of eight children. His father worked in the shipyard, and his mother was the local midwife. He had experienced a frugal childhood and appreciated the good things in life. Like Nick, he was interested in sports, eagerly competing with Nick for their knowledge of the players and teams of various sports.

A few weeks after Nick arrived at Combermere Barracks, he finished his basic training. Elsie, Dick and Joyce stood in the crowd proudly watching the troopers passing the parade. Led by a military band, it started from St George's Chapel, through the gate of Windsor Castle and down into the town. Later on, they met with Nick on a bench by the river.

"I was so proud of you, Nick," said Elsie, glowing.

"Can't believe you're at Windsor now," said Dick, "It's a relief for your mum. Hopefully, she will get some sleep now!"

Elsie opened her bag and produced a small brown paper parcel, "I brought some sandwiches, Love, would you like one?" she said, offering Nick the open parcel.

They fed the ducks with a few bits of leftover crumbs and spent the rest of the day in beautiful spring sunshine content to catch up on news and laughter at the latest stories and jokes.

June 1942

The battle of the Coral Sea, the Java and the Medway dominated the headlines in May and June 1942. The attack on

Pearl Harbour by Japanese aircraft in December 1941 led to the United States' entry into the war. It resulted in a major naval battle in the Pacific Ocean between the Imperial Japanese Navy, the United States and Australian air forces. It began in May 1942, lasting just four days. It was an unusual sea battle because at no stage did the aircraft carriers exchange fire. All attacks were made from the air. It resulted in a huge loss of life on both sides but was successful if only to stop the Japanese advance. Four weeks later, the Battle of the Midway began in the Pacific. Fought almost entirely from the air, the United States succeeded in destroying one of Japan's major aircraft carriers with most of its best naval pilots, thereby ending the threat of further Japanese invasion in the Pacific.

Entering Manzies on the High Street while home for forty-eight hours leave, Nick closed his eyes, inhaling the pungent smell of pie and mash, "Cor, how I miss that smell!" he said.

"Me too," said Kenny.

The boys felt at home in the clean, bright eating place with white tiled walls and snug seating booths. They found a seat and slid along the bench.

"Nothing changes here, does it, Kenny?"

"Nope, and I hope it never does!"

"What you 'aving then?" asked the waitress.

"Pie and mash and loads of that lovely parsley liquor," said Kenny.

"I'll have stewed eels, darling," Nick said to the blushing waitress.

"So, how's it going then, Kenny?" asked Nick.

"Yeh, it's all going well! Like you, it's mainly square bashing and training, but there's loads of written work, too. Have you heard about the new Lancaster Bomber that's replacing the Wellington? It's heavier and has four engines."

The steaming plates of food were placed on the table, and the lads tucked in.

"So you're training to be a pilot then?" said Nick with his mouth full.

"Nah! Rear gunner. I've done the training as a wireless operator, and I'm training to be a gunner now."

"Sounds exciting!" said Nick.

"Exciting, maybe, but bloody dangerous, too!" retorted Kenny.

"Yeh, well, things will be better now that the Americans have come into the war. Did you get to see the Pathe News at the cinema?"

"What, the Japanese bombing of Pearl Harbour?" Kenny took a swig of tea, "Yeh!" he added.

"It was bloody awful!" exclaimed Nick.

The two friends continued their conversation and finished their meal. Leaving Manzies, they walked in the warmth of an early June day, deciding what to do for their short time together.

"What about the pictures?" said Nick,

"Nope!" replied Kenny. "I'm not spending that last few hours of leave in the cinema! Let's go up West!"

Amid the bomb-scarred West End of London in June 1942, the air of optimism and hope that the two friends experienced the last time they were there seemed stronger than ever. Arriving at the exit of Charing Cross station, the lads had to jump out of the way of a gang of scruffy small boys precariously steering a large wooden wheelbarrow filled with newspapers between them.

"Sorry, guv, it's paper for the war effort," they called back before crossing the road.

They hurried down a side street, once overshadowed by tall buildings but now flattened in a pile of rubble and open to the sunshine.

Fortunately, Trafalgar Square experienced minor bomb damage. An air balloon hung, suspended high above Nelson's Column. The huge black lions dominating the Square had an air of defiance as they sat on their plinths, majestically guarding the grand monument. Pigeons flew amongst the crowds of people and servicemen of all ranks weaving in and out of the crowds. A young uniformed sailor stopped to alter a white carnation in his girlfriend's jacket lapel as she looked dreamily into his eyes. A huge double siren replaced one of the fountains around which scores of people sat in every possible space listening to a band playing an arrangement of Glen Miller music on a raised wooden platform erected at the base of the steps outside the National Portrait Gallery. Two American soldiers entertained the crowds, jitterbugging with their partners. The boys hung around, soaking up the atmosphere. Nick took the opportunity to open the newspaper pages he had bought outside the station. They walked on.

"What's the headlines then, Nick?" Kenny asked.

"Looks like the Americans have beaten the Japs in the Midway, that's good!"

"Bet that was a hellova battle!" responded Kenny, "Worlds gone mad!" he added.

Nick sniffed, "Yyeeeup!" he said, "And there ain't much we can do about it!"

He folded the newspaper and tucked it under his arm, "We are wasting time, mate," he muttered. They pushed through the crowds, heading towards Piccadilly.

"Whatchit!" exclaimed a young woman.

Fixing her dislodged hat, she turned an angry face to the boys, "Is there a fire or sommat?" she shouted.

"Sorry," said Kenny.

He touched his forehead politely and walked on. Nick turned on the charm.

"Sorry darling," he said, but it didn't work.

"Oi!" said another young woman, "It's not funny!"

Two other girls stood by watching. "Leave 'em alone," said one, "they didn't mean any 'arm,"

"Think they own the place in their uniforms!" continued the angry girl.

"Don't be so miserable. There's enough of that already without you pickin' on 'em!"

"Fancy a drink with a couple of careless louts?" Nick called to their rescuers.

"Don't mind if I do,' said one of them cheekily.

Turning to her friend, she dug her elbow into her, "Coming?" she asked.

The girls caught up with the two soldiers and walked on together.

Nick was frantic the next morning when he realised his revolver was missing. Hopping around the bedroom, he shared with Joyce when he was home. He pulled on his trousers and pushed his feet into his shoes. Grabbing a shirt, he flew down the stairs and rushed through the living room into the scullery and out of the back door.

"Where's 'e off to in such a rush?" asked Dick.

"Trouble! 'E's in trouble!" exclaimed Elsie dramatically. She sighed, "'ope, there's nothing wrong!"

"That's it, Love, always look on the bright side!" teased Dick.

Cissie came to the door of the Packham household, tying up the belt on her dressing gown.

"Hello, Cissie," Nick puffed anxiously, "Is Kenny up?"

"Not sure. What's up then? Is somebody sick?"

"No, no!"

Kenny came into view at the top of the stairs.

"Is this what you want?" he said casually, dangling a revolver with his finger in the trigger ring.

Nick gasped! "Cor, thanks, mate!" he said, "I'd have been in deep trouble if I'd lost that. Where d'you you find it?"

"Under the table at the pub. Serves you right for showing off to them girls!" Nick gave a sideways wink, "I got a date out of it, though."

Cissie looked up and said, "You don't have to go to those lengths to get a date with me, Nick."

Nick screwed up his face and said, "You're Kenny's sister! Anyway, you're going steady with whatshisname!"

Cissie blushed, "A girl gets lonely when her man's away fighting the war,"

"You hussie Cissie!" Nick quipped. He paused, curious, "Seriously, you want a date with me?" he queried, "Tell you what, I'll take you out for a drink next time I'm home."

Patting Kenny on the shoulder, Nick said, "Thanks again, Kenny, you're a pal!"

As he opened the door, Cissie called out, "Promise, Nick?"

"What's all the noise about?" called Mrs Packham, carrying a huge basket of washing into the scullery. She placed her load on the copper boiler. "You'll wake the neighbourhood!"

"Too damn right," called a voice from outside. Nick leaned out the door to see Mrs. Smith in her dressing gown and her hair gathered up in a net. She bent her great frame to pick up the milk from her doorstep. "Sorry, Mrs. Smith, you, of all people, need your beauty sleep!"

"An' you can shut your row up too!" she retorted angrily.

"That's enough, Nick. I have to live with my neighbours. Either come in or go on out." said Mrs Packham. "Bye Mrs Packham.

See you when you're home next, Kenny. Stay safe!" called Nick.

....

After his initial panic over the missing gun, Nick began to appreciate the bright, fresh morning that had welcomed the beginning of another warm June day. He sat reading his newspaper in the shade of a tree in the small family garden. Dick took a break from hoeing the weeds around the vegetable plot. He leaned the hoe against a runner bean post; lifting his cap, he pulled a handkerchief from his pocket to wipe his brow. "See if Mum's got the kettle on, son. I could do with a cuppa right now."

A few minutes later, Elsie put the tea tray down on an upturned box outside the scullery door, "Tea up!" she called, "I'm off down the High Street to see if I can get some sausages for dinner and if I go now the queue might not be too long. Mrs Cohen needs something for her bronchitis, too poor ol' soul! See you later."

The rhythmic sound of a train along the track at the side of the garden clattered by, leaving a trail of smoke in its wake. The silence followed; only the gentle rattle of a mower from a neighbour's garden and the distant sound of children's voices could be heard playing in their gardens as father and son sat relaxing together in the sunshine. A bee buzzed nearby, and a blackbird chinked across the garden, chasing an intruder.

"What's in the news?" Dick asked, tipping his cap to scratch his head.

"The battle-for-the-Midway in the Pacific," said Nick, still engrossed in reading.

"Did you read about the fall of Singapore?" Dick added.

Shaken out of reading, Nick said, "Yes, and did you know Dad that my old regiment, the Norfolks, were in Singapore?" He frowned thoughtfully, "They were all either killed or captured, and some of them were my old mates."

"Gawd blimey!" exclaimed Dick, "Don't tell yer mother, she'll 'ave a fit!"

Nick went back to his newspaper.

"They sunk the Prince of Wales too," murmured Dick, "and a cruiser, um, er,..."

"The Repulse?" asked Nick.

"That's the one!" remarked Dick.

"It was good to read about the sinking of the bloody Bismark," rejoined Dick. "Seen enough sea battles to last a lifetime!" he mused. He pulled out his tobacco pouch and began to roll a cigarette, "I spent Christmas Eve 1916 on a raft in the middle of the North Atlantic; did I ever tell you that one?"

"Yes, Dad," murmured Nick, "and you served on HMS Engadine on the Russian Convoys!"

A goods train rattled by that seemed to go on forever.

"Did I ever tell you about the time I swapped ships with my mate then?" Dick said above the clamour and billowing smoke that followed.

"What?" exclaimed Nick. Silence returned as the train moved along the track, "I said, did I ever tell you about the time I swapped ships with my mate? I forgot his name?"

"Stan, Dad!" Nick said wearily. He shook out his newspaper.

"That's 'im!" said Dick. "I was lucky. Poor sod went down with his ship in the Atlantic! What annoyed me was that 'e owed me five bob!"

Nick chuckled half-heartedly. Closing his newspaper, he said, "Sorry, Dad, I just wanted to finish reading about the Midway. D'you want a hand?" he added, trying to look interested.

"Nah! I'm finishing now."

Nick stood up and stretched, "Right then, I'm going up West. I'll leave the paper for you."

Dick licked his fag paper and frowned, "wot Again?'

'Yep, I've got a date!'

'Stone the crows, it don't take you long!' Dick called after him.

Opening the garden gate, Nick entered Church Path. His mother was hurrying toward him. "Good news, Nick," she cried, "Danny Smith has been found. I met Mr Smith in Sainsbury's and he told me. The poor chap was crying."

"So, is he coming home?" asked Nick

"I doubt it. He was taken prisoner somewhere in France,"

"He never made it to the beaches then," said Nick thoughtfully.

"It's good news anyway, isn't it, Nick?"

"' Course it is, gives the Cohans a bit of hope for Eli too."

Nick's relationship with Mrs Smith wasn't very good; he found her spiteful and nasty. Even so, he hesitated outside the Smith's white-wickett garden gate before opening it and knocking on the door. Mrs Smith opened it, her eyes red with crying.

"Mum just told me your news. I'm glad Danny's been found."

"Thank you, Nick," said Mrs Smith. With a sob, she turned to go back in the house. Looking over her shoulder, she said, "Thank you for coming," and then closed the door.

Chapter 11
Somerset, 1942

Nick returns to Windsor to join the Regiment in Somerset in 1942

On his return to Windsor barracks, Nick learned that he and his fellow Troopers were to join the Guards Armoured Division in Somerset. Climbing into the back of canvas-covered army lorries, more than sixty young troopers made themselves comfortable. The convoy left the outskirts of Windsor and sped noisily off on the long journey to Trowbridge. Passing through the streets and lanes, girls giggled and blushed at the wolf whistles resounding from the back of the open canvas. The lads chatted and laughed as they wobbled about in the lorries, trundling their way through towns, villages, and sun-dappled lanes.

"Give us a go on yer horn, Basil mate," Nick asked.

"Oh, no, not that again," grumbled Archie Golding.

"What did yer 'ave to bring that for?" he snapped at Basil.

"I dunno!" said Basil, holding it up to admire it, "I like it! It's a kind of mascot. I used to sound it when I rode with the hunt."

Archie gave a sarcastic laugh.

"Huh!" remarked Nick, "You hunted with the hare and hounds then?"

"I did!" replied Basil proudly. "Give us a blow on it then." Basil wobbled to the open exit and blew on the horn. To the delight of his fellow troopers, the sound came out as clear as a bell; cheering resonated into the street.

"Give us a go," Vic Jenkins asked.

"Huh," said Basil, handing the horn to him, "You won't get a sound out of it, mate!" he said.

Vic returned the instrument to its owner, conceding to Basil's comment.

Archie grunted and grabbed the horn, "I'll get something out of it!" he said.

"Okay, who's gonna lay bets," Nick asked.

"Two bob," said Benny, rummaging in his pocket for change.

Nick spent the next ten minutes collecting money while the lorry swayed and bumped towards its destination. Archie failed to get it to make a sound and threw it viciously back at Basil.

Laughing, he said, "It's busted!"

Stunned, Basil yelled, "What did you do that for?"

Benny jumped up from his seat and, grabbing Archie by the lapels, pinned him to the wagon's side with his fist in his face.

"You're gonna get it one of these days, you bastard!" growled Benny.

"Leave it, Benny, it ain't worth it," said Basil.

With the confrontation over, the competition resumed to see who could get a note out of the horn, keeping the Troopers amused for the best part of the journey to Trowbridge.

Trowbridge June/July 1942

The Regiment was billeted on various farms and homes in the area and in commandeered hotels. As they approached their billets, the lads were surprised by the hundreds of armoured cars and tanks of varying sizes and shapes lining Trowbridge's peaceful lanes and streets. Women hung around in little groups while children, distracted from their games, watched curiously as soldiers busied themselves on the vehicles.

"Crikey, we gonna be part of this lot?" Nick remarked, dropping to the ground out of the lorry.

"It's what's called a regiment!" Wilf quipped sarcastically.

Nick gave him a shove, flicked his beret off and ruffled his hair.

"Get off!" said Wilf, replacing his beret.

The sun hung low in the sky when Nick and Wilf strolled along the hedge-rowed lane of resting vehicles.

"Hey," shouted Nick, pointing, "That's a 'Daimler Dingo!"

The lads took a closer look at the little armoured car, "It's a neat little thing," he added.

"It's built for a different job," came a voice from behind, "Here, have a look."

The little armoured car was low enough for the lads to lean over the top to see inside.

"See, it has pre-select gears with five gears forward and five gears reverse and two steering wheels, one at each end."

"Yeh, that's so you don't have to turn it around to reverse," interrupted Wilf. "Correct," said the guardsman,"

"And it's only got a Bren gun," Wilf said.

"Correct again," the guardsman added, "That's about its limit when it comes to artillery because of its size." He began to walk away but turned to say, "It's not to be underestimated, though; it's going to be worth its weight in gold for speed and manoeuvrability when it's needed!"

The soldier left the group to their thoughts and comments, and as the evening drew to a close, they could be seen, under a darkening sky, strolling back to their billets.

The next day, the troopers were split up into groups. Amongst the gathering of troopers, Nick stood together with his closest comrades to listen to Squadron Leader Captain Ward instruct them in the role they would play.

Four squadrons, A, B, C, and D, formed the Armoured Reconnaissance Second Household Cavalry Regiment. Each Squadron had 5 troops consisting of four vehicles: two Daimler armoured cars and two scout cars. The Heavy troop attached to each squadron consisted of an A.E.C. Mark lll Matador and two White Cars, commonly known as the 'blood wagons,' carrying supplies and medical equipment. Altogether, over a hundred vehicles formed the Second Household Cavalry Regiment.

"You will be assigned to B Squadron under my command, your Squadron Leader," Major Wignall said with a wry smile. A ripple of laughter ensued. "The aim of the reconnaissance squadrons," concluded the Major, "is to find a route ahead, safe and clear of the enemy, for the tanks and infantry to follow. Any questions?"

There was no response.

Nick and Wilf were allocated a Daimler armoured car attached to 5 troop in B Squadron. The Troopers spent the next month studying the forms and performance of the various guns, ammunition and vehicles they would use in action. Included in their education was the use of the unfamiliar No 19 wireless set and, not least, the various uses of the shovel that hung on the side of the armoured car!

"Stone the crows!" Nick gasped, "We 'ave to sleep on the ground?"

Wilf shrugged his shoulders, equally bewildered. "That's what we were told. We dig trenches for our safety. It ain't gonna be fun!"

Overhearing the conversation, Charlie said, "If we're very good, we may be allowed to sleep under a bivouac with a bedroll."

"Yeh, I heard about them," said Nick, "Like little tents. Why do we 'ave to dig holes, then?"

"I told yer! Safety." Assured Wilf

The next day, Nick found himself in a crew of three in a modern Daimler Armoured car, travelling in convoy with the Regiment en route deep into the heart of Somerset. This was his first experience of a complete divisional training scheme with a 2 pounder anti-tank gun and a Besa machine gun in the discomforts and difficulties he might meet on the battlefield.

With no room to stand, there was just enough space inside the Daimler for the three occupants to sit. To the right of Nick sat the Troop Leader Palmer, who had room to stand only when the turret was opened. Nick sat beside the Besa Machine Gun as a wireless operator / gunner. Wilf, the driver and gunner, was in his seat lower down in a well at the front of the car. Surrounded on all sides and between them were the many controls, tools, equipment and armoury required for an armoured vehicle.

By midday, the division came to rest in a field near Cheddar in the heart of the beautiful Mendip Hills. Driving into the harbour the Troop Leader said,

"Remember what you were taught about forming a circle, Trooper Grant," "A laager Sir,"

"Correct!" Wilf steered the vehicle into position with the other vehicles already drawn into the harbour for the night. Troopers set to work immediately, digging slit trenches. Nick pushed his beret back on his head and pulled a handkerchief from his pocket to wipe the sweat from his face. Leaning on the shovel, he turned to see what Wilf had done.

"Deeper Trooper," came a commanding voice from behind. He turned to face the Troop Leader. "Deeper," he repeated and walked on.

Nick threw a glance of irritation at Wilf, who was sitting on the edge of his slit-trench with his feet in the neatly dug hole. He glanced down at Nick standing in his half-dug trench, shrugged his shoulders and lit up a fag. Frustrated, Nick lifted the shovel and plunged it into the earth!

The young troopers settled down for the night as best they could in full uniform, ready, if necessary, for action. Nick was the last to retire. Groping his way in the dark, he kicked a clod of earth into the trench of the sleeping Wilf, who responded with an angry verbal outburst closely followed by an additional barrage of offensive adjectives and requests for silence from other sleepers! "Aw shuddup!" Nick retorted

Early the following day, the crew of the Daimler awoke to begin their first divisional trial. This was a serious time for nineteen-year-old Nick Clayton. The noisy enclosure of the armour-plated vehicle allowed no idle banter. Headphones were donned, and the only communication between the crew was referred to directions.

Sliding down into the driver's seat, Wilf positioned himself at the wheel, opened the throttle and started the engine. Keeping close to the car in front, the Daimler bumped easily over rough ground. Nick listened to the wireless to hear the squadron leader giving directive orders. They advanced all day and into the night when the car in front suddenly came to a grinding halt. The Troop Leader, Lt Palmer, sent a message over the radio to the leading car, "What's the problem?"

"We should have turned off back there," came the reply.

The four vehicles halted in a quiet country lane. Spreading the large map over the front of a car, the Troop leaders bent their heads to study a map in the bright glow of a torch. Tempers began to fray as directions were rejected and arguments ensued.

This was just one of many incidents that held up the crew of the Daimler armoured car. Worse was to come when the crew were directed to switch roles. The Troop Leader took control of the wheel, Wilf took the wireless set, and Nick studied the map.

He directed the four armoured cars in entirely the wrong direction. His good sense of direction was better than his map reading skills. He was later pleased to report that he instinctively found a clear route.

"Instinctively?" bellowed the Second in Command Captain Ward, on their return, "Instinctively? Well, let's throw away the maps, and you can lead the Regiment safely through the war in Europe!" he shrieked in the lad's face.

Schemes and trials followed one after the other. The Regiment faced many more problems on these exercises, from wireless communications and mechanical breakdowns to petrol shortages and lack of replacement tyres, often causing exercises to fail completely. They later learned that while the schemes were often over-ambitious and mistakes were made, they proved invaluable training for war.

In July, an order came for an exercise at London Docks where loading tests on various vessels were to take place. A month later, a small battalion of vehicles were chosen for the task, one of which was the Daimler from 5 Troop, B Squadron. It included Trooper Nick Clayton. Leaving Trowbridge, the convoy of cars travelled along the roads and lanes of Somerset and Wiltshire, passing through towns and pretty villages and arriving in London later in the day. The vehicles drove into Knightsbridge and past Hyde Park Corner. They went along Constitution Hill, jerked and clanked their way slowly around the statue of Queen Victoria, past Buckingham Palace, down the Mall and under Admiralty Arch, passing safely around Trafalgar Square and then to the base at Woolwich.

The next day, the vehicles were driven to the King George V docks, where Troopers were shown how to load and unload the vehicles onto crates and then onto a ship. Nick looked up from his work to watch as the vehicles dangled precariously in the air, swinging from side to side,

Standing beside Wilf, Nick joked, "Wouldn't mind being up there. D'you reckon I could get a chance to sit at the wheel?"

Wilf frowned and sighed! "Idiot!" he muttered.

He shook his head in despair and rummaged in the toolbox for a spanner. Suddenly, there was an almighty bang as the vehicle dropped forty feet into the ship's hold. Surprised, Nick glanced up and saw the heavy chains that held the Matador crate dangling and clanking together at the end of the crane. His mouth dropped open, "Stone the crows!" he gasped.

All the tyres on the vehicle had burst, and, on inspection, the steering wheel had shot off its column. When they heard the news, Wilf directed a look of satisfaction at Nick, who pointed his spanner at the ship.

"Huh! That proves that I am being watched over and will return home safely from the front line when we finish off the Hun!" rebuked Nick.

Wilf shook his head in disbelief.

The exercise at the docks coincided with news of the disastrous British and Canadian attack on the French coast, where thousands of British and Canadian troops and US Rangers died in a failed attempt to secure the French port of Dieppe. The purpose was to open a second front in North West Europe to relieve the pressure on the Russians after the German advance on the Soviet Union. The operation also allowed the opportunity for a practical trial beach landing in the event of real opposition for which the British Chief of Combined Operations was agitating and which, under pressure, the government agreed to.

On the return journey to Trowbridge, the convoy passed through the East End of London towards Blackfriars Bridge. Standing in the turret next to the Troop Leader, Nick smiled at the cheering crowds.

"Seems a bit over the top, sir," he said, adding, "Huh! We're heroes already, and we ain't done nothin'!"

"They must think we're returning from Dieppe," the Troop Leader replied.

In the Autumn of 1942, the Regiment went to Linney Head Ranges in Pembrokeshire. Drafty Stackpole Court accommodated the soldiers in its large, spacious rooms.

"For those of you who are new to this great 'ouse," boomed the Corporal Major, "The drafts and the cold are all part of your learning.' It will 'old you all in good stead for the forthcoming European visit when you wish you were 'ere instead of there!" Tucking his baton under his arm, he turned to go. "Ah!" he said, suddenly wheeling round again. Glancing down the spacious room lined with grey iron bedsteads, he added, "One other thing; you may be wondering where the nearest place of entertainment is. Well, I can tell you it is in Pembroke nearby and, a few miles further, the seaside town of Tenby is very nice too! You may find time to visit it."

Nick grinned!

"That is," continued the Corporal Major, "If you still have energy left after the daily, gruelling exercises you will experience on the ranges." He gave a sarcastic smile and turned his portly, upright frame to leave the room.

Nick groaned as soon as he was gone, "At least we don't have to dig trenches!"

Bob lay on his bed thinking, "Wonder what they're doing back home."

"I'm wondering what Germany is doing right now," said Wilf. "If Jerry is in Russia, as the newspapers claim, then they won't be invading Britain for a while."

Nick lifted his head off his arms and rested on his elbow, "Yeh, you're right, so why are we 'avin' to train so bleedin' 'ard?"

"They've been in Russia for the last year," Wilf added.

"Yeh, well, there's no way Hitler and his henchmen can invade England at the same time."

There were many early mornings when the Autumn mist lay like a blanket of down over the fields, where dozens of tanks and armoured cars were seen to set off on yet another manoeuvre, grinding their way through the lanes, villages and coastal roads of Pembrokeshire where the mixed emotions of the local people were made evident. Farmers glowered from their fields; shopkeepers stopped what they were doing to search the window in an attempt to see the traffic pass by. Curious faces peered from behind curtains; women stood gossiping on doorsteps. Some waved and wished them luck; others glared and called children to stop their games in the streets to clear the way for the noisy vehicles while young women sauntered coquettishly along the pavement, giving provocative side-long glances to the troopers who responded accordingly!

Out in the open fields, rudely interrupting the tranquil scene of the beautiful countryside, the sound of mortar bombs, Besa machine guns and other ammunition resounded mixed with raucous voices yelling instructions. Occasional rest stops in a remote village created an interesting diversion. Local people were sometimes only too pleased to meet and greet the Troopers. Curious boys in short trousers and caps searched the vehicles lining the narrow streets while women dressed in simple frocks covered with neat pinafores handed out what they could afford in home-cooked preserves and cakes. Pretty young girls eager to help coyly enjoyed the winks and flattering comments as they assisted the women.

"Butter's rationed, so it's gotta be margarine!" a lilting Welsh voice was heard to say.

Nick grimaced! "I wonder if they've got any sandwiches without butter," he thought as he graciously smiled and accepted the food.

"Thanks very much," came numerous grateful replies.

Gathered in a small group with his friends, Nick spotted a newsagent's shop, "I'm off to get a newspaper," he said, pointing across the road. Stuffing a scone in his mouth, he went toward the newsagent, hastily digging into his pockets for some money.

The girl behind the counter smiled and handed him his change, "Thanks, Love," he said. Then, placing his hands on the counter, he lifted himself up, leaned forward, and kissed her on the cheek. Quick as a flash, her hand came across, and Nick felt the sting on his face!

"She didn't appreciate it!" he told the boys, covering his throbbing face with his hand.

Wilf laughed, "That'll teach yer!"

Nick finished the remains of his scone and opened his newspaper on a low stone wall. He devoured its pages until the order came to remount. The men returned to their armoured cars and tanks, and their tasks bent on finishing yet another scheme. The excitement over a small group of people stood in the centre of the village chatting in the late afternoon sun while others resumed what they had been doing as if nothing had disturbed their day.

1942 Christmas

While it was no surprise to hear that leave was to be granted, it was certainly a relief for the Troopers to hear thay they would be going home for Christmas.

Nick and his mates boarded a train at Tenby and crammed into an empty carriage. They bustled about removing coats and hoisting duffle bags onto the racks above the seats into which they finally settled for the long journey home. Satisfied exhalation of smoke filled the carriage as those who chose to lit up a cigarette. The train rattled and shuddered, and then a burst of steam and smoke belched noisily out of the engine funnel. Steam spurted out from the wheels billowing up, obscuring the view from the window until the train picked up speed. The boys fell back in their seats, visibly relieved at the thought they were going home. The rhythmic sound of the train as it swayed along the track blended with the lowered conversations passing between the lads. They glanced around but carried on their conversation as the door slid open, and another passenger entered to claim the last vacant seat. He hoisted his small brown suitcase onto the rack and made himself comfortable. He produced a pack of cigarettes out of his pocket, of which he took one. Tapping it on the cigarette box, he crossed his legs, struck a match and inhaled deeply. The conversation reduced, and soon, the carriage fell silent apart from the distinctive sound of Nick turning the pages of his newspaper. A few minutes passed before one Trooper broke the silence, "Not sure what I will find when I get home, what with the bombing and all," he muttered.

"Are you going home on leave then?" said the latest arrival.

He was about thirty years of age, wore civvies over his tall, slim frame and spoke with a Welsh accent. One or two of the boys acknowledged that they were.

"'oome for Christmas then?" he sang. "I've been 'oome for the last six months," he added, "convalescing after an injury I received in Tobruk."

Nick smacked his newspaper closed and gasped, "Tobruk, did you say?" All eyes were now on the stranger, keen to hear more. "Yes, I was injured just before Rommel's second offensive when the rest of the Coldstream Guards were captured."

"Coldstream Guards?" Nick fired another question.

"Yes, the 3rd Battalion."

"We're all Royal Horseguards, part of the Guards Armoured Division," said Wilf.

"2nd Household Cavalry! I guessed that by these, the 'Ever Open Eye,'" said the passenger, pointing to Wilf's shoulder flashes.

"I'm in the 1st Household Cavalry!"

"You were lucky then," said Nick.

"Don't know about Lucky," he replied. "If getting meself nearly killed is lucky, then I guess you could say I was!"

The interesting stories the Welshman offered kept the lads occupied for the rest of the journey to Swansea, where they changed trains and separated to their various destinations. Late in the afternoon, Nick boarded the train to Paddington Station along with other servicemen who struggled to get their bulky luggage onto the train and down the crowded corridors. Carriage doors clunked shut all along the station platform, and the train pulled slowly out of the station, groaning under the weight. Nick made himself as comfortable as he could in the corridor, moving when necessary at train stations for other passengers to pass along. An air of lively cheerfulness came from both ends of the train as it went on its journey. As night fell, dim blue lights, fitted to avoid being seen by enemy planes, lit up in the carriages, giving the passengers a ghostly, indistinctive appearance. Songs and laughter spilled out into the corridor, and Nick sang lustily along with the other servicemen in the packed corridor.

Elsie and Dick Clayton had waited up for their son late into the evening before deciding they could wait no longer and retired to bed.

Bleary-eyed, Elsie opened the back door, "O my gawd, what time do you call this then? Yer father's asleep upstairs." she hissed.

"Hello, Mum," said Nick wearily. He stepped into the unlit scullery.

"Gotta be careful with the lights, or I'll 'ave the air-raid warden yellin'," whispered Elsie.

She lit a match and, reaching up, pulled down the chain attached to the gas lamp set in the center of the ceiling. Gas hissed out of it, and she deftly lit the mantle, giving off a dim light.

"Good to have you home, Son," she said, flicking the dead match into the still-warm embers of the fire grate,

"Bout time you had electricity installed," said Nick, dropping his duffel bag onto the floor.

"Don't get me on that," Elsie grumbled, "They're talking about knocking down the cottage to make space for the museum next door."

"Really?" exclaimed Nick. He undid his coat and slumped onto the chair, "I'm really tired, Mum, so talk tomorra. I'll kip down on the chair here rather than disturb Joyce. You go to bed, and I'll see you in the morning." He stood up, cupped his mother's head, and kissed her forehead. "G'night Mum."

The warm smell of toast and the muffled chink of a cup as it was placed on a saucer roused Nick the following day. He yawned, pulled the blanket over his shoulder, made himself comfortable and dozed again.

"Nick." Whispered Joyce.

"Don't wake him, Love," said Elsie

Nick opened one eye. A hand signal from under the blanket was enough for Joyce to run, jump onto her big brother, and settle by his side.

"You've got a job to do today," she chuckled.

"O yeh and what's that?" Nick replied.

"We're making Christmas decorations, and we need your help."

"And who's we?"

"Margaret and me and Mum and Mrs Green,"

"Is Cissie Packham helping?"

"Nope," said Joyce, slipping to the floor. She giggled knowingly and began to drag Nick out of the chair, "She's got to work, then she's going to the pictures with you-know-who."

"Struth, you've got a lot of energy," Nick groaned.

Dick was just finishing breakfast, "Well, I'm off Love," he said, getting up from his chair. "Nice to see you, Son, but I gotta rush now to get down to the butcher, or we're gonna 'ave no meat for tomorrow." Dick slammed the door as he left.

"Stone the crows," said Elsie, frowning, "That door's gonna come off its 'inges one of these days!"

The next day was spent as Joyce hoped, with Margaret and her brother helping Elsie make Christmas decorations. Nick wobbled on a chair to hang the paper chains across the ceiling while Joyce and her mum helped Margaret dip holly in a solution of Epsom Salts. The results were just as the magazine predicted. When it dried, the holly looked frosted and beautiful.

"The holly's really nice, Joy. Where did you get it?" asked Nick.

"Me, Margaret, Billy Mellor, and some of the other kids from School went over the 'oller Pond, and we picked loads. Yeh, I got really prickled when I went blackberry picking, didn't I, Margaret?"

"Yeh and Billy Mellor's mum was really cross when we got back," said Margaret, rubbing her nose.

"Why?" asked Nick, "'Cause she told him not to go an' e did an' e trod in some dog pooh….."

"Ugh!" remarked Elsie, "that's not a nice thing to say, Margaret."

Sniggering, Joyce and her friend got up from the floor and added a paper Chinese lantern to the Christmas tree.

Full of mischief, Margaret looked at Joyce and added, "Well, it's true, and she didn't 'alf clip him one round the ear!"

Joyce put her hands on her hips and lifted her chin, "Well, you'll be pleased to know that we went round to everyone and gave them some holly," she remarked.

Elsie sighed, wiped her hands on her apron and got up. "I can't help anymore," she said, "I've got other things to do before we go out."

"Me too," said Mrs Green.

Nick followed the two women into the scullery out of earshot of Joyce and Margaret, "That reminds me, Mum," he said, "what's this about you not getting electricity?"

"Oh!" said Elsie, surprised, "'e's selling the land to the Museum."

"Whose sellin'," the landlord?'

"Yes, all four cottages will go. Breaks my 'eart just thinking about it!"

"They've started putting electricity in the other cottages," said Mrs Green, buttoning up her coat. "Mine's on the list to be done. It makes me feel really bad for your mum."

"Where're you and Dad gonna go then?" asked Nick.

"I dunno, some council flat somewhere," Elsie added, "Anyway, I don't wanna talk about it, Nick, not now anyway."

Mrs Green brightened and changed the subject. She looked at the Christmas decorations they had made and said, "I'm looking forward to decorating my room with these. Come on, Margaret."

Handing Margaret some bits to carry, they left the cottage.

To Elsie's delight, Dick returned with a whole chicken. "Where the 'eck did you get that from?" she gasped. "I had the luck to bump into me brother Harold. He was on his way round here with it."

"Gawd blimey, where'd he get it then?"

"Don't ask!" He said, "I reckon it was from one of the customers at the Ritz, you know, where he does his lift attendant job."

"How come he's working there then, Dad?" asked Nick.

"He lost an arm, didn't he?" remarked Dick.

"Yeh, I remember, a couple of years ago, working in that factory,"

"That's right. Thought he'd never work again, but he got lucky, I guess. It's not much money, but he gets some fair-sized tips and chickens, too!"

Dick tied his scarf tighter around his neck, "Can't stand around here gossiping, got to go to work now, see you later,"

Elsie braced herself as the door banged shut and shook her head with frustration, "'Spose, I gotta find something to make stuffing now!" she said, patting the plump chicken.

Elsie spent the rest of the morning and well into the afternoon preparing food for Christmas day with her few meager ingredients.

The fog that came in with the dawn on Christmas Eve had cleared, revealing a bright sky and a crisp, cold day. Nick wore his thick army coat and walked to the corner shop to buy a newspaper.

"Hello, Nick," called out Mr Cohan, coming from the opposite direction, "Home for Christmas then?"

"Yeh! Lucky, there's not much going on for the Regiment right now. I'll be off back in a day or two. Have you heard any news of Eli?"

"Nothing lad." Mr. Cohan lowered his head, "It's the missus I worry about. She's not eating and seems to be in her own world."

"I'm sorry," said Nick, "'s'pose it's no good telling her not to give up hope?"

"I've tried everything, Son, but she just seems to get further and further away. Yer mum's been kindness itself and other neighbours too, but it don't seem to 'elp!"

At that moment, Mr Green came round the corner; he tipped his hat politely and strolled on by.

"You on your way to the Nag?" called Mr Cohan.

"Yep! you comin' then?"

"Don't mind if I do," replied Mr Cohen.

Falling into step with Mr Green, he threw Nick a backward glance, touched his cap and said, "Nice to see you, Nick. Take care of yourself."

Nick selected a newspaper from the rack outside the newsagent. He opened the pages and joined the queue to pay for it. He stood buried in the pages of his newspaper.

"Any good news then, Nick?" Nick glanced around to answer the question,

"Not much, Cissie," he said, closing the paper. "Hey, I thought you were working today. Joyce said you were."

"I've got half an hour off for lunch. I saw you looking at the newspapers, so I followed you in."

"Good, I'm glad," said Nick.

"Really? You seem pleased to see me!" remarked Cissie.

Nick hesitated, "Well, er, I can ask you how Kenny's getting on, can't I?" he said awkwardly.

"Me Mum had a letter from him last week, and he seems okay, but reading between the lines, I think being a gunner is taking its toll. Did you know he's been on sorties?" she asked.

"Has he? No, I didn't, but I'm not surprised; I suppose it had to happen sooner or later!"

"You payin' for that paper or not?" came an irritated voice from behind Nick.

"Keep yer 'air on, lady," retorted Nick.

He paid for his paper, took hold of Cissie's arm and led her out of the shop. In the winter sunshine, they strolled along the road toward the High Street, "I haven't got much time, Nick. Manzies is really busy right now."

Nick stopped and looked at Cissie, "You ain't working at Manzies?" he said grimacing.

Cissie shrugged, "Haven't got much choice, and anyway, it's not such a bad job. I really want to do some war work, but Mum's not happy about that. I'm too young anyway."

"So what you going to see tonight at the pictures?" asked Nick

"Holiday Inn," said Cissie. "I s'pose Joyce told you that an' all," she said, dropping her eyes.

"Is 'e taking you?" Nick said with a biting tone.

"Don't say it like that, Nick. Alan's a nice chap,"

"Say it like what?"

"Well, sounds like he isn't good enough," said Cissie quietly.

"He's not!"

Cissie gasped, "Who says? Nick Clayton? He's a darn sight better than you, and if that's all you've got to say," Cissie paused, "You can……. push off."

Cissie flounced off, leaving Nick grinning.

He caught up with her, "Aw Cissie, I didn't mean any 'arm. It's just that I like you,"

"Well, I don't like you," Cissie retorted and continued alone.

Nick let her go. He shrugged and turned thoughtfully back toward home.

Chapter 12
Christmas Day 1942

The day dawned cold and foggy. Nick awoke to the excited voice of his twelve-year-old sister sharing the contents of her pillowcase with their parents in the bedroom. Joyce saw him peering round the open door, "Look, Nick," she cried, holding up a multi-colored knitted jumper, "Isn't it lovely?"

Elsie raised her eyebrows, "sat up 'till two this morning to finish it," she murmured. "I think there's something under the tree for you too, Nick," she said.

Clambering off her parent's bed, Joyce ran down the narrow, steep stairs; Nick followed.

Joyce put down her precious jumper and grabbed the gift addressed to Nick, "Open it then, Nick," she squealed, "Go on, open it."

"What's the rush, Joyce?" said Elsie, entering the room from the stairwell. "Sorry, it's wrapped in newspaper, but well….."

Nick looked at his mother, "What's to be sorry for Mum? I'd've been surprised if it were wrapped in anything else."

"It's the best I could do," called Elsie from the kitchen.

"What's this then?" said Nick, pointing to a pattern on the paper that held the gift.

"It's a Christmas tree, well it's s'pposed to be anyway,' said Joyce. "Don't you like it? I tried to make it really pretty with potato prints, but the paint wasn't very good."

Nick turned the paper around to decipher the pattern. "I love it and can see that it's a Christmas tree now. You are so clever to make it."

Joyce beamed. Nick finally opened the gift to reveal two bars of precious soap, "Thanks, Mum, it's just what I need."

"Well, I know how difficult it is to get nowadays. Use it carefully,"

Elsie had saved a couple of eggs from her allowance, which she boiled for Nick and his dad. Joyce tucked into her bread and milk, looking on as they ate their eggs, willing them to give her just a spoonful.

Nick handed his sister a piece of bread, "Here, you can dip the bread in my egg."

Dick offered her another piece of bread, and she dipped it again. They chuckled as she relished the taste.

The rest of the morning was spent enjoying the warmth of the fire and listening to Christmas programmes on the wireless. Elsie packed all the food and gifts she had prepared and ready to take to the family gathering at her mother-in-law's home.

The day did not disappoint the family. The bottle of port wine Dick managed to procure from the licensee of the Nag's Head was eked out into each glass and saved for the toast following the King's speech; games, songs and entertainment followed. The young adults of the family disappeared to a quiet area to discuss the war, current affairs and the latest films, to the disapproval of Elsie,

Opening the door to another room, she asked, "What are you doing here then? Aren't you coming in to have a sing?'

"Aw mum, give us a break," moaned Nick, "I ain't seen me cousins for months, and we've got lots to catch up on."

"Well, I think you're being rude, " Elsie snapped. She turned and exited the room, closing the door firmly behind her. The day ended as it always did on Christmas Day. Joyce and her younger cousins and their mothers retired to bed at a late hour. Meanwhile, the men were engrossed in their traditional game of cards.

Spartan Feb 1943

Nick returned to his regiment at Linney Head before the year was out, pleased to meet again with his fellow soldiers.

Over their pints of beer, local people gave intermittent glances and nodded toward the troopers as they entered the village pub. Counting some coins into his hand to pay for a beer at the bar, he asked, "Hey Wilf, did you have a good Christmas then?" Taking their drinks to a table, the lads spent the next hour sharing their different stories, exaggerating and elaborating accordingly.

"I was a bit bewildered," commented Trooper Dave Brewer, who accompanied them from A Squadron,

"Why?" asked Nick. "Well, when I arrived home, I opened the door and another man was there,"

"And?" Questioned Nick.

Well, it was a bit odd 'cause he was sitting in my armchair, very comfortable. It turns out he was a cousin of my wife's, but I had never heard of him before. The best of it was he was wearing my bedroom slippers!"

Nick sniggered.

"What's funny then?" Dave asked indignantly.

"Sorry mate!' I er...," stammered Nick. "You don't think he was a lover or something, I 'ope!"

Dave declared, "My wife's faithful, and anyway, he was very polite and left soon after I arrived." Dave frowned and whispered, "But he shouldn't 'ave bin wearing my slippers."

The regiment moved back to Somerset at the end of January 1943 and had more gruelling schemes but none as gruelling as Spartan.

Standing to attention on a cold late January morning, Troopers from B Squadron learned their fate.

"At ease," came the commanding voice of Captain Ward.

Boots resounded carelessly, and shoulders dropped as the Troopers of the Second Household Cavalry relaxed.

"This exercise will be the hardest you have experienced yet," he roared. "Its purpose is to test the vehicles and your endurance ready for the real test in Europe. The exercise will cover an area that will stretch from Land's End to John O'Groats and will be constantly on the move. There will be nothing to cheer you; no sneaking off to farms for eggs to fry for breakfast and no football or cinema's to take your mind off the gruelling discomfort of the exercise. You will be alert and ready for action at a moment's notice."

Once the young troopers were dismissed, an air of anticipation resulted, buzzing with conversation amongst the groups of troopers as they went to their billets.

Nick sucked in the cold air and blew out, "Gawd struth!" Rubbing his cold hands together.

Wilf raised his eyebrows, "You can say that again!"

The lads went off to join another group of troopers.

"Hey Nick," called Bob, "You 'eard that; no wenchin' neither!"

Arms locked around each other's shoulders, the young men walked off, deep in conversation.

Nick broke from the group laughing, "I bet yer ten bob I'll find me a beau'iful girl who is willin."

Good-natured shouts and jeers followed as they arrived at the door of their billet.

On a cold February day in 1943, the one hundred armoured cars of four sabre squadrons fanned out on surveillance in the narrow lanes of Somerset. A column of tanks and armoured cars of the Guards Armoured Division ground their way along, following at a distance. Enclosed in the dank air of cramped conditions, Wilf sat at the wheel while Nick and the Troop Leader Lt Palmer kept a constant listening ear tuned into the wireless.

Alert, they awaited orders for their next objective. The suspense of hiding in the woods or ditches of tree-lined lanes, not knowing what was around the next corner or wondering where the enemy might be, created nervous agitation even before anything happened.

"You think this is suspense? Wait 'till you're in the thick of it facing the real enemy." Said the Troop Leader.

"Thanks," thought Nick.

Exercises carried on through the night with no rest. When rest did come, the exhausted Troopers slept soundly in the warmest, most comfortable place they could find, only to be rudely roused soon after and off again.

"It's bloody cold," whispered Nick, blowing on his fingertips, "What time is it, Wilf?"

Spread out on the straw-filled barn floor lay other weary troopers sleeping. Wilf sat next to Nick, his eyes closed, resting his head against the side of the barn. He sighed and drew back his sleeve to look at his watch.

"Can't see in the dark," he murmured, moving his arm about to get a better view, "I think it's two am,"

"D'ya think we might get a lie in?" joked Nick.

"Shut up and let me get some shuteye, will ya!" Wilf snapped. Plumping up the little straw he had, he made himself comfortable and fell asleep.

The lads were woken that morning before daybreak to hear bellowing commands to return to their vehicles. A discordant movement saw B squadron leave the warm barn and head out into the cold night air, each to their car.

Almost too weary to talk, Wilf said, "We're in the lead today, Nick, and you're driving."

"Right," Nick replied. He climbed into the Daimler through the side door and wriggled into the seat.

Just before leaving Windsor, Nick had taken a few brief driving lessons and passed a simple test on the High Street. Now, he was ready to manoeuvre the Daimler armoured car in a major military exercise. Taking a deep breath, he opened the viewing slit and started the car.

The morning dawned frosty, bright and clear. By late morning, the reconnaissance exercise had been cautious but uneventful; there was even a chance to crack a joke or two.

Passing a junction in the road, they carried on when suddenly the Troop Leader yelled, "Hold it!". Pointing in the direction of the horizon, he added, "Something is coming over the top of that hill."

The Daimler came to a halt, as did the other three cars of 5 Troop.

"Reverse, reverse," yelled the Troop leader.

In haste, Nick shot the gears into reverse at speed and ended up in a ditch on the side of the road.

Climbing out of the turret, the Troop Leader yelled, "Get the bloody thing back on the road." It was too late! The troops had been spotted by the enemy tanks and taken prisoner. Wilf shot Nick an irritated glance.

Nick shrugged his shoulders, "You should be grateful," he said, "You can sit back now and enjoy the scenery!"

Once again, the Troopers from 2 HCR stood at ease in the field that served as a parade ground.

"Well, lads," bellowed the Squadron Leader, "I am obliged to inform you that 'Spartan' is at an end. It has been a success, with only a few technical problems reported and one or two casualties. Well done!"

"Where's me ten bob then?" Basil whispered to Nick!

"What for?"

"You said you'd get to lay a girl!"

"Go blow yer horn!" said Nick.

Chapter 13
Norwich Again
March 1943

In March 1943, the regiment moved from Somerset to Wolterton in Norfolk, where the officers found comfortable rooms in Wolterton Hall or Nissan huts, and everyone else slept under canvas. Day after day, rigorous training and exercise became part of the Trooper's routine. The days grew warmer and extended; trees hung heavy with new growth. Enclosed in a tent taking a well-earned rest Nick lay on his camp bed reading a letter.

In contrast, the rest of his fellow Troopers occupied themselves in recreation. Wilf cleaned his boots while Basil sat at a table reading.

Nick sat up and, leaning on his elbow, exclaimed, "Hey me mate, Kenny's been made Staff Sergeant in the Royal Air Force."

Only Basil glanced up and nodded acknowledgement. Nick read silently on:

…………Mrs Packham's right proud. Dad and I are thinking about you and wondering where you are and what you are doing. Will you send us a line soon? We haven't heard a word since you left at Christmas. Kenny's mum's got three letters since then. I have to lie to her when she asks if I have heard from you. Dad and Mr Green are sharing an allotment

so we can get some nice fresh veg. The ground's a bit hard at the moment, but they will dig it over as soon as they can. Joyce had a nice birthday. I managed to get her a new pair of shoes. She's got such big feet now. The sirens still go off now and then, and we never know when, so I am still living off my nerves. Mrs Cohan is poorly with her chest again. Still no news of Eli. We are just about managing the food rationing, trying to make it all stretch. Gran is poorly, too, and she'll be 90 in a couple of weeks. We had to call the doctor again, and he said we mustn't stop her daily brown ale and bath bun as he said it would kill her. I hope you're alright. I pray for you every night. Don't forget to write soon.

Your loving Mum

Putting the letter aside, he flung his legs over the side of the bed. He sat for an idle moment, scratched his head and yawned, 'Me mother's complaining 'cos I don't write,' He said.

"Nah, you're always too busy doing other things," sneered Bob.

"Yeh," Wilf said, spitting on his boots. Rubbing them vigorously, he added, "Which one's it gonna be today then, 'Mary from the Dairy' or 'Honeysuckle Rose'?"

A ripple of laughter ran through the tent.

Nick stood up and stretched, "Me and letter-writing don't go together!"

1943 Mid- March - July

During the next few months, occasional schemes relieved the boredom of the parade ground in order to keep the Troopers familiar with the vehicles, ammunition and wireless sets.

On one of these exercises, the route passed through the village of Stifkey. "Stifkey," murmured Wilf thoughtfully, "Aint this the village where that vicar used to take prostitutes?"

Nick's eyes widened, "I dunno!"

"I'll tell you!" said Lt Palmer. His name was Harold Davidson, and he was defrocked for immoral practices with prostitutes in London. I think it was about nine years ago."

Wilf threw back his head and laughed, "Reckon Harold prayed with 'em then laid with 'em! He was looking after their spiritual needs!" he chuckled.

"That's not all," came the voice from the turret, "He ended up in the mouth of a lion; killed him!"

Nick snorted, "Blimey! Poor sod didn't deserve that!" he said thoughtfully. "How did he end up in the mouth of a lion then, sir?"

"He got a job in a circus!"

"Phew!" said Wilf, "You'd better be careful, Nick," he added.

"Why?" asked Nick.

"You don't want to upset God!"

"Yeh right!" exclaimed Nick, "You'd better not be seen at the racecourse tomorrow either!"

....

Nick and his fellow Troopers were in high spirits as they climbed into an army lorry where another half a dozen Troopers were already seated comfortably, "You lot going to Newmarket?" asked Basil, settling down for the ride. "Yeh, hop in," a friendly voice called. The conversation and raunchy humour that followed continued for the hour-long journey until the lorry stopped near the race track. An invasion of men in khaki poured out from behind the canvas covering, clattering to the ground in highly polished black boots. Nick pulled himself up to his five foot eight size and straightened his hat; rubbing his hands together, he said, "This is gonna be good!"

The day wore on with relentless cheering to encourage a winning horse and the frustrations and moans at losing a race. As they went off to get their winnings, Archie, Wilf and Nick were suddenly stopped in their tracks. Straightening up, they jerked their hands to a salute as Major Wignall and another officer passed by.

"Carry on, Troopers," said the Major.

"Blimey," said Archie once they were out of earshot, "didn't expect to see him here!"

"Why not!" interjected Basil, "They are human, you know, with human feelings!"

The lads moved on, laughing.

The last race was over, and people began to filter out through the gates. The lads followed the crowd into the lane where the lorry waited to take them back to camp.

"I aint doin' this again," moaned Archie.

Nick slapped him on the back and laughed, "Couldn't have happened to a nicer guy. Better luck next time, mate."

"I'm tellin' yer. I aint doin' this again,"

Hauling themselves onto the lorry, it soon disappeared down the road vibrating with voices singing 'Show Me The Way to go home, I'm tired, and I wanna go to bed....'.

August 1943

Time passed, and it seemed the Regiment would never do anything but everlasting training and exercise. Overnight stops in the depths of the countryside were made easier since the Troopers were finally given bivouacs to sleep under.

"Wondered when these were going to arrive," said Wif.

"Gonna get a good night's sleep under the bivvy with you keeping me warm, darling," remarked Nick.

Wilf rolled his eyes and, taking a last draw on the stub of his cigarette, threw it on the ground.

People in the villages and towns had long since become used to the sight of tanks suddenly appearing out of hedgerows, followed by troops of infantry clattering across the lanes and firing volleys of gunfire at any given moment. Net curtains continued to lift from windows as the convoys passed through, and children came out into the street to run alongside their cars.

Nick continued his newspaper reports on Hitler's progress and whatever sports results he could find. In August, he was disappointed to read that a one-day match at Lord's Cricket Ground between an England XI and a West Indies XI ended in a draw despite Trevor Bailey taking 6 wickets for only twenty-seven runs in the first innings.

"It's only a game," Wilf commented, "Meanwhile, Hitler is bombing the brains out of Britain. Put it into perspective, man!"

"No luck there then," Nick remarked, closing the door on yet another newsagent shop. "' er old man's glaring at me over the top of 'is glasses. You'd think I had ideas!"

"Well, didn't yer?" asked Wilf.

Nick opened the pages of his newspaper, "She was a looker!" he murmured. "'Ere," Nick suddenly exclaimed, "This is lookin' good! It says 'ere Mussolini's been taken prisoner and Italy's surrendered and coming over to our side." Excited, Nick closed the paper and slapped Wilf on the back. "Reckon the war will be over before we fire a shot," he said.

In 1936, Italy's fascist dictator Benito Mussolini signed a document allying Italy with Adolf Hitler and joined the war in 1940, fighting alongside Germany on several fronts, including the North African campaign. Now, in 1943, after the first major bombing of Italy, Italian leaders deposed Mussolini and later signed an armistice with the Allies. However, Germany invaded Italy immediately, occupying towns and cities and seizing control of local governments and fighting to liberate Italy continued for another year.

Norfolk November '43

When Nick fell ill with a chest infection, winter was beginning to set in. It started after some particularly bad weather when the Troopers spent several cold, wet nights holed up in slit trenches. Arriving back at the billet, Wilf and Basil bowled in.

Wilf bent to undo his bootlaces, "How're you feeling, mate?" he asked.

"Missed a good route march today in gale-force winds along the flippin' coast." Rubbing his feet, he added, "Me feet are killing me!"

Others came noisily in, out of the cold, giving Nick a hard time for being sick.

"Some people will do anything to get out of a route march!"

With that two orderlies came in and went over to where Nick lay. "I'm off to hospital," Nick said weakly.

"Yep!" said an orderly as he busied himself, removing Nick from his bed, "His temperature's up through the ruddy roof; I think he's got pneumonia!"

"Bad luck!" exclaimed Basil.

Hospital

Nick spent the next month in hospital, still able to look for a pretty face with whom to tease and flirt. Lying between the clean crisp sheets in neat surroundings, winter sunshine poured through the windows onto the highly polished floors. Nick had an unexpected visit from his Squadron Leader, Major Wignall.

He came to see how the trooper was progressing. With an air of importance, Matron, followed by a young nurse, led him to Nick's bed. Dismissing any formalities from Nick, he shook him by the hand, expressing his hope that the lad was feeling better.

"I'm feeling a lot better, thank you, sir. The nurses and matron here are looking after me well enough."

"Good to hear," came the terse reply. "Hopefully, you will soon rejoin your unit."

"What should I do when I leave here, sir?"

Don't worry about that. We'll see you are delivered safely back to your unit."

The Major and Matron moved away from Nick's bedside and stood in a short discussion. Nick watched as they left the room. Reaching the door, the young nurse opened it for the Major and Matron, who left the room; turning to Nick, she gave him a flirtatious wink. Faintly smiling, Nick raised his eyebrows in acknowledgement and slid down between the bed sheets.

As it happened, Nick didn't return to his unit immediately; instead, he was given two weeks' leave. He packed his bag and began the journey home to Walthamstow.

Standing idly at Waterloo Station, he caught the eye of an elderly man with a walking stick watching him. Nick scowled and moved towards a newspaper stand. Browsing through the magazines and papers, he looked around furtively and saw the man still hanging around. He bought a newspaper and walked away in the opposite direction. The pungent smell of cheap aftershave caught Nick's attention, and suddenly, he was aware of the suspicious-looking man standing just to his left, leaning on his walking stick. Nick frowned as the man moved closer to him. With a swift movement, Nick kicked the stick and swore at the man who crumpled unsteadily.

Moving quickly away, Nick yelled back, 'I know your sort. Get lost!'

People stopped what they were doing and turned to see what the disturbance was as the man hurried away. A slightly flustered Nick joined the queue of young soldiers to buy his train ticket home.

1943 Late November, early December

The blackout curtains were securely fastened when Nick sat with his family at the dining room table. Elsie brought in tea on a tray and laid it on the table. She wiped her eyes with her apron skirt, and Nick felt an atmosphere. "You all right, Mum?"

"Thank gawd you're 'ome. You 'ad me worried!" she brusquely said, "I s'pose they're looking after you at them barracks?"

"'Course they are Love," said Dick, "You know 'ow 'is chest is and always 'as bin!"

"Yeh well 'e shouldn't 'ave gone in the army then!" she argued. Removing the lid of the teapot, she stirred the tea.

"Come to think of it," Elsie continued, "They shouldn't 'ave passed you 'ealthy neither!"

Nick gave his mother a wink, "Too late now, mum! Anyway, I'm fine now and looking forward to resting and relaxing."

Joyce sat close to her brother with her face against the sleeve of his coarse army jacket. "Your jackets prickly," she said, lifting her head and grimacing but continued leaning against him.

"It's time you were in bed, Young Lady," said her father.

"Dad," whined Joyce, "I'm nearly thirteen and Nick's only just arrived."

"I don't care. It's late, and you have school tomorrow. Up the apple and pears with you,"

Reluctantly, Joyce left the room, returning almost immediately to plant a kiss on her brother's cheek.

"G'night, Little Sister," said Nick, "See you in the morning."

"G'night," called Joyce from the bottom of the stairs.

Dick finished his tea and stood up, "I think we'll talk in the morning Son," said Dick. "It's late, and I'm tired."

Elsie frowned, "Wait a minute, you 'aven't……".

"In the morning, love," Dick interjected. Again, Nick sensed something was not right but brushed it aside.

Joyce had gone to school by the time Nick went down for breakfast. Elsie and Dick were sitting at the dining table just as if they had not been to bed.

"Som'inks's wrong!" said Nick, pulling out a chair and sitting down.

"Yes," said Dick.

Instinct made Nick say, "It's Kenny, isn't it?"

Dick sighed deeply, "He's dead, son,"

Nick was stunned into silence. For a brief moment, he put his head in his hands. "How, when?"

"His plane came down in the Med, lost at sea, the telegram said." Elsie sobbed.

"His poor mum and dad,' she said. She began to get agitated. "And what with the Marsdon's losing Bobby at sea, where's it all gonna end?" she cried.

Dick touched her hand and gently said, "Now then, Love, don't get yourself upset."

"Well, I can't 'elp it," retorted Elsie, blowing her nose into a clean hanky. "It'll break my 'eart if I lose you, Nick," she said, now weeping bitterly, "Poor Mrs Packham," she wailed.

Cissie answered the door to Nick dressed in a short grey woolen cardigan, neat white collared blouse and pale blue linen skirt, "Oh," she sighed, "Come in, Nick."

He followed her into the living room. "Mum is upstairs, and Dad's gone to work," she said quietly. "Would you like a cup of tea?"

"No thanks," said Nick. Cissie sniffed, "I s'pose you've heard the news?"

"Mum and Dad told me this morning, I'm so sorry." After a short silence, not knowing what to say, they both spoke together.

"When did....?" said Nick.

"Are you....?" said Cissie.

"Sorry you go first," Nick added, smiling gently.

"I was going to ask you how long you are home for?"

"A couple of weeks." Nick sighed deeply, "When did you hear um a-a-about, Kenny?" he stammered, fiddling nervously with his jacket cuff.

"Four days ago."

"So recent!" exclaimed Nick.

It seemed like a long silence before Nick blurted out, "Gawd, I'm gonna miss 'im!"

Cissie's eyes welled up, "Me too," she said.

She pulled out a chair from the table and sat down. Nick followed suit.

"Mum and Dad are devastated. That bloody awful telegram!" she spat, "I just hope to God we don't get another one about Joe; it will kill them both! Bloody stinking war!" she said angrily.

Nick touched her hand across the table and gently said, "There are times when I think it's just an adventure, but when you get this kind of news, it brings you down to earth, and you wonder why."

Cissie responded to Nick's touch and laid her other hand on his. They sat silently together before Cissie said, "You've not been well. How are you?"

"I'm fine now," Nick replied.

Another silence ensued before Nick said, "I like your hair. It's different."

Cissie smiled sweetly, "Thank you," she said, "I'm glad you're here." I miss your cheeky face and that familiar smell you have."

Nick frowned, "What smell?" he questioned, lifting his arm to sniff his armpit.

Cissie giggled, "I don't know, but it's not a bad smell," she added quickly.

They were interrupted by a sound on the stairs, "O, here comes Mum," said Cissie, quickly withdrawing her hand.

Mrs Packham entered the room looking tired and naturally sad. Nick pushed his chair back and stood up, "Don't get up Nick" she said softly, adding, "Have you had a cup of tea?"

"I'll have one if you're making one," he said, adding, "erm, I'm sorry to hear about Kenny,"

"Thank you, Nick," replied Mrs Packham. "You must be feeling it also,"

"He was a good friend, more like a brother," Nick said almost inaudibly.

Cissie stood up to comfort her mother as tears came into her eyes, "I'm alright, love, don't fuss!" she said, turning to the steaming kettle on the hob.

Taking a sip from the tea, Nick asked Cissie, "Do you think you're up to seeing a film or perhaps not?"

"I don't know," she replied, shaking her head.

"You thinking of taking her," Mrs Packham asked.

"Yes," Nick replied.

"That's if your boyfriend doesn't mind," he said to Cissie.

"He's away right now," she replied.

"He won't mind. You should go, dear," said Mrs Packham.

The following Saturday afternoon, Nick met Cissie at her gate on Church Path. Wrapped up warm in a green coat that showed off her trim waistline and a perky little hat over her shoulder-length chestnut brown hair that threw out gentle curls, Nick thought she looked lovely. There was little to choose from at any of the local cinemas. They varied from war films to 'Titanic' or 'Girl Crazy' with Judy Garland and Mickey Rooney, which Cissie said she would rather not see now. So they chose to go to the Granada where the recently released film 'Madame Curie' was showing, starring two of Cissie's favorite actors, Greer Garson and Walter Pidgeon.

The lights were dimmed when they entered the cinema, but an usherette led the way to their seats by torchlight. Nick's heart began to race as he sat next to Cissie. He really liked her and would have taken advantage of her had she been any other girl but that, and under the circumstances, he checked himself and behaved like the perfect gentleman. Cissie warmed to Nick and thought she wouldn't mind if he made a pass at her. When he didn't, she was slightly disappointed, but realising they had grown up almost as siblings, she was not surprised. The film ended and, as always at the last film showing, everyone stood until the National Anthem finished.

Coming out of the cinema, Cissie thanked Nick for taking her, "I enjoyed it," she said, "It was interesting!"

It was late when they began the walk home. Cissie shivered and pulled her coat tightly around her.

Nick finally gave in to his instincts and put his arm around Cissie's shoulder, "Don't worry," he said politely, "I'm only trying to keep you warm."

"Thank you. I don't mind," replied Cissie.

She walked closer to him, warming them both.

Nothing was said, but the tenderness between them was palpable. As they drew near Church Path, Cissie stopped and turned to Nick.

"You can kiss me if you like," she said sweetly.

Nick gazed at her. He saw the sadness in her pretty face. He grasped her shoulders gently and brushed a kiss on her waiting lips. Cissie felt her legs give way. Nick held onto her, and they stood together in the darkness, holding each other.

"Oh, Nick," Cissie whispered, "I really can't bear the thought of not seeing Kenny again. I miss him so much," with her face against Nick's coat, she began to sob.

"I miss him too, Cissie," he said, tightening his arm around her.

She looked up at him, and he bent to kiss her again. This time, with the passion that Cissie needed. Nick's warm, soft lips gently opened her mouth, and they knew it was right.

The couple met again and again in the next two weeks of precious leave that Nick had. They walked in the parks and strolled down the busy Saturday market hand in hand, not caring who saw them. They stole away in discreet places to give way to their passion for each other. Nick had never felt like this with any other girl and was cautious about allowing his feelings for her to go further than kissing. But when they were alone in the park late one evening, Cissie encouraged him to touch her body, and he could no longer contain himself. She undid the buttons on her coat, and taking Nick's hand in hers, she lifted her jumper and placed it on her bra-covered breast. He slipped his hand behind her back, pulled the clip together, and released the bra. Cissie flinched.

"It's okay," said Nick, "I'll stop if you want."

"No! Don't stop." she breathed.

Nick let his hand stroke the softness of her back, and then he bent to kiss her midriff, kissing it until his lips reached her small, pale breasts. His loins burst with longing for Cissie, who felt the same, her body willing him to go on. A surge of deep desire went through her body when he touched her nipple. She felt the strength of Nick's masculinity against her leg; then she knew they had to stop!

"Nick, Nick, stop!" she cried.

He lifted her head, looked at her and smiled. He took a deep breath and said, "Yes, or I will ruin you here and now."

He kissed her and helped her tidy her clothes. They kissed several times as they walked quietly home, saying nothing, each deep in their thoughts about what had just happened. The last kiss was taken at Cissie's gate, and when the door opened, Mr Packham came out.

"Okay, Nick," he barked, "that's enough; say goodnight and take yourself off now!"

Nick let go of Cissie's hand and said goodnight to her.

"G'night, Mr Packham," he called as he crossed Church Path and went to his gate.

Both families watched as the relationship developed. Mrs Packham confronted Cissie, "You're already promised Love," she said.

"But I really like him, Mum," whined Cissie, "I think I always have, and I never felt like this with Alan. What am I going to do?"

Shaking her head in despair, Mrs Packham said, "Well, you'll have to make your mind up. it's one or the other." Cissie sat with her elbows on the table, covering her mouth with her fists, tentatively watching her mother dry the dishes. She turned to speak. "Nick's family agrees this should never have happened."

Putting away the last plate, she hung the tea towel over the door handle and continued, "D'you know what? I always hoped you and Nick would get together one day but never thought it would happen."

"Neither did I, Mum," murmured Cissie sadly.

In the Clayton household, Dick took Nick aside, "I've been talking to Mr and Mrs Packham, and we all agree that your friendship with Cissie has gone too far. You know she's already spoken for, don't you?"

"Yes Dad!" Nick said brusquely.

"It's no good, you taking that attitude son. It can't go on."

Nick turned to go, "Well, I'm leaving here soon, so she can do what she likes then, can't she?" he said bitterly.

The two weeks they had together passed quickly. During that time, many people attended a service held for Kenny in St Mary's Church, after which Nick and his father went off to the Nag's Head for a drink along with other mourners. Cissie and her parents declined and went home.

"Come on, Lad, you've had enough to drink, we should go home, come on now," pleaded Dick.

"Kenny's dead, Dad!" slurred Nick, "'e's dead!"

"I know, I know, but drinking yourself silly won't bring 'im back."

Mr Cohan helped Dick take Nick back home.

"Gawd struth," gasped Elsie as they entered the scullery, "I've never seen 'im this drunk before! Get 'im upstairs Dick," she added.

All too soon, Nick and Cissie were saying goodbye. Standing on the platform in the station, Nick looked smart in his uniform and beret. Cissie cuddled into the warmth of his coat, "I think I love you, Nick Clayton," she said. Tears welled up in her eyes, "I'm gonna miss you."

"What you gonna do about Alan then?" Nick asked.

"I s'pose I'll have to tell him," she said thoughtfully. "He's a nice enough chap," She paused and sighed, "It's not going to be easy, but what can I do? I don't feel for him like I do for you. He's coming home for Christmas, so I'll tell him then."

Cissie gave a long sigh, "I wish you were staying."

Chapter 14
January, 1944

Before long, Nick found himself back with his unit, this time in Weymouth, where two Squadrons - A and B of the Second Household Cavalry were in the process of waterproofing the tanks and armoured cars in preparation for the proposed landing on the European beaches. On a cold day in January, military vehicles lined the wide promenade bumper to bumper. Dozens of soldiers were busily working on vehicles between the barbed wire beach defences. The feeling that the Regiment might soon be sent to Europe became a reality as the Troopers worked.

Basil's spanner clattered to the ground; he sighed, "I have an awful feeling of foreboding in my gut," he said, resting his elbow on the side of the armoured car.

"Okay, so what's the feeling about then," commented Wilf, adding, "Let me guess, we're all going to die on the French beaches?"

Fixing the canvas waterproof cover on the other side of the vehicle, Nick looked up sourly from what he was doing. He pointed his spanner at Basil and said, "You might, old mate, but I ain't! So shuddup, pick up and get on with the job."

"What's wrong with you, mate?" asked Wilf, "You ain't normally so snappy. You've been in a mood ever since you arrived back. What did they do to you in that hospital?"

Nick gave no reply and carried on working. Wilf shrugged his shoulders and walked away.

"Search me!" said Dave in reply to Wilf's questioning body language.

Dave Brewer from A Squadron was a familiar character to the lads. He was a short, dapper older man with a long, thin face. He found Nick to be moody and reserved. Wilf told him that Nick was usually the life and soul of the party, "But he seems to have changed since he had pneumonia and went into hospital."

Nick's frequent trips to London when he got leave began to answer a few questions for Wilf. Bewildered, he said, "What again?"

"I reckon he's got a girlfriend," Basil commented as he, Archie, Wilf and Taffy went for a pint at the local pub.

"What's new?" commented Wilf, "he's never without a girlfriend or two!"

Basil pursed his lips and shook his head, "This is different. I reckon he's got it bad this time. Haven't you noticed he's not as interested in girls as he used to be?'

Wilf shrugged, "Yeh, you're right, I s'pose," he said, "What the heck, we've got better things to talk about. Let's have a beer!"

Cissie told Allan how she felt when he came home for Christmas. He took it badly and got angry. He was not prepared to be dumped by Cissie in preference to a cocky bastard like Nick Clayton. He wouldn't leave when she asked him to, and when he finally did, he threatened to get Nick the next time he saw him. Nick laughed when she told him.

"Who does he think he is then Walter Pidgeon?"

'I wish!' said Cissie with a glow in her eye.

Nick whisked her into his arms, turned her so that her back was to him and cupped her breasts in his big hands.

Cissie gasped, "Stop it, Nick, you know I can't resist when you do that, stop it!" She smacked his hands, but Nick held on.

"I know," he teased. "Who's best then, me or Walter Pidgeon?"

"You, Nick, you," she cried.

Whenever he could get leave, it was spent with Cissie. Nick waited inside and outside Manzies until Cissie finished work. They wanted to spend every minute together.

As the days grew brighter and spring began to throw up crocus and daffodil, new emerald green canopies of buds burst on the trees, and birdsong just got merrier; the couple felt happier about having to spend their time together in better weather. They walked to the Hollow Pond, where they talked, laughed and made love as far as they dared to go.

1944 Late March

Waterproofing and maintenance continued at Weymouth, along with forty armoured cars of the two squadrons, various vehicles including tanks and lorries, some as large as Ford 3-toners were boxed in with canvas sheeting attached to the sides and back of the vehicles just above the tracks and wheels. The beach and harbour were jammed as ever, with vehicles bumper to bumper along the promenade. A collection of amphibious and other vehicles could be seen floating about in the water, having been driven down a pontoon ramp and into the sea to test the waterproofing. Returning to the beach, the waterproofing was blown off with a loud bang.

With everything going on around him, Nick stood idle for a moment, reading a newspaper.

"Anything interesting then, Nick?" called Wilf from the top of a Cromwell tank.

"The Eighth Army, second air invasion of Burma," murmured Nick, picking his teeth. "They've landed gliders behind Japanese lines,"

"That's as far as they've got yet 'aint it?" remarked Wilf, "I guess," murmured Nick, turning the newspaper page.

Upon hearing the conversation, Basil approached and said, "I've just been told we're going back up to Yorkshire to join the rest of the Regiment!"

Nick's shoulders dropped. 'Damn!' he spat.

Knowing he would not see her for a while, he scribbled a quick note to Cissie and added it to the pile of letters waiting to be collected.

Wilf asked Nick, "Last letter to your girlfriend then?"

"Yeh! I've got it bad, mate! She's lovely."

The next day was spent loading the Squadron cars, and the 2nd Household Cavalry lorries to return to Yorkshire.

The next six weeks were spent on the firing ranges high up on the Yorkshire Moors. The fields once blooming with wheat and barley were now just blackened earth caused by the work of belching flamethrowers practising their skills, along with rifles and guns varying from the heavy tank guns to the 15-mm Besa and the 75-mm guns of the AEC Mk III armoured cars of the Heavy Troop. The armoured vehicles struggled to keep up with their larger companions in heavy rain. Negotiating the churned-up tracks over the moors left by the tanks in front slowed them down to a standstill. With boots squelching and sucking, the Troopers worked in thick mud. Tying ropes to the vehicles, they heaved and pulled them clear in order to continue the exercise.

"I'll be back in the hospital if we 'ave to do much more in this weather," Nick complained,

"You and me also," quipped Bob.

"Cleaning them boots and polishing your buttons will warm you up. Gotta look our best for Monty," Wilf said.

Inspections were commonplace but not as important as three major visits in a short time. General Montgomery himself arrived in February and, in March, a visit from the King and Queen with Princess Elizabeth. A few days later, Mr Winston Churchill came, escorted by the Commanding Officer Lieutenant-Colonel Abel-Smith and other dignitaries. Preparation for the visits on these occasions was strenuous, with the Troopers working their fingers to the bone spitting and polishing every nut, bolt, button, and toe cap. The sun glinted on every bit of polished metal!

Returning to the tent that served as a billet for the troopers of five troops, Nick commented, "Never realised Monty was so short,"

"Me neither," said Wilf, "powerful with words though."

"Makes you feel better and more like a soldier with a mission hearing his talk," said Bob.

"Yeh, rather than a glorified mechanic and boot cleaner," Nick grumbled.

"It ain't that bad," said Wilf, "I'm proud of what I'm doing and look what we've learned!"

"I liked that comment he made: 'We're going to knock 'em for six!" Said Archie.

"Together, you and I will knock the enemy for six!" interrupted Bob.

"Makes yer proud to be a soldier," added Nick

22nd April 1944 Move to Brighton

By the end of April, the Guards Armoured Division, with the rest of the British, American and Canadian forces, were steeped in speculation about the coming invasion of Europe. All over Britain, plans were being put in place for D-Day, not least the plans for the Regiment to move south to Brighton.

On a fine late April day, over a hundred vehicles of the 2nd Household Cavalry Regiment at full war strength prepared to leave Selby in Yorkshire and another two hundred and forty vehicles of the tank divisions that formed the Guards Armoured Division. The three occupants of one of the Daimler Armoured cars were in high spirits at the prospect of their new destination.

"Brighton!" yelled Wilf.

"Ere we come!" added Nick.

The Troop Leader Lt Palmer of Five Troop B Squadron was not impressed, "Get yourselves sorted out, you incompetent lot, or I'll put you on a charge!"

"Miserable bastard!" grumbled Nick under his breath.

The journey took the whole division down the Great North Road towards London, stopping at Stevenage overnight. People stood open-mouthed with awe at the magnitude of vehicles that passed by. It was nearly a mile long. Children covered their ears, and crowds cheered and sang as they passed noisily through the center of London; car horns sounded, and even the traffic lights changed for their convenience. Police directed traffic and cleared areas to let the convoy pass Hyde Park Corner and over Vauxhall Bridge without hindrance. Leaving London, they passed over the Sussex Downs and on to Brighton, where the Divisions separated; some to Eastbourne, others to Crawley and the 11th Armoured Division as far away as Aldershot.

High-ranking officers were billeted in hotels in the Preston Park area, while the troopers were given addresses at private homes and guest houses.

The bright evening sun cast long shadows when the Troopers were discharged to their lodgings. Leaving their vehicles parked on the curb of the road, they went off in high spirits. Nick and Wilf were the last to find their address.

A short, stocky woman opened the door to them, "Oo, that sun," she said, shading her eyes with her hands.

"Never mind the sun, Love, let the lads in!" said her husband cheerfully.

"All right, all right, Mr Kelly," she quipped, "come in, boys, we were expecting you."

Nick and Wilf whipped off their berets and followed Mrs Kelly, carefully negotiating the narrow hallway with their bulky kit bags to avoid scraping the decorated walls. Leaving their bags in the hallway, they were shown into a cosy sitting room.

"Sit down, lads," said Mr Kelly, "' spect you'd like a cup of tea,"

"Yes, please," said Nick politely.

"Now, Paddy," interrupted Mrs. Kelly, "it's late. Let the boys, er, so what's your names?" asked Mrs Kelly.

"I'm Nick, Nick Clayton,"

"And I'm Wilf Grant,"

The couple shook the lads warmly by the hand.

"Nice to meet you, eh Paddy?" she said, nodding approval to her husband.

"Yes!" he answered. "I was going to say it's late, and you both might like to settle in while I make you a cuppa. I'll show you your room,"

"Thanks," replied the boys in unison.

Mrs Kelly waddled her short round frame out of the living room to the stairs in the hall, "I hope you'll be comfortable," puffed the kindly woman on the stairs.

"If you saw some of the places we've had to sleep, you'd think this was a palace, Mrs K," replied Wilf.

"You poor lads," said Mrs Kelly, opening the bedroom door.

Nick and Wilf entered the room.

"If you don't mind me asking, how old are you?"

Nick dropped his bag on the floor alongside one of the single beds, "I'm supposed to be 21, but I'm only 20. Put me age up; I did!"

"How long have you been in the army then?"

"Me? Since June 1940."

"I joined up the same time, but I am 21," said Wilf.

"Four years!" gasped Mrs Kelly, "and you were only 16 when you joined up!"

Shaking her head in despair, she left the room.

Standing in the doorway, Nick called after her, "You got any kids then?" he inquired.

"No, we were unlucky," replied Mrs Kelly, "Then again, would I have wanted my boy to be going off to war right now?"

"We're a bit of a handful for you then," Nick said.

"Only too pleased to have you," sang Mrs. Kelly warmly, and she began to descend the stairs.

Wilf threw himself on the bed and breathed a deep sigh. Nick looked around at the small, sparsely furnished bedroom.

A small wooden chest of drawers separated the two beds above, which hung a small picture of a curly-haired Jesus in a white shift dress standing with his arms outstretched while a squadron of aero planes in formation passed over his haloed blonde head. Against the wall by the open window stood a large walnut wardrobe where the edge of a white net curtain billowed gently out onto the darkening street below; in the corner stood a chair over which Nick laid his coat. He stood gazing out onto the street for a moment and thought of Cissie and home.

He woke the following day to the smell of bacon, "Oy, Wilf, can you smell that bacon?"

Wilf moaned, turned over, and wrapped the blankets around his body. In no time, Mrs Kelly placed a plate of bacon and egg in front of Nick and Wilf.

"Tuck in boys," she said, "and enjoy, 'cause you won't get this every day; it's a treat for your first day here."

"Seen me cap Love?" asked Mr Kelly.

"I think it's where you left it," replied his wife kindly.

"I know, 'anging on the 'anger in the 'all!" he chuckled.

"What do you want a cap for on a hot day like this?"

"You would if you had this much hair," said Mr Kelly, stroking the shiny top of his bald head.

"Dinner'll be ready by six o'clock," called Mrs Kelly as her husband left the house.

"Hope that's okay with you, lads," she added quietly to Nick and Wilf.

"Yes, thanks," the two lads answered in unison.

To say that the invasion of the Regiment's arrival disrupted the equilibrium and mundane atmosphere of Brighton would be an understatement! Nick and Wilf met with Basil and Bob on that first day to explore the area. Vic and Archie joined them later, and before long, Benny, Charlie and other Troopers from A Squadron swelled the gang of young men, who mingled in groups on the streets and beaches of Brighton where dozens of other soldiers and sailors of all ranks and divisions gathered. Cafes burst at the seams, and street vendors left their sites early after selling out of food and drink. Girls turned out at the end of the working day only too pleased to link arms with their visitors and take them off for a drink or two at the nearest pub. Nick enjoyed the company of the girls as much as his mates, but he longed for the company of Cissie, and before long, he was at Brighton station to enquire about trains to London.

Mr and Mrs Kelly were only too happy for her two guests to bring their friends back to the house for a game of cards. Dusk was falling when the card game finished. Vic and Basil left for their own lodgings, and Wilf and Nick made themselves comfortable in the armchairs that were part of the furniture that made up the snug little living room of the terraced house.

Old family photographs hung randomly on the dull papered walls; two little white ceramic figures of children in Edwardian dress dangled on tiny swings strung from the picture rail on either side of a huge Welsh dresser on which was displayed a complete china tea-set decorated with red poppies. A large dining room table filled the centre of the room, covered with a red velour tablecloth similar to that in Nick's family home, and a huge Aspidistra in an equally large brass container stood in one corner.

"I reckon it's gonna be nice here," Nick thought.

April - July 1944

The anticipation and expectation of an imminent invasion fizzled out as the days passed by. Waterproofing and maintenance continued along with drilling and exercises. Free time was spent in the cinema or at the dance halls.

The lads had no trouble finding a partner to take to the floor, but competition with the Yanks and their wild dance routines proved a distraction for the girls, who abandoned the boys in preference and were keen to learn the dances from their American guests.

"Bloody Yanks!" huffed Archie, "I was just getting to know her. She smelled nice, too!" He looked around for another partner, and finding one, he said, "And if another Yank takes her off, 'e's gonna be in trouble!"

Nick raised his eyebrows and huffed, "You might meet your match, mate!" he said.

"And you can get lost too, you big nancy!" Nick's brow furrowed; he grimaced,

"What did you say?" he snarled.

"Ah, get lost," replied Archie.

Grabbing him by the collar, Nick clenched his fist and came face to face with his rival.

Wilf pushed between the two soldiers, "Pack it in, Nick. I keep tellin' you he aint worth it!"

"The mood I'm in right now………" said Nick between his teeth, "I'll bloody kill 'im!"

"What are you so mad about, Nick?" asked Wilf, adding, "What happened on your last leave?"

Nick thought for a moment before answering. "It's Cissie! I've known her for ages, ever since she was a little girl. She's the brother of Kenny, my best mate…... he died a couple of weeks ago…. his plane came down in the English Channel." Nick put his head in his hands. Cissie and I, we……"

"You what?" said Wilf.

"I dunno, it doesn't make sense, really…..we just found out we like each other."

"Do you love her?"

"I dunno. I don't want to be away from her. I suppose so."

Nothing was said for a few seconds, then Nick added, "We both miss Kenny so much. We were like brothers."

Wilf sighed, "Sorry about your mate Nick." he gently said.

Nick lifted his head and looked around the dance hall, "Come on mate, we're waistin' time. Let's get a pint."

"Good idea," replied Wilf, patting a friendly hand on Nick's shoulder.

***

Cricket matches were played at Preston Park, where Nick excelled in the adoration of girls who hung around to watch him play. He enjoyed the attention but always had Cissie on his mind; every opportunity to see her was tantamount. Day passes were given, but all weekend passes were cancelled. The long journey from Brighton to Walthamstow often meant only an hour or two with Cissie and his family before returning to Brighton ready for any last-minute orders to leave England.

"Why don't we meet here at Waterloo Station next time?" called Cissie to Nick one day as she watched him go through the barrier to board his train.

"Are you sure, sweetheart?" said Nick, "It would give us a bit more time, but you'd have to get from Walthamstow to here on your own,"

"I've gotta get back home from here on my own, Nick, and I'm a big girl now,"

"Just don't speak to any handsome men on your way,"

"Oh Nick, I love you!" exclaimed Cissie unashamedly into the crowd.

***

Early in June, news spread quickly that an invasion was imminent and that one of the Marshalling areas would be Portsmouth. With strict instructions to avoid Portsmouth Docks, Nick and his friends took a train to Cosham. The boys laughed and joked together as the train steamed down the track. Suddenly Nick leaned forward and whacked Reg Murphy, one of the troopers, on the legs with his folded newspaper, "Lucky you live in Cosham Reggie," he said, "Never 'eard of the place 'till you said you lived there."

A few days before, the young soldiers had discussed the possibility of going to Portsmouth, curious to see what was happening there. It wasn't until Reg Murphy from 'C' Squadron mentioned that he came from a village near Portsmouth that hopes began to rise.

"You're from down south?" exclaimed Wilf, "but you're Irish, ain't yer?"

"I was born in Ireland, but me dad joined the navy, so when I was nine me mam uprooted and moved to Portsmouth to be near him, but she didn't like the city, so she moved out to Cosham." said Reggie, "Reckoned it was more like the village she left Ireland."

"So you reckon we could take the train there?" asked Nick.

"Yes," said Reg, adding, "It's a couple of hour's journey though."

The journey from Brighton was long past when the four young lads in uniform stood on Portsdown Hill watching hundreds of aircraft fly over the coast to Europe, creating a dark cloud, "It looks like a starling murmuration," said Basil.

"What the heck's a starling murmuring?' enquired Nick.

"Murmuration!" corrected Basil. "It's when starlings mass together in a huge flock. Haven't you ever seen that?"

"Nope. But I bet they don't make that loud sound!"

"You'd be surprised," added Basil

The sight and sound of so many aeroplanes left the lads speechless with awe. Gradually, the planes disappeared into the horizon, leaving only scudding clouds in a calm sky. The silence that followed left them stunned. The warm breeze gently stroked their faces, and the grass beneath their feet felt firm and soft. The rooftops of the houses below gave them an aura of safety, and the sound of a dog barking and children's voices nearby brought them back to reality. "Struth!" gasped Nick, dropping to the ground. Wilf sat down beside him. They gazed across the harbour, where a fleet of vessels of various sizes waited at anchor. Reggie broke the silence, "Those planes have gone out to bomb the bridgehead to clear the way for that lot when they get over there," he murmured.

Nick sat with his forearms dangling over his bent knees, "Reckon, you're right!" he said.

Reg drew in a deep breath, "Anyone for a cuppa at me mam's?"

Nick smiled and, clapping his hands together, stood up and yanked Wilf to his feet. "Sounds like a good idea to me!" he said, "unless there's a pub where we can get a pint!"

A few days later, on the fifth of June, roads and beaches around the coast of Britain were packed with military vehicles and infantrymen waiting in pouring rain to board the landing craft that would carry them on the first leg of their journey across the Channel to the Normandy beaches. The following day, the landing craft, with their cargo, slipped their moorings and went quietly out to sea.

Soon after D-Day, word spread that the Regiment would follow, but no movement could be made until the Normandy bridgehead was cleared of fighting.

Back in Brighton, the air was tense with expectation and activity. The young soldiers were kept busy with any work they could find! Nick, Wilf, Basil and Bob were given paint and brushes and ordered to paint anything that didn't move! Taking a break from work, the lads sat leaning against a half-painted fence.

Basil offered a cigarette to Wilf, who took one from the pack, and then to Nick, "Go on 'ave one; it'll calm yer nerves,"

"Nope! Not interested in spending me money on fags!"

"Please yerself!" said Wilf, lighting his cigarette from the match Basil held out to him. He drew on the cigarette and said, "Did you hear that A Squadron 1 Troop 'ave already left for Normandy?"

"Yeh," remarked Nick and Basil in unison.

"Lucky they don't have to face a battle on the beaches, thanks to those poor sods who arrived on D-Day," said Nick.

"Yeah," murmured Basil. "A week earlier, they wouldn't have bin so lucky!"

13th June

The three friends heard the sound at the same time. It was different. They saw a peculiar object flying at speed across the sky. Soldiers going about their business stopped and looked up.

"What the hell is that!" exclaimed Basil.

"Whatever it is, I don't like the look of it," said Wilf, scrambling to his feet.

With its odd-shaped wings and red-hot tail, the evil-looking thing zoomed noisily over the rooftops, belching out flames as it went.

"Sounds like a ruddy motorbike!" exclaimed Basil.

Nick was thoughtful. "I read sommat recently about a new weapon the Germans were making," he said.

"D'you reckon that's it?" asked Wilf as the first drop of rain fell, "I'm going inside."

"Oh, no, you're not," came the booming voice of Corporal Palmer, "Get over to the drill 'all with the others,"

Paint brushes and pots were stored randomly inside a building, "At the double, you lazy lot," bellowed the Corporal.

"Did you see that thing go over sir?" Nick asked, trotting backwards away from the building, drawing his chin in and his chest out. The Corporal stood erect and replied, "That lad was Hitler's latest invention to try to destroy the spirit of the British people. Now get yourself off, at the double!" he yelled.

"Sir!" coughed Nick and, with a quick salute, ran after the others.

It was the last week of June when Nick got a letter from his mother to say Dick had had a heart attack and was in Whipps Cross hospital.

Nick was given seven days of compassionate leave to go home.

"Jammy sod!" declared Basil.

"That's a bit heartless! said Wilf, "The guy's dad is at death's door."

"Sorry," Bail said sympathetically, "You know what I meant."

"Sure, no offence taken," said Nick "Just hope he's okay, 'specially now just as we're going off," he added, "That's all me mum needs!"

On a dark, wet afternoon, Nick arrived at Walthamstow station and headed straight for the hospital. The ward was well-lit, bright and airy; White iron bedsteads lay in rows, mirrored in the highly polished brown linoleum floor. A table with equal reflection was set in the middle of the long, narrow ward. Only two nurses were on duty when Nick opened the door. No sooner had the door closed behind him than it opened again, and Matron entered, recognised by her crisp white bat-wing headgear and starched white collar that seemed to restrict her neck movement. She gave Nick a curious look.

"I'm here to see me, Dad, Mr Clayton," said Nick.

"Oh," responded Matron, "Oh, right," she hesitated, "I'm not sure which bed he's in. One moment."

Nick waited while Matron went over to one of the nurses who, in turn, directed Nick to a curtained off area in the ward behind which was his father's bed.

"Thanks," said Nick and gave her a habitual wink!

The Matron glowered!

The drama and anxiety Nick felt when he read the letter from his mother disappeared when he saw his father. Apart from looking a little tired and drawn, he was cheerful. They greeted each other warmly. Dick released his hold on his son's hand.

"So, Dad, what have you been up to for this to happen?"

"I guess I overdid it on the allotment and just keeled over!" Replied Dick, "Mr Green was with me, frightened him to death! Anyway, quick as a flash, he went off to find old Joe Burns. Lucky, he was nearby. He contacted the hospital on one of them police box phones, and then they sent an ambulance."

"Lucky Mr. Green was with you. You'd have laid there for ages and... well!"

"Yeah right!"

"I'll go and see Mum when I leave you. How is she?"

"Not taken it very well, I s'pose. How long you home for?"

"I've got seven days leave, so that'll be good to help Mum out visiting."

"That's good."

Elsie was visibly relieved to see her son arrive, "It's good to see you, son," she said, adding, "I've been that worried about Dad, and you don't know what I went through when I 'eard that buzz bomb landed on the Guard's Chapel."

"Now, what would I be doing in a chapel, Mother," laughed Nick.

"Well, you never answered my letter to tell me you were safe, did yer? Me nerves won't take much more, what with one thing and another."

"Sorry, Mum, I should've written. You're getting yourself in a state now. Sit down."

The scullery door flew open, and in rushed Joyce. 'I saw you coming up Church Path,' she puffed and threw her arms around Nick's waist.

He responded to her hug and then gently pushed her aside.

"What's the matter, Nick?" said Joyce, a little hurt by his action.

"Nothing," Nick sighed, "I'm sorry," he added and took her hand, "I'm just a bit worried about Mum and Dad, and I'm tired right now."

"That's okay. Do you want a cup of tea?" she asked Nick.

"Later," Nick replied.

"I can make it," Joyce insisted.

"I forget that you've grown up, Joyce," Nick said apologetically, "Go on then make me a cup of tea and I think Mum could do with one too." Nick added, looking at his worried mother, "I've been in to see Dad."

"Have yer?" questioned Elsie. "How is he then?" asked Joyce, swilling the teapot round with hot water,

"I thought he looked okay and didn't expect to find him that good!"

"That's a relief," Elsie said, blowing her nose into her handkerchief. "Gawd he scared me!" Mrs Green called in later to see the family, "So how long you home for then, Nick?" she asked.

Nick looked up from his newspaper absently,

"What?" he asked.

"Seven days," interjected Elsie.

Nick went back to his newspaper.

"Yeh, he's gonna help Mr Green finish off the digging on the allotment!" added Elsie, frowning in Nick's direction.

"You're being rude," hissed Joyce at her brother.

"Sorry, Mrs Green," Nick said, folding the newspaper pages, "You know me….."

"Mr Green is just the same, can't get a word of conversation out of 'im once 'e gets 'is nose into the newspaper!"

"I've made some bread pudding," called Elsie from the kitchen, "Would you like some?"

"Yes, please!" Came a chorus of voices from the living room

Nick woke early the next day with one thing on his mind: to see Cissie. It was hard for him to contain his eagerness without seeming disloyal to his family. Visiting times at the hospital were in the afternoon from 2-4 pm so it seemed okay to Nick to find an hour in the morning to meet up with his girlfriend.

"I don't mind, Nick; there's nothing for you to do here. You know she's at work?" Elsie said. "But do go and help Mr Green with that digging sometime!"

"I will, I promise! I'll pop in to see Mrs Packham first and see if Cissie's got half an hour lunch break."

"Oh, it's you, Nick," said Mrs Packham, opening the door, "'Ow are you Love? Sorry to hear about your dad. Have you seen him?"

"Yes I have. I saw him yesterday. He's looking good. I guess it wasn't a bad heart attack. Me and Mum are going to see him again this afternoon," said Nick, "I'm going to see if Cissie can get time off for lunch but I called to see how you are first." he added.

"Thanks, Nick, I'm okay, I s'pose." She shook the gingham tablecloth out of the open window to remove the crumbs. "It's hard for me, but Mr Packham 'es gone into himself. I'm worried about him. He's just not interested in anything and sits in the chair lookin' at the walls when he's home."

"I'm sorry," said Nick.

"Anyway, enough about us. You've been in hospital, how are you?" said Mrs Packham cheerfully. She didn't wait for an answer, adding quickly, "That Alan has been a real nuisance to poor Cissie, not that I don't feel a bit sorry for him, but in a way, it's good they broke up 'cause he's really showing 'is true colours now!"

"What do you mean?" Nick interjected, "How's he been a nuisance?"

"Well, when he's home, which is too often if you ask me, he calls round banging on the door calling for Cissie. She tries to be kind and calm him down but he loses it when she closes the door. He shouts and hollers through the letterbox and up at the window that he won't give up."

"Well, that can't be good for Mr Packham either."

"You know what, he only needs to do it once too often, and I think he'll thump him!"

"I feel kind of responsible," Nick said.

"Go on, it's not your fault you finally realised Cissie was for you. 'No one's surprised!"

"Really?"

"You didn't know?" Mrs Packham smiled, "Go on, get off to Manzies and make that date before she plans something else today."

Just as Nick hoped, he managed to get a seat in Manzies without attracting Cissie's attention, and a waitress came over to serve him.

"Do me a favour," he said quietly to the girl. I'm here to see Cissie Packham but don't tell her. I just want to sit and watch her for a while."

The girl frowned, "You a bit of a weirdo?" she asked rudely.

Nick winced, "No, she's my girlfriend!" he hissed.

The girl opened her mouth with surprise, "You must be Nick then?" she gasped.

"Shhhh! Yes, and I'll have a coffee, please." Nick replied.

The girl turned and sighed, "oh, how romantic," she said to herself.

The waitress returned with Nick's coffee.

"Thanks," said Nick,

"Do me another favour?"

"I'd do anything for you," she said weakly.

"If she doesn't notice me in five minutes, let her know I'm here."

The waitress could contain herself no longer, and before the five minutes was up, she said to Cissie, "Who's that good-looking chap sitting in the corner over there? He's trying to hide, but every now and then, he gawks at you!"

Cissie squealed with delight when she saw Nick. She put down her tray and said to the waitress, "It's him, my Nick, I told you about!"

"I know," said the waitress, "Lucky you!"

Cissie looked around furtively, pretending to be taking an order. "What are you doing here, Nick?" she hissed.

Nick grabbed her hand and drew in a deep breath of air. "You heard about my dad?" he replied.

Trying to wriggle her hand free, she hissed, "Let go of my hand, Nick!"

Nick chuckled and reluctantly did as Cissie asked. The girl pulled away from Nick and made to look as though she was taking an order. She cleared her throat,

"Yes I did hear. So you've got leave then, how long?"

"Seven days!"

"What?" hissed Cissie, hardly able to contain herself. "Can you get any time off for lunch?"

"No, we don't get lunchtime breaks because that's when the place gets bustling, but maybe twenty minutes after two 'clock."

Disappointed, Nick said, "That's no good. Me and me Mum will be at the hospital then."

Cissie frowned and screwed up her face, "How long have you been here anyway?"

"A few minutes," said Nick with a grin.

"Watching me?"

Nick winked, "You look really sexy in that outfit!"

"Stoppit, Nick, you're embarrassing me!" Cissie said. "I have to go now, or I'll get the sack,"

Sliding out of his seat, Nick stood up, "I'll call round your house later then," he said.

"Who says I'll be in then?" teased Cissie.

Nick spent the next couple of mornings helping Mr Green finish the heavy work on the allotment, visiting his dad in the afternoon and with Cissie in the evenings.

Late one night, there was a knock on the door. Elsie opened it to find Joe Burns standing there, "Hello, Joe?"

"There's been a call to the station for Nick," said the policeman.

Elsie looked worried. "He's not here right now. He's with Cissie. He's not in trouble, is he?"

"No, no, it's from the army. He needs to come down to the station to take a call."

Elsie went with the policeman to get Nick.

"I'll be back," Nick called to Cissie

Nick picked up the phone at the Police Station, "But I've just been given seven days leave sir," Nick said to the caller,

"I wouldn't call you back unless it were urgent," came the reply.

Nick returned to Cissie, where she and his mother waited for news. "I've got to leave first thing in the morning," he said to the bewildered faces looking at him.

"It can only mean one thing," said Mr Packaham.

"Oh no!" said his mother, clapping her hands to her mouth, "you're going to war!"

"Oh, Mum, don't be so dramatic! I'm going to have to go, whatever!"

"It's alright for you; you ain't sitting at home worrying, and what about dad?" she snapped.

Mrs Packham sat down next to Elsie. "There's no point in worrying, Dear. It's not going to help Nick; just let him go," she gently said.

Tears were welling up in Cissie's eyes, but after seeing Elsie's reaction, she sniffed and controlled herself.

Later in the evening Nick stood at Cissie's gate to say goodbye. "I'm leaving on the early morning train and don't know when I'll see you again."

A solitary tear ran down Cissie's face as she lay her head on Nick's chest. "I don't start work until 8.30," she said, "I'll come to the station with you, and we can say goodbye there. Oh Nick, I'm going to miss you so much," she sobbed.

Nick felt tears pricking but squeezed his eyelids to stop them from coming. "I love you, Cissie Packham," he said.

Cissie sniffed. "It took you long enough to say it," she giggled, wiping her nose on her hand.

"You will wait for me?" Nick asked.

"You dope, of course I will. I'll wait forever if I have to!" She thought for a second, then added, "but don't let it be too long. I want your babies!"

Nick chuckled. "If we're not careful, you'll have dozens!"

Elsie finally let Nick go at the door of the scullery. She patted his jacket and said, "Take care of yourself, Love."

Looking at all the soldiers he had been trained for, Nick walked down the garden path to the gate. He turned and smiled, opened the gate and waved to his mother. Elsie wiped her nose and waved the handkerchief she was using. "I'll give Dad your message when I see him later," she called as she watched him disappear along Church Path hand in hand with Cissie. Soon, Cissie stood, sad and alone, on the station platform as the train disappeared out of sight.

Chapter 15

Nick arrived back in Brighton later in the day. Gathered shoulder to shoulder in the large tent that served as a drill hall, the young troopers heard that orders had finally been given for the regiment to move out of Brighton to the concentration area at Paddockhurst Wood East Grinstead. A silent wave of anticipation swept through the lines of soldiers.

"That's the lot," said Wilf, stuffing the last item of clothing into his canvas duffle bag.

Nick was tying his bootlaces, "Let's hope we get the same decent accommodation as we got here!" he said.

Picking their heavy bags off the kitchen floor, Nick and Wilf said goodbye to Mr and Mrs Kelly. Mrs Kelly dropped her shoulders and tipped her head to one side.

"O we are sorry you're going, lads," she said sadly.

"Yeh, we've really enjoyed 'aving you," Mr Kelly added.

"You've bin no trouble," Mrs Kelly said, wiping her nose, "You will keep in touch and let us know how you are doing, won't you?"

"'course we will, and you, be sure to keep safe too," said Wilf. It'll be over quickly now that we're going over there."

"Wilf's right," chuckled Nick, "So keep yer chin up."

The couple stood at their door until the lads were out of sight.

Paddockhurst Woods was a great disappointment for the lads who were now once again living under canvas with no home-cooked meals and comfortable beds. All leave was cancelled, though that didn't stop the Troopers from sneaking out to the local Royal Army Ordnance Corps dumps to steal extra equipment. Aware that if they got caught, there would be consequences, their expeditions continued.

"Boy, that was a close one!" Nick puffed when he returned with the spoils. "Thought we'd got caught on our way back, but the Corp just turned his back on us. Don't think he saw us."

"He saw us alright," said Basil.

"Watchyer got this time then?" asked Harry.

"Another stove, better than the one we've got," said Basil.

"Two's better than one anyway," chuckled Nick. Twenty-four hours later, Basil and Nick were seen sporting extremely short haircuts!

"Ha!" laughed Wilf. "He did see yer both then and sent you off to the barber."

'Bastard!' spat Nick.

Another day came, and the skies were again black with rain clouds. The afternoon plans to spend time playing cricket on the local cricket pitch were scuppered because of torrential rain.

"Blimey never thought I'd hear meself say I'm glad they called off the cricket match. Never bin so bleedin' wet for so bleedin' long!" complained Nick.

"Yeh, we'll be growing webbed feet soon!" added Basil

"Then we'll be able to swim across the Channel; couldn't get any wetter," muttered Nick.

It hadn't stopped raining since the day they arrived in Paddockhurst Woods, adding to the misery of the tedious day-to-day cleaning equipment and training, which only served to pass away the anxious waiting hours for the inevitable call to arms. These were tense days of anticipation and apprehension, knowing that the Regiment would be off any day now.

The Troops paraded for inspection on a field that served as a barrack square; brightly polished buttons and toe-caps glistened as Major Wignall took the parade.

"Where's the Colonel?" hissed Nick.

"'eard he got the shingles, di'n't you know?" Wilf hissed back.

Captain Firth was seated under a makeshift tent at a trestle table the following day, over which an army blanket was spread, sifting through a pile of coins. The sky hung heavy with more rain clouds as the Troopers stood waiting for ten shillings of allocated francs. Captain Firth repeated the same thing to each one:

"Remember, there is a penalty for any trooper taking more than ten shillings worth of French francs into France - Good Luck!"

Nick, Wilf, Archie and Basil strolled away from the table, inspecting the French coins, "Wonder how much a franc is worth then?" Nick muttered.

"Haven't a clue," Wilf said thoughtfully.

The young Troopers, along with the rest of the division, were ushered into the drill hall tent, where they stood to listen to what the Padre had to say:

"What I am about to say to you is not something you will want to hear, but it is necessary all the same. There will almost certainly be an occasion when you will have to dispose of a dead body on the field of battle. However, I hope and pray you don't. All the same, you will need to know what to do."

The silence was tangible! All eyes were fixed on the Padre, and all ears were attentive as he told them the necessary procedure.

"You will find a decent place to bury the body in the ground. But before you do so, remove one of the two dog tags from round the neck and submit it to your Commanding Officer with as much detail as possible of the location. The information will then be sent to the medical crew who will find and place a white cross on the grave. This routine will apply to any person you find, even those who may have lain dead for a considerable time. This will not be an easy task and one you will not easily forget."

The Padre paused and moved to the side of the table he was leaning on. You may have already seen the pamphlets posted around warning of the importance of good sexual health and the dangers of sexually transmitted diseases.

"You will all be issued with preventive information and contraceptive sheaths. Remember this: most prostitutes have got a disease of some sort."

The last and final orders were given regarding the dangers of the potency of local wine and Calvados, "Should you need to use it, Calavados is equally good for lighting fires!" At these last words, a ripple of laughter ensued

The lads hovered in the doorway of the drill hall tent, looking out at the rain. Troopers jostled and pushed past them.

"Struth!" gasped Wilf, "don't like the sound of all we just heard."

"Comes home to you, doesn't it," murmured Basil.

Archie gave Basil a gentle shove, "Keep away from the prostitutes, Basil, or you'll get a dose!" he laughed.

Basil scowled, "I ain't that sort!" he snapped, adding, "I'm a married man!"

"I'm a married man; O I'm a married man," mimicked Archie sarcastically.

Both Bick and Wilf shot him a glare. Archie grinned and shrugged his shoulders.

Stepping out into the rain, Nick called back over his shoulder, "Grow up, you idiot!" Archie was about to respond when Wilf elbowed him hard and glared!

"What?"

"You can be such a bastard sometimes!" "Why? I was only joking!"

"Yeh, well, you and your jokes ain't always funny!"

"Ow, get lost," responded Archie. He left the tent, pulled up their coat collars, and straightened their berets. The lads followed, returning to their billets through the rain and mud.

Two days later, on the 9th of July, the regiment was placed at six hours' notice to move.

"Get your letters written today because you won't get another chance this side of the Channel!" boomed Lt Palmer.

"Me mum's not gonna love this one, that's for sure," said Nick,

"Don't suppose my mum's gonna get a laugh out of mine either," added Wilf.

Later that day the tent that served as a barrack room for the lads fell quiet, each young trooper lost in his thoughts of news to their families.

The letters were written, but there was still no movement until the morning of the 11th of July when an order came through to move to a Marshalling Area near Gosport.

The journey from Crawley was slow but without incident. Nick sat in the cramped bowels of the Daimler armoured car, the No 19 wireless set hung around his neck resting on his chest. The only visible parts of Lt. Palmer's body were his legs standing on his seat next to Nick, the rest exposed to the warm summer drizzle outside. Sitting in the driving seat surrounded by instruments and controls Wilf kept his eye on the rear end of the vehicle in front through the observation window; the speedometer flickered between fifteen and twenty. Surrounded on all sides of the vehicle were the many necessary articles of equipment, from gun cartridges and Bren Gun magazines to smoke dischargers and containers of drinking water, leaving space only for the crew to sit in their seats.

People stopped to wave and cheer as the convoy of armoured cars rumbled and clattered through the lanes and streets along the south coast. Arriving in Gosport, the crew of the Daimler was just three of the many who clambered out of the armoured cars and clattered into the narrow street of terraced brick houses.

Doors opened all along the street, and women gathered at their entrances. Children stopped what they were doing to stand and gawp at the long line of new arrivals lined up on the side of the road. Nick and Wilf met with Basil and his fellow crew members Vic Jenkins and Archie Gorman. With nothing to do, the Troopers left Wilf and walked idly along the pavement to chat with Troopers from the rest of the 'B' Squadron. Wilf was finishing his cigarette when a woman came out of the house carrying a tray of mugs and a plate of cakes.

"Here you go, Tommy, love," she said, "Reckon you could do with a nice cuppa right now."

Wilf stubbed out his cigarette and wiped his hands down the front of his jacket with eager anticipation, "Thanks very much," he said,

"Oy Nick here's a kind lady with a cuppa tea for us," he called.

The lads needed no second invitation; they hurried back to join Wilf.

"Thanks," said Nick, "that's all right. Love, drink it while it's 'ot!" she said.

"You off soon then?"

While Wilf answered the woman's question Nick was distracted by the appearance of a pretty young girl who appeared in the doorway of the house. With all the charm he could muster, he said, "Hello, Love, your mum's a good cook – nice cakes."

With that, a tall, stout man appeared with his thumbs hooked in his braces. With a look of contempt, he stood in front of the girl.

"Inside Lass," he growled.

The girl obeyed her father's order and disappeared back into the house. Nick quickly looked away. Raising innocent eyes to the sky, he strolled closer to Vic.

"Can't win 'em all, mate," whispered Vic.

".......But you don't know exactly when then?" said the woman in response to Wilf's explanation.

"No," he said, "but I think it won't be long now."

"Bloody maniac," murmured the woman.

"What?" exclaimed Wilf.

"That bloody Hitler, I mean – not you, Love," she chuckled. "Well, it ain't no laughing matter. Each one o' you is a mother's son!" Lifting the corner of her apron and screwing it up in frustration, she added, "Makes me mad!" She paused, "Would you like another?' she asked, pointing to the mug in Wilf's hands.

"No thanks, that was really nice and welcoming."

"Well, I wish you good luck, and God bless you," she said.

Taking the tray and contents back into the house, she hissed something to her husband, blocking the doorway. "Yeh! Well, I was a soldier once, you forget!" he said loud enough for the troopers to hear. "Huh, those were the days!" the woman retorted.

There were erratic moves forward over the next few hours. The boredom was relieved by more offerings of refreshments and friendship. Children curious for information bothered them with questions and the attention of the local people and young girls in pretty dresses amused them until the armoured cars moved closer to the beach.

Late in the evening, the remaining sections of the Guards Armoured Division filled the beach and seafront with many vehicles and soldiers. Nick and Wilf watched to see what landing craft awaited in the bay.

Suddenly, Nick pointed and yelled, "There is an American Landing Tank. See the stars and stripes? Ha! I knew there would be!"

"Yeh, well, all we have to do is make sure we get on it!" commented Wilf.

Nick rubbed his hands together with glee. "Yep, they've got pork chops and ice cream. Woohoo!"

At 10 pm only two of the three Squadrons left on designated Landing Ship Tanks. B Squadron was not one of them. None of the Troopers got much sleep while waiting on the shingle beach for the tide to turn. Low conversations ensued from their homes and families to the time they joined up and the changes to their lives since then.

Suddenly, at 3 am, they were jolted to their feet when indistinct voices shouting orders broke the dark silence. Sailor's forms moved eerily about in the dark, urgently encouraging the Troopers to get ready to move. A last-minute call from an officer dishing out luggage labels to anyone who hadn't written their name, rank and number cut through the air. Lt. Palmer climbed onto the armoured car and down through the turret while Wilf and Nick scrambled in through the side door and moved with the vehicles towards the cavernous mouth of an American LST.

Nick breathed deeply, trying to control the surge of excitement that welled inside him, "This is it, Wilf me lad!" he said under his breath.

***

The sea crossing was calm and gentle, with no enemy aircraft in sight and plenty of time for the Troopers to enjoy the company of their American hosts, including a good meal and welcome shower. Nick and Basil were two on guard duty below deck, breathing in the acrid smell of smoke and sulphur. They stood together, speculating thoughtfully about what might lay ahead in Europe until they were relieved to hear the voices of visitors.

"Gee Guys," drawled an American soldier appearing from the upper deck, "You gotta put up with that smell?"

Nick soon got into light-hearted conversation with the GIs.

"Hey Nick," called one of his new acquaintances, "give yer a tenner for that 38 pistol yer carrying."

"Huh! No way, mate," called Nick, "It ain't mine to give yer," he chortled, "And what am I gonna do without it over there?"

Basil looked bemused, "He just offered me twenty quid for my Tommy Gun," he hissed.

Two hours later, Wilf and Nick went up to the mess room, where they met up with more American soldiers and enjoyed a meal of hamburgers and chips and a huge bowl of ice cream before retiring to snatch some sleep.

A scraping jolting sound shook the men out of their sleep as the Landing Ship Tank ran aground on a French beach code-named 'Juno'. One by one, the vehicles drove onto the beach, exiting through the huge mouth of the LST that they had entered a few hours earlier.

"Gawd blimey!" gasped Nick,

"What?" spat Wilf.

"Look at them, white crosses," his mouth hung open as the Daimler rolled out of the Landing Ship tank and drove onto the beach.

Dozens of white crosses dotted about marked the places where the bodies of those who were killed when they landed on D-Day. "They didn't stand a chance, poor buggers." It seemed to Nick almost irreverent to see a couple of sailors kicking a football around the area.

All the hours and weeks spent waterproofing proved unnecessary as the ramp of the Landing Ship Tank dropped down into shallow water. However, once the vehicles were ashore, the Troopers set to work blasting the waterproofing away from the sides of the vehicles.

Driving up the beach and onto the road, Nick looked out to sea. Out of the huge open mouth of the Landing Ship Tank, the last of its cargo trickled onto the sandy beach. Various ships, lorries, and amphibious tanks lay rusting, broken and mangled. By contrast, the sea was now busy with all kinds of anchored ships of varying description. Small naval craft were going about their business, weaving in and out of the traffic, while amphibious vehicles moved back and forth from ships to shore, depositing supplies. High in the sky hung a barrage balloon, keeping watch, it seemed, over the activity on the sea below. Stirred by the sights and sounds the young trooper was overwhelmed to think he was part of this huge military operation.

***

The Troopers were acutely aware that though the beaches were cleared, the enemy was not far away, and Caen was still in enemy hands.

"Quiet," Wilf said.

"Yeh!" said Nick, "This is it! We're not playin' games now. It's nerve-wrackin'! Me heart's pounding!"

"You and me too."

"If you weren't scared," called Palmer from the turret, "There would be something wrong with you."

The convoy of armoured cars ground their way towards the first assembly area at Brecy, passing grey, stone-built farms, buildings and villages along leafy lanes, past orchards and cornfields that once depicted peace and tranquillity but which now lay scarred and burnt-out. Along the way on the side of the road, here and there, a lone white cross marked other shallow graves. The convoy travelled on with no incidents, and by midday, it noisily entered the village of Creully.

The drone of planes in the distance caught their attention, and the convoy stopped. Unsure of what was happening, Nick waited for the next order to be given. Suddenly, the rat-a-tat-tat of ack-ack guns rent the air.

"Enemy planes," whispered Wilf, straining through the front vision slit.

"Dismount and take cover," came the urgent command from the lieutenant.

Nick and Wilf scrambled through the door in the side of the Daimler and dashed to the side of the road to reach the cover of the hedgerow.

"Shit!" said Nick in a loud whisper and fell to the ground as the first bombs resounded in the field nearby. On his hands and knees, he scuttled to the safety of the hedgerow, desperate for some safe shelter.

Terrified, he found himself digging the ground with his hands as bombs exploded all around. Wilf lay on his belly, trying to subdue his racing heart, along with other Troopers lying on the ground, equally petrified. Then, just as suddenly as it started, it stopped, and those planes that survived the attack droned away into the distance. Visibly shaken, the Troopers clambered back into the armoured car, sighing in relief. Engines revved up, and the convoy roared off again in a cloud of dust towards Brecy.

Nick was quietly preoccupied with his thoughts. Wilf glanced at him from time to time. "That gave us a bit of a scare," he said.

Nick remained silent.

"You okay, mate?" Wilf shouted to Nick.

Nick lifted the headphones from one ear to listen. "Yep, I'm fine," he snapped. "I'm concentrating!"

Just after midday the convoy had reached the forming up area. Following the vehicle in front, Wilf drove the Daimler into a field where the two squadrons, B and C, were to spend the night—the last twenty-four hours had been wearisome.

"Well done, men," said Lt. Palmer. "Rest up now and make the most of it. We'll be off again at first light tomorrow."

Nick was quiet as he took off his beret and undid his jacket. He slid down at the side of the Daimler and dropped his head.

Wilf gave him a playful slap on the side of his head, "What were you trying to do back there in that village?"

"Don't want to talk about it," "You looked right scared!"

"We all were, you were!"

"Yeh, but I thought you were digging to Australia," joked Wilf. "Shuddup, I don't wanna talk about it."

"Nothin' to be ashamed of, mate," said Wilf blowing out a puff of cigarette smoke, "I was shitting myself too!"

Overhearing the conversation, Basil called, "We ain't playing games now. It's the real thing!"

'Yeh! Yeh! All right, I know,' commented Nick impatiently, 'Just drop it, will ya?'

"Come on, mate, we're gonna see if we can get a beer somewhere."

Nick brightened and looked up, "Where you gonna get a beer then?"

"Thought that would cheer you up," laughed Wilf.

No beer was found, but a rough football game, albeit with only half a dozen players, helped lighten Nick's mood.

Tired out after a long day and very little sleep, Nick and Wilf retired early under the bivouac while late in the evening, small pockets of men sat together conversing in low voices. Like so many fireflies, the glow of cigarettes moved about in the darkness; now and then, a guffaw of laughter echoed through the air until finally, apart from the distant sounds of battle and the intermittent sound of footsteps from those on guard duty, all fell quiet.

In the light of a beautiful summer day, the village of Brecy appeared to have been bypassed by the events of the war. A feeling of anticipation swept through the division at the sight of a flourishing farm nearby with the possibility of fresh eggs. After a breakfast of porridge and a mug of strong tea, the lads prepared to leave for the next stage of their journey to Bayeux.

"You're getting good at cooking porridge, Wilf me ol' mate," said Nick.

"Yeh, well, the dual-burner you nicked from the R.A.O.C dump made the difference,"

'Wilf, do ya wanna swap my sugar ration for your butter ration?'

"Why?"

"You know I hate butter!"

"Yeah, alright!"

"Anyway, that wasn't one of my burners. That was Basil's, and he got an even shorter 'back and sides' for that," chuckled Nick.

He slapped Basil on the back, and the two of them wandered between the array of stationary armour to the edge of the field overlooking the village street. Local women gathered in little groups by a village pump. One young girl separated from the group when she noticed the young soldiers peering in her direction over the top of the hedge. She immediately diverted her eyes and went on her way. Nick let out a quiet whistle.

Basil looked at him and grimaced. "Huh, you never know when to stop, do you?"

Flicking his butt end into the hedge, he turned to leave.

"No 'arm in lookin," Nick retorted.

"Bonjour," one of the women called.

Nick removed his beret.

"Bonshore, ma'am," he said politely. The woman spoke again in her native language; Nick lifted his shoulders and hands in bewilderment. Before he could blink, the rest of the women approached the hedge, jabbering excitedly.

"Vous Englataire soldat?"

"Hey Basil," called Nick, "Do you know any French?"

"Nope!" Basil replied and walked on.

"Sorry, Darlings," Nick said to the group of women with his usual flair and turned to go.

"Boch casque!" called a woman. Laughing, she held up a German helmet filled with water from the pump. Nick turned and smiling broadly, he lifted his thumb in agreement. The women scattered in all directions only to return shortly in excited droves to welcome the English soldiers. Generous gifts of food and brandy were handed out to grateful men with open hands!

"This is all right," chuckled Nick.

"Yeh!" added Basil, "We can feast tonight!"

"Gotta be better than canned chicken," Wilf remarked.

"Take it easy with that brandy," called the Car Commander, "It's not what you're used to and can be lethal!" Nick gave Wilf a sly wink.

As the sun went down the bottle of brandy was shared out between the troopers, loosening their tongues with jokes and stories.

"Do you remember the first time you got drunk?" Nick asked Wilf.

"Huh! Yeh! I was fourteen, I think. I pinched a couple of bottles of my dad's homemade wine, and a couple of friends and I went to the park and drank the lot. The local Bobby found us pretty paralytic and helped get me home. I can't remember much after that, but me old man took the belt to me the next day. I hated him!"

"You 'ated your dad?" enquired Nick. "I remember my first cigarette. I got a belting for that too, but I don't 'ate me, Dad!"

"If you had my dad you might feel the same as me! He used to get drunk regularly on that wine and then hit my mum. Tell you what I'll never do that to my wife, nor my kids!"

As the brandy bottle emptied, the voices got louder and laughter more raucous late into the evening.

A rather subdued, overhung rabble of men climbed into their vehicles and drove off the following day to continue the journey to Bayeux.

Gathered in a field in the forming up area of Anguerny, two hundred men of all four Sabre Squadrons of reconnaissance armoured cars stood together on a bright but damp day to hear their Squadron Leader, Major Wignall, report on the next plan of action, codenamed "Operation Goodwood". They learned that having driven the German army off the beaches, they were now putting up fierce resistance in the stronghold city of Caen.

Raising his voice, Major Wignall spoke on: "A forty-four-kilometer recce from here will get you to the town of Benouville in two hours. There, you will cross the Orne River, now safe in

British hands thanks to the tanks and bravery of Major John Howard and the British Airborne Troops. You will then reconnoitre south to secure the villages east of Caen and an area known as the Bourguebus Ridge. Two Sabre Squadrons A and B will follow the Welsh Guards' reconnaissance tanks."

"That's us!" whispered Nick.

"Yeh, shh!" responded Wilf.

The Colonel continued, "Three tank divisions, the 11th Armoured, Guards Armoured and the 7th Armoured, will also participate in the operation. The tanks of the Welsh Guards and the Canadian forces will then rout the last German-held bastions of Caen."

A subdued cheer went up as the last words were spoken.

"Now, men," added the Major, "I wish you all the best of luck. Stay safe, and let the battle commence!"

Late in the evening on the same day, A and B squadrons were moving out of Anguerny following the bulky tanks of the Welsh Guards. In their wake came a caterpillar line of tank divisions and infantry lorries. The convoy passed through villages, whipping up dust clouds as they went.

"Can't see a bloody thing for darkness and dust!" Moaned Wilf, his eyes squinting behind his goggles to get a better view.

"Just keep your eye on the car in front, Trooper," Corporal of Horse Palmer called from the turret.

"Ain't the dust that I'm having trouble with," hissed Nick, "it's sleep deprivation!"

"I heard that, Trooper Clayton," called Lt Palmer, adding, "You'll be on guard duty if and when we stop while everyone else sleeps!"

"That ain't fair Sir!"

In the early hours of the morning, the convoy drew to a halt. The occupants of the tanks and other vehicles slept wherever they could make themselves comfortable. Nick, Wilf and Palmer prepared to sleep under the bivvy tent at the side of the armoured car. Littered on the ground they noticed the remains of leaflets dropped by the RAF on D-Day.

"Sommat about surrendering," said Nick, studying the leaflet, "Yep, asking the Germans to surrender," he clarified.

Screwing up the paper, he threw it down.

"Where would we be now if they had agreed?" asked Wilf, settling down for the night.

Nick lay awake. Opening the side of the bivvy, he looked up at the leafy silhouette of the apple trees against the ultramarine sky and murmured, "Probably out on some cold moor in Yorkshire!" He lay with his hands clasped behind his neck, his thoughts taking him back to Cissie and home; "They'll all be in warm, comfortable beds sleeping," he murmured.

"What?" asked Wilf.

"Nothin" mate! Why? Do you want me to read you a story?' "Shuddup!"

It was still dark when the drone of allied planes woke the Troopers. Ack ack guns added to the noise.

Nick grabbed his helmet and put it on, "I ain't takin' no chances," he said, burying himself deeper under the rough army blanket that covered him.

"They're bombing Caen," said Corporal Palmer thoughtfully.

He was standing with another officer, both with binoculars, watching the dust rise and the fires burn as the bombs hit the ground in the far distance.

As dawn broke, the silhouettes of the two officers could still be seen against the sky standing together.

Nick heard them talking. "O well, that's that. Let's hope that does it," said the officer.

"That's the plan, and hopefully, the way will be clear for us," said his companion, discarding his butt end and squashing it in the ground with his foot.

No more sleep was had that night. Nick lit the dual-burner stove undercover and out of the rain, quickly boiling a saucepan of water for tea at the Lieutenant's orders. Soon after, the convoy of armour began its journey again in the direction of Caen. Nick put down his mug of strong tea and attached his headphones. Wilf started up the Daimler, and Nick grabbed his mug before it spilled; that and a handful of dry biscuits served as breakfast that morning.

The armoured car crew concentrated on their tasks as best they could.

A pencil dropped onto Nick's head from Lt. Palmer's hand. "Damned bumpy road," he yelled from the turret.

Nick bent to pick up the offending pencil. He reached up to hand it to Palmer, who took it just as the vehicle turned a sharp bend, throwing Nick to one side and spilling his tea.

"Bloody waste of time that was," he said, discarding the cup.

He replaced the wireless set and straightened his headphones.

Making their way slowly along the wet, narrow road, various army vehicles passed them in droves. In contrast, Red Cross cars carrying the wounded squeezed past in the opposite direction, building up a congestion of traffic that threatened to come to a standstill. Added to the traffic noise, the continuous drone of hundreds of planes overhead made it hard to think! Dull explosions ensued as they expelled their cargo onto German-held Caen, where clouds of dust billowed up as bombs hit the earth.

Amidst the rubble and debris of destroyed homes and buildings, local people resolved to stop, wave and cheer as the convoy passed.

"Bienvenue soldats Anglais, Bienvenue," they cried in chorus.

Children were hauled to safety at the side of the road to let the convoy pass, and weary older men, excited by the sight, summoned the energy to trot behind the young boys as they ran joyfully beside the tanks and armoured cars.

Leaving the villages behind, the convoy weaved through the lanes and traffic until they reached a road bridge over the Orne Canal. As the Daimler reached the bridge's other side, the crew could see two gliders that lay broken and buckled nearby. Clothing was hung out to dry on a line between the two gliders. A few soldiers relaxed on the grass; some stood to acknowledge the passing convoy.

Leaving the bridge behind, the convoy snaked its way forward. Sometime later, the crew of the Daimler was shaken by an explosion that shook the ground. Grinding to a halt, they soon learned that a vehicle behind them had gone over a mine and the crew killed.

"Shit!" exclaimed Wilf, "We drove over that mine!"

"Bloody hell!" breathed Nick. His mind flew back to his home, his parents and Cissie. "Am I really going to get back home again? Will there be another mine with my name on it?" he wondered.

Left to his thoughts, he and Wilf remained in the armoured car, waiting until the damaged vehicle was cleared and the crew picked up by the White Medical Car. The convoy moved off again, carefully wending between the white safety tapes lining the mine-filled roads. They later learned that three troopers from A Squadron died in the blast.

By late afternoon, the tanks of the Welsh Guards had engaged the enemy before any more reconnaissance was needed. B Squadron of the 2nd Household Cavalry halted on the Bourguebus Ridge. In the distance, the outskirts of Caen could be seen, and the tank battle was already raging.

"The job's done. We're not needed anymore," said Palmer.

With the 'Goodwood Operation' over, the Squadrons were ordered into the harbour near the village of Demouville. Soon after their arrival, the troopers sat relaxing with tea, cigarettes, books, and cards while others went about their business.

Suddenly, a bombardment of shells and mortar rained so close that the tea in the lads' cups rippled. Shaken to their feet, they moved to see what had happened. Soldiers appeared from every direction to find two injured troopers from 'A' Squadron and another lying dead in the middle of the harbour area in a mass of rubble. The Troopers stood back and watched in horror. Harry Parks fled to a corner and threw up.

Someone cried out, "Medics, medics!"

Stunned, they continued to watch as medics hurried to the spot with stretchers and medical supplies. An air of disbelief gripped the troopers, who silently returned to their occupations and thoughts.

Late in the day, the clouds burst, and a thunderstorm raged, settling the dust but bringing out a swarm of mosquitos. There was no shelter other than the confines of the armoured car. Avoiding the leaks of water that trickled in through the turret, the lads sat miserable and wet trying to make sense of the incident that took place earlier. "That's another two men from A Squadron, dead!" murmured Wilf.

"Yeh, and we 'aint bin 'ere five minutes!" Nick said. The cheerful face of Charlie Smith opened the door in the side of the armoured car.

"They're erecting a tent for something!" he called.

Nick and Wilf joined the other Troopers as they crossed to the tent in the rain.

Gathered in the steam-filled tent along with dozens more bare-chested troopers in their underpants, the troopers stood together. Steaming wet clothes hung on ropes tied from one side of the tent to the other.

By nightfall, the tent was crammed with soldiers hoping to get a decent night's sleep, but the constant sound of bombs exploding and rain resounding on the canvas roof disturbed any peace; added to that, their conversations about their first experience of war casualties kept them awake.

"That was Eddie Earnest killed," said one.

"Yeh, he was a decent sort, got a wife and three kids, too."

"Think the youngest is only a few months old," added another thoughtfully.

Though Nick felt the grief and incomprehension of what had happened as deeply as his fellow Troopers, he was grateful for the distraction of a conversation in another corner of the tent.

He and three other troopers strolled over to the Troopers, "What yer talking about then, you lot?"

"We've seen a Tiger Tank," gasped Charlie. "Bloody huge they are!"

Benny Osborne was relating a story of how the crew of his Matador had watched the battle between the Cromwells and the German Tiger tanks and then lost sight of the rest of the convoy.

In the middle of his story, Basil interrupted with, "Shhh, I can hear a nightingale!"

They fell silent.

Nick grimaced in Basil's direction. He sighed and asked, "Really?"

"That is a nightingale," said Basil.

"So what," snapped Archie.

"I can hear it?" Charlie said.

"Anyway," grumbled Nick. Wanting to hear the rest of Benny's story, he asked, "Then what happened?"

Benny continued the story relating how the crew drove through a cornfield and into a lane where they came across a lone Tiger tank. "It was just there on the side of the road,"

"Yeh, and there was a dead German," said Charlie, adding, "he was standing against a low wall with his head blown off! At least, I think he was dead! The lads laughed! "Pretty grim really!"

"Bloody hell," Archie whispered, "Yeh, well, that wasn't the end of it," said another Trooper, "Tell 'em the rest of the story, Benny."

Benny then told how they heard another Tiger Tank coming along the road and escaped by putting down a smokescreen and racing away to safety. "They're bloody huge! We fled down that lane like a bat out of hell."

The group continued their conversation, and Nick's thoughts returned to Eddie Earnest.

Drawing in a sigh, he said, "Well, that's me done," he said, "I'm gonna get some shuteye!"

As they returned to their sleeping quarters in the tent, Nick jostled with Basil, "Nightingale!" he sniggered and began quietly whistling the tune of A Nightingale Sang in Berkeley Square.

Charlie shoved Nick and said, "Shuddup, I heard the thing too."

The next day, two troops from the B squadron were ordered to patrol the area surrounding Demouville. They set off in pouring rain, grateful that the German guns were silent.

Struggling to drive through the muddy, broken roads churned up by tanks and bombing, it was not until early afternoon that the vehicles came to a halt at the side of the road. Nick listened to the conversation between the lieutenant and other troop leaders.

"Think we're being withdrawn," he hissed to Wilf. Sure enough, the command was to return to the harbour.

Half a dozen troopers stood together on wet grass beside the parked vehicles, avoiding dripping trees and muddy puddles at the side of a field.

Wilf lit a cigarette and said to Nick, "It's your turn to make the grub."

"Great!" Came the grumpy reply.

Called to order later that evening, the Squadron Leader announced: "The news is that there's been an attempt to assassinate Hitler. A murmur of speculation rippled through the troops momentarily before they were drawn to attention again to hear that the next objective would be Caumont-l'Evente.

On a damp but bright morning, the two Squadrons began the journey toward Bayeux. The route took them through the recently liberated, broken and destroyed southern area of Caen, passing groups of refugees with what belongings they could carry. German prisoners of war tramped along the road in bedraggled groups accompanied by Canadian despatch riders. One or two broke away from the line of prisoners, still with their hands on their heads, desperately crying, "Hitler Kaput only S.S. wish to fight."

Like a row of beetles crawling along a narrow track between the tall shells of bombed-out buildings, the armoured cars ground their way through the devastation of Caen. No sound came from within as Troopers looked aghast at the hundreds of civilian dead bodies and animals that still lay amongst the rubble, the result of the allied bombing of the city. Rescue squads could be seen beating off swarms of flies that obstructed their work. Nick held his nose against the smell that penetrated the enclosure of the Daimler. Suddenly, Wilf braked, bringing the car to a halt behind the leading vehicle.

"What's the problem?" Palmer called on the radio.

"Animal carcasses blocking the way," came the reply.

No further advance could be made until the way was cleared. Troopers left their cars and approached the scene.

"Looks like they're bloody moving!" exclaimed Nick to Wilf.

On closer inspection Wilf said, "Seems like it, but I think you'll find its maggots crawling on them."

Nick squirmed, "Ugh!"

"Just get stuck in Trooper Clayton," called Palmer. Under the rubble of bricks at the side of the narrow clearing of road, a row of bodies of men, women and children lay where they died. Palmer could see the look of bewilderment on Nick's face.

"They've been shot!" he said, "Why didn't they just leave?" he murmured.

"The Germans wouldn't allow them to! Simple as that!" said Palmer. Once the sickening task of clearing the dead animals off the track the journey towards Bayeux resumed.

Camilly 23rd - 29th July Stay 6 days compulsory training trips

Warm, bright sunshine greeted the lads as they exited their vehicles in a leafy orchard on the southern edge of the Calvados region of Camilly. The whole regiment had converged on a large area of farmland. Dozens of vehicles, from tanks of the various divisions to the little scout cars of the Household Cavalry, littered the area. Dozens of soldiers milled around in safety. Cooking pans were bubbling away on stoves around which little groups of men hovered.

Nick stood by watching Wilf prepare the food when Vic and Archie arrived on the scene.

"What you gotta eat today then?" enquired Archie.

"Roast beef and Yorkshire pudding," joked Wilf.

"Yeh, with horseradish sauce and roast potatoes!" chuckled Nick.

Archie raised his eyebrows, "Well, we've got homemade shepherd's pie and runner beans freshly dug from the allotment!"

"Cor, I wish it was true!" commented Vic.

The meal was over, and the pans cleared away. The lads settled into a quiet evening of conversation and card games.

The next day after their first decent night's sleep for a while and the arrival of a mobile shower unit, hot showers and clean dry clothing refreshed the troopers. With no further orders, they idled away the next few hours lounging in the warm sunshine, watching the few team players that Nick could muster at a game of cricket until early evening when they saw a canteen lorry arrive. "Could this be our meal tonight?" Wilf said in expectation. The lads stood and watched as the truck drew to a standstill. Lt Palmer crossed in front of it.

"Sir," Nick called. !Is that the supply lorry with our meal tonight?"

"Wait to find out!" came the curt reply.

"Bastard!"

"' e's a miserable sod!" said Wilf.

As the lads hoped, they enjoyed a proper hot meal from the supply lorry that evening and spent the rest of their time in quiet conversation.

The occasional outburst of laughter drowned out the distant sounds of war when Palmer interrupted the tranquillity of the warm evening."Make the most of the evening and get a good night's sleep, you'll be on training exercises tomorrow!"

The lads groaned in response. Looking up at the silhouette of the officer's shape against the setting sun.

Wilf asked, "How long we here for then, Sir?"

"As long as it takes for the bridgehead to clear."

"Do you know what's happening then, Sir?" Asked Basil

"As far as I know, both the British and American armies are still packed into the area of Normandy. The Americans will be the first to leave for Falaise to do battle with Hitler's Seventh Army. The bombing of Caen didn't deter the enemy. They've regrouped south of Caen in Falaise.'

While waiting for the breakthrough, compulsory physical training exercises were ordered. In the early morning mist that spelled another warm sunny day, a long line of troopers, dressed in P.E kit and carrying route maps, left the harbor area. The exercise, while uneventful, proved fascinating. Running through the lanes and byways, they passed open entrances to small farm buildings where chickens foraged, vegetables grew in open fields, and cows grazed alone in meadows. Curious deviations were made en route, and the troopers returned to the harbour with armfuls of illicit produce.

While the majority of local people were delighted to meet and greet their liberators, some were not so pleased when they found their chicken runs raided, other produce began to go missing, and cows were milked. Angry farmers shook fists at the fleeing thieves.

"Verlass mein land," they yelled.

Get off my land.

After reporting the offenses to their Officers, embarrassed Troopers were later seen with hair cut so short that just a circle of hair was left on their heads! Rather than give up, the troopers dreamed up a new devious strategy to bargain with the local people, ensuring the continuation of fresh eggs, milk, cheese, cider and the odd chicken in exchange for cigarettes and chocolate.

"I can't believe you managed to get a bit of the other in the five minutes you were gone, Benny!" said Archie.

'She was willin'," and came on to me. "I can't 'elp it if I'm born irresistible!" chuckled Benny.

"You'll get the pox if you're not careful," said Basil, stroking his moustache.

"She was nice-lookin too," Benny said thoughtfully.

The sound of a despatch motorbike put smiles on their faces. Jumping up, the lads walked quickly to meet the driver, who dropped a mail bag beside the bike. Corporal-of-Horse Davis appeared from a tent bent on collecting the mailbag. Nick winked at the lads and went to look as though he was about to open the bag.

Sniggering, the lads waited; a high-pitched voice yelled from a distance, "Leave it!"

"Leave it!" mimicked the boys in unison and in the same high-pitched tone.

After a meal of locally acquired sausages, new potatoes and fresh peas, the lads read their mail.

Nick recognised Cissie's writing on the envelope and soaked up the smell of her perfume.

"Cor!" He sighed, holding the letters against his chest, "What I wouldn't give to feel her lips on mine right now!"

"If you ask me, you've lost it, mate!" Wilf muttered.

"She loves me!" Nick added. Hugging the letter, he began to hum the tune of Embraceable You."

"Go on, then give it a blast, mate," called Charlie.

He didn't need to be asked a second time. An audience of men listened as, in full voice, he sang the song to the end to great applause.

"You cocky bastard Clayton," Archie said sourly.

'You missed your vocation mate," said another.

Apart from a few words about her family, Cissie's letters mainly spoke of her love for Nick and how she prayed for him to stay safe and longed for him to return home. His mother wrote about her fears and anxieties for Nick's safety and her worries about Dick's health and the vegetables that failed. Joyce added a few words with news of her successful school sewing project and how she cried when she saw the film 'Lassie Come Home' "and isn't Elizabeth Taylor so beautiful I wish I had black hair like hers!"

To their relief, the next day, leave was granted for the Troopers to go into Bayeux, just over fourteen miles away. Boarding a three-ton lorry, the troopers were in high spirits. Within an hour they were wandering the streets of Bayeux, surprisingly untouched by any bombing. It was a city not unlike any other city but with the addition of a huge twin-spired cathedral.

The town was in a carnival mood; red, white and blue striped French flags hung from windows fluttering in the breeze, and the lads were overwhelmed by the reception they received from the local people. Stopped at every corner, they were joyfully embraced and kissed by young and old, male and female alike, handed flowers and bottles, the lads enjoyed every moment.

"This is alright," laughed Nick, hanging on to the last kiss from a pretty girl. Wilf bent to pick up a child clinging to his trousers. To his embarrassment and jeers from his mates, a woman motioned to him to kiss the child while she took a photo. Avoiding more embraces and loaded with gifts, the lads moved on, passing shops and hotels in whose doorways homeless and despairing refugees from Caen sheltered with what possessions they could carry.

Suddenly, Basil exclaimed, "Yanks!"

Coming from the opposite direction, a group of American soldiers swaggered towards the lads in the middle of the brick-paved road, "Hey Limeys," called one, "Heard you arrived!"

"We're lookin' for somewhere to eat," announced Wilf,

"We'll show yer," drawled one. Two of the American soldiers joined the lads, and chairs were soon drawn up to a table covered with a blue-chequered tablecloth in a neat cafe,

"I'm Steve, and this is Eddie," said Steve, holding a friendly hand. The lads shook hands warmly. "Where you from then," drawled Steve.

"I'm from Walthamstow in London, and Wilf's from Clapham in London. Basil here, he's from a posh home up north somewhere," said Nick. Basil laughed, "The Cotswolds are stupid in the mid-west!"

"Was never any good at geography," Nick chuckled.

"We were stationed in Kent near Canterbury," Eddie said, "Nice place!"

"Nice people too, and the kids, well, we took to them!" added Steve, "I'm originally from Texas and Ed's from Dallas."

"So what's with the trumpet then?" inquired Ed, opening a cigarette packet and offering the pack to his friend.

"It's not a trumpet. It's a hunting horn!" Basil replied.

"Oh, yeh, for fox hunting?"

"Yes," The new found friends inspected the horn closely.

"See if you can blow it," said Wilf with a grin.

"Nah, not in here!"

Ed took another drag on his cigarette and blew the smoke out of the corner of his mouth. "If you can get a sound out of it, I'll give you ten bob!" added Wilf.

Steve looked at Basil inquiringly.

"Go on, then you heard him!" chuckled Basil.

Ed put the horn to his lips and blew. To the listener's surprise, a sound ensued!

"'E did it!" cheered Nick. "Cough up, Wilf," he added.

While Wilf dug into his pocket to produce the ten bob. "What's ten bob in French francs?" he enquired.

Steve looked at the horn and said, "Give it here."

Flicking his cigarette into the ashtray, he took the horn and blew hard, but no sound came. Bewildered, he returned the horn to Basil, who said, "Ed was lucky. There's a knack to it that comes with practice."

Meanwhile, Nick's attention is diverted to a pretty waitress who is only too willing to accept his advances and plant a kiss on his lips! Basil deliberately blew on the horn, distracting Nick. Annoyed, Nick spat, "You daft bugger!"

"Non, non!" said another waitress, frowning and wagging a finger at Basil.

That night Nick lay under the canvas bivouac brooding over an invitation he received from the girl in the cafe who invited him to her home. Archie and Benny took up an offer and stayed out overnight. Can't blame them, Nick; sleeping in a bed with sheets and a blanket was temptation enough but the comfort of being in the arms of a woman would weaken any man's willpower.

Nick reached for his jacket and pulled the love letters from Cissie out of the pocket. He turned them over in his hands. He missed her. He remembered her lovely form in the pretty dress and cardigan she wore on their first date and how they both felt after the death of Kenny. Soul mates, he thought to himself. It's not the same when I meet other girls, he thought, but with so much temptation, it's hard.

Chapter 16
From Camilly To Caumont

With another exercise over, Nick lounged carelessly on the grass in the sun beside the armoured cars along with other Troopers when Benny came over with the news that the breakthrough was imminent. "Just heard we're on the move!"

"Told yer!" said Wilf, gloating! Jumping up, he brushed the grass from his trousers, "I caught the end of a conversation to say that the Americans and Canadians have finally liberated Caen."

"Yeh, yeh, alright," Nick replied irritably.

Distracted, Nick looked round to see the Troop Leader, Lieutenant Everard, approaching them. "Ere he comes now to give us the news, I reckon!"

With his usual air of importance, the Troop Leader marched up to the lads and snapped, "All leave's been cancelled. Get to the Squadron Leader's tent, and he will fully inform you." He looked at the other troopers hanging around, "At the double!" he snapped.

The lads jumped to attention, tidied their uniforms, and replaced berets before jogging across the grass towards the tent. Groups of troopers appeared behind armoured cars and from other corners of the field to join them.

Under cover of the tent, they stood together to hear the Squadron Leader inform them that with the help of a five thousand bombing raid, the Americans and Canadians had fought a hard battle to liberate Caen, leaving the way clear for the next objective for the Allied Forces to move south and gain control of a clear road towards their next objective.

He continued: "Today I have been informed that we are to move immediately to St Martin-des-Besaces via Caumont-l'Evente. From here on, the squadrons will split up," he said, adding directions for each squadron to recce a safe route.

Nick and Wilf learned that B Squadron would operate under the 15th (Scottish) Infantry Division.

"Infantry?" hissed Nick.

"Yeh! But the Churchill tanks will be following," reassured Wilf.

Stripped to the waist, under a clear blue sky in the warmth of the mid-afternoon sun, the lads were later busy cleaning and maintaining the armoured cars. Taking a break, Nick and Wilf stood together behind their vehicle, out of sight.

"I'll be sorry to leave 'ere," muttered Nick,

"Yeh, me too, it's been good." Wilf ground the last of his cigarette into the grass and chuckled.

"What's funny?" asked Nick.

"I just remember that farmer who chased me off his land red-faced when I picked up one of his chickens!"

For the next few minutes, the lads shared the stories of their escapades while on compulsory exercises, stealing what they could from the local farms and then chased off by angry farmers with any weapon available from clods of earth to blunderbusses while their wives followed, shouting and waving brooms about.

Still laughing at the memories, Nick took off his hat, releasing a lock of hair. Brushing it back and replacing his beret, he glanced to his left.

"Look out!" he said, "'ere 'e comes again."

Eyeing the paint pot the Lieutenant carried, his heart sank!

"Petrol tanks filled; oil checked?" The officer snapped as he strolled along the line of vehicles.

"Yes sir," came the repeated replies.

Walking slowly around Nick and Wilf's armoured car, his eye rested on an obstruction to the turret.

"Sort it," he snapped "and get that spade secured!"

Handing the pot of paint to Nick, he added, "Orders to paint out the Corps sign; security reasons, and when you've finished, pass it to the next car!"

Nick looked at the paint pot and brushes and sighed; this late in the day, he asks us!

Stoves cooled after the evening meal, and the last tea dregs were emptied onto the grass. Conversations reduced to murmurs, and once again, the familiar glow of cigarette ends moved about like so many fireflies dancing in the cool of the evening. Bivouacs were erected, bedrolls came out, and the men settled down for another night, oblivious of the constant thud and crump of guns in the distance, continuing the nightly bombardment they were becoming used to.

Goodbye to Camilly

At three in the morning, the throbbing of a motorbike arrived in the harbour and, immediately, much to the chagrin of the sleeping troopers, came the sudden call to move out. Dazed and sleepy, Nick moaned, "I knew that motorbike engine spelt trouble!"

"Me too," Groaned Wilf, rolling up his bed.

Overhearing the conversation, Lt Everard said, "Tough! You're leading the convoy!"

Nick baulked, "Oh well, guess it's our turn. Let's hope the way is clear."

With another two or three hours of darkness, the lads settled in their seats. Wilf hit the starting motor, adding to the noise of dozens of revving engines, "Here we go, Nick!" he chirped, turning on the headlights.

"No headlights; the order is no headlights," the Troop Leader bellowed from the open turret.

One by one, the vehicles negotiated a sharp bend in the murky darkness and out into the lane, the Matadors bringing up the rear with their noisy London bus engines.

The early morning sun slowly dawned, turning the sky from ultramarine to pink and orange, waking the land. The temperature was high by midday, beating down on the Daimler metal chassis.

Out on the open road, the landscape changed quite dramatically. Instead of the streets that wound through wide open fields as they did in Normandy, the lanes now dipped between high hedge-rowed banks overhung by trees in an area known as the Beny Bocage.

Coming within five miles of Caumont, the peace they had enjoyed on their journey was disrupted. The leading cars ground to a complete halt as they came across more damaged and abandoned vehicles and dead animals still harnessed to broken-down carts blocking the way. Suddenly, shots were fired at them from within the woods lining the road. Detours proved impassable as mines were found to be everywhere. Behind the convoy of armoured cars, Infantry fell out of their trucks and ran cautiously along the road, dropping to the ground on the edge of the woods to discharge their rifles. Others battled with snipers moving in the woods like shadowy spectres, while others set to work to remove the debris and clear the way. For the first time, Nick heard the rushing sound of flame-throwers. In the chaos came the distinct sound of another explosion. An unfamiliar sound came over the radio, and Nick overheard Lt Everard gasp in horror.

"A Churchill's gone up!" He murmured.

"A Churchill tank, sir?" Nick enquired

No reply came from the Troop Leader. In the silence that followed, Nick watched as Wilf and the officer lit up a cigarette, sucked in the nicotine, and blew out the smoke with satisfaction.

"Give us a drag," he asked Wilf.

His friend passed him the cigarette. Nick drew on it and coughed.

"Have one Trooper," said the Troop Leader, handing an open packet to Nick.

"It'll steady your nerves," said Wilf.

Nick's head began to spin at each inhalation of the cigarette. He felt quite light-headed and relaxed by the time he had finished. He thought over, with horror, the things he had just seen and heard: the sight and sound of the wasp flamethrower lighting up the woods; above the noise and chaos, the faint screams of the victims; the speed of every movement; the sound of another tank going up and the thought that another tank crew may not have escaped.

"Sir," he said, "what was that strange sound we heard earlier?"

"A tank went up as I said," began the Troop Leader, "Sometimes when that happens, the radio is still netted, so when the tank gets hit, the radio controller's hand stays pressed on the communication button so you get to hear the cries of the men inside as the tank burns up,"

Wilf gave a low whistle.

Nick grimaced, "Bloody hell!" He said and drew on another cigarette, glad that he was in the reconnaissance division, he thought, and not in the tanks or infantry fighting it out with the enemy, "Poor bloody infantry," he whispered.

Tired out after a sleepless night, the crew of the Daimler passed the time dozing as best they could with little comfort, their minds anticipating an imminent forward command.

With the area cleared and safe, the order came to move out again. Putting the car into gear, Wilf set off, followed by the rest of the Squadron cars. Struggling against the desire to sleep, they drove on through more debris that lined the roads, dead animals, and rough ground. Detouring through suitable gaps in the hedge and across fields, they dipped down to negotiate narrow streams before finding one safe enough for the tanks and infantry trucks following. Successfully negotiating a tiny hamlet filled with more curious onlookers, they pushed on another mile towards the village of Caumont. Sitting in the close confines of the armoured car, Nick puffed nervously away on his newfound relaxant, wondering what danger there might be around the next bend in the road. Behind them, the other cars followed at a distance, ready to decamp at a moment's notice rather than engage in any battle should they confront the enemy.

The small village of Caumont came and went, hardly stirring the community. Only a few people emerged from their homes to welcome the convoy that was soon on its way to St Martin des Besaces.

At St Martin-des-Besaces (France)

St Martin-des-Besaces was a small village on an important road towards the French town of Vire, the next objective for the Allied forces. The main street, lined with neat, red-roofed cottages bordering the road, ran from one end of the village to the other. One large farm dominated the street corner, extending out and beyond into agriculture fields under a clear blue sky.

Onlookers gave tentative waves, wary of the enemy snipers who fired at the convoy as it passed through the village. Moving swiftly on and out of the town, the lads later heard the guns of the Churchill tanks once again dealing with the enemy that occupied the village.

End of July

Rounding a sharp bend in the lane, the leading Daimler came face to face with an 88mm gun not long after leaving the village behind. In the next second, the gun fired and hit the car. Flames burst through the vehicle. Nick jumped quickly through the side door, but Wilf didn't follow.

"Wilf, Wilf, get out, Wilf," he yelled.

Immediately, the second Daimler went into action and took out the 88mm. In the chaos of gunfire, flames, and smoke, Nick scrambled back into the vehicle to find his mate unconscious in his seat. He hooked his arms under his old friend's armpits and pulled violently to try to release him from his seat. In no time at all, flames and smoke engulfed the unconscious Trooper. Pain shot through Nick's leg, and, realising he could do no more, he leapt to safety out through the door. His leg was alight with burning petrol. Horrified and groaning with pain, he frantically beat it with his hand, which in turn caught fire. Two infantrymen came to the aid of the Troop Leader, who was struggling to douse the flames.

"Chuck him in the ditch," yelled a voice from a distance.

Throwing the trooper into a ditch, they smothered his burns with earth. In pain and shaking badly on the grass verge of the lane, Nick noticed the damaged German gun emplacement and enemy corpses that lay about on the ground. The Daimler was burning furiously. Suddenly, he gave a howl of grief for his friend. His head was spinning; he felt the cool breeze on his face and heard the confusion of voices around him before inhaling deeply from the cigarette held to his mouth by an infantryman kneeling beside him. Troopers had dismounted from their armoured cars and gathered to the spot, each one contemplating what had happened.

Basingstoke Hospital End of July - 1st September

Two days later, after temporary care from army medics

at an aid station and on a warm summer day, Nick boarded a ship from the Mulberry Harbour that served as a temporary port, bound for England. Seagulls dipped and soared under a clear blue sky; their cries cut through the air as the hospital ship slipped away, cutting through the calm sea.

Below deck, Nick lay on a bunk staring at the ceiling. Alongside him lay a row of other injured soldiers, bandaged and broken. Nurses moved between the bunks with armfuls of equipment, from bandages and medication to bowls and trays of teacups. Recurring flashbacks reminding him of the horrors he experienced dominated his mind. Tears fell down the side of his face and behind his ears, and he began to sob.

A voice spoke gently from the bed beside him, "You wanna talk about it, Tommy?"

Nick turned away from the voice.

"It's tough!" added the voice, "I lost a buddy, blown to bits! I was lucky. I just got a head wound and a hell of a headache!"

Some time passed before Nick roused and turned to look at the speaker. "

My best mate got burned up in an ambush," he murmured.

The soldier introduced himself as Mac and, reaching across, held a hand out to Nick, who gave his left hand in response, his other being heavily bandaged.

"Nick!" He said, adding, "You're a Yank!"

"Correct, from Baltimore. I was injured when my platoon was advancing somewhere towards Falaise."

The two carried on talking when another voice rudely interrupted them, "Nick! Nick Clayton?"

Nick turned to see Charlie Smith from Heavy Troop hobbling on crutches towards him, smiling broadly.

His voice grew serious, "Hey Nick, I heard about Wilf. Sorry!"

"What about you then?"

"Broke me bloody leg a week ago! Fell off the turret!" He chuckled, "Not exactly a war wound! Anyway, lucky; fed up with me hoppin' around on one leg, they said I could heal at home."

Nick was silent. He wanted to end the conversation.

"Hey Yank, you ok?" Called Charlie.

Mac said he was fine. Nick groaned inside. He lay looking at the complicated, bulky, white-painted pipes that laced the low deck ceiling. Charlie continued his chat with Nick.

"Heard you got shot up in a village - hit the petrol tank and …"

"Don't wanna talk about it,"

"Must've been bad,"

"Don't wanna talk about it," Nick snapped.

……………………………...

Arriving at the hospital in Basingstoke, Nick was transported in a wheelchair to a bright ward, grateful for peace and the quiet. Saline bandages were applied to his wounds for the next couple of weeks.

A nursing sister opened the bandages at the request of the examining Colonel, who said, "Hmm, second-degree burns, eh? Lucky, it could have been worse," the Colonel said.

He sniffed, "Hmm, It's a bit high!"

"We like 'em high, don't we sir?" Sister responded gleefully.

The doctor smiled and shook Nick's hand, telling him that the wound should be much better soon, and then he could return to the regiment.

While Nick was relieved that his wounds were only superficial, he was still tormented by the death of his friend.

"I couldn't save him!" He sobbed when a pretty young nurse came to change the bandages.

The days passed, and with the help of crutches, Nick

could go out on the hospital grounds. On a warm, sunny day in mid-August, Nick sat on a bench with his parents, Joyce and Cissie.

"It's healing well," came Nick's sombre reply to his father's question.

"What do you think of dad then, son?" said his mother cheerfully.

Nick lifted his head to speak, "Yeh, it's good to see you lookin' so well, Dad."

Dick produced a newspaper, handing it to Nick he said, "Have you got one today?"

"No, Dad, thanks," He put the paper on the bench beside him.

"Did you read about the American's success in Caen?" said Dick trying to encourage his son to talk. "They're in the thick of another major battle now to take Falaise."

"Hm," Nick grunted.

Elsie sighed. Cissie stood up and held a hand out to Nick, "Come on, Nick, let's walk."

Leaving his crutches propped against the bench, Nick took Cissie's arm.

Elsie watched as the couple went across the lawn. "What we gonna do, Dick? He's broken. He just ain't the same. Poor Cissie."

"We just have to give 'im time, love,"

Sitting with her elbows on her knees and her chin in her hands, Joyce murmured, "She looks so pretty an' all."

The young couple wandered the lawn and sat on another bench under a large yew tree.

"I'm glad your leg is improving," Cissie chirped.

Nick bent forward and looked at the ground.

"Not sure you should wait for me, Cissie," he murmured.

Cissie's heart missed a beat. Lifting her head to the sky, she let the gentle summer breeze brush her face and ignored the comment.

"Margaret and I went to see 'Mrs Miniver' at the pictures again. I heard it was Mr. Churchill's favourite film."

"Yeah, well, maybe you can find a way to marry Walter Pidgeon," said Nick sarcastically.

"Nick, don't!" Cissie whispered. Tears began to prick her eyes.

"You heard what I said." snapped Nick.

Holding his face in her hands, she turned it to look into his eyes, "I don't care; I will wait for you,"

Nick freed himself and got up to leave, "Why waste your time? It might be me who gets killed next time."

"Don't let your mum see us quarrelling, Nick,"

Exasperated, Nick grasped Cissie's arm firmly and led her through a gap in the bushes at the back of the bench, where they stood for a moment looking at each other in the shadow and privacy of a building. Nick sighed deeply, lowered his eyes, and let a tear run down his face. Cissie closed her eyes with sorrow and drew him to her.

"Hold me, Nick," she whispered.

He felt the warmth of her body and suddenly gave way to sobbing bitterly. Cissie murmured gentle words of comfort and covered his face with kisses.

Nick looked at her face, "Don't you understand?" he cried angrily, "I don't want you!"

In a moment of anguish, he grabbed her upper arms and kissed her passionately; Cissie responded warmly and there, in the privacy of the shrubs, their two tormented hearts abandoned all caution and made passionate love. Joyce's gentle calling jolted them into action.

Picking her way through the gap in the hedge, the young girl found them coming away from the building, fumbling with their clothing. "What yer doin' here?" she chuckled.

Red-faced Cissie uttered some incomprehensive words.

Bemused, Joyce grabbed her trembling hand to leave. "Have you been fighting?"

"Not really," replied Cissie, "We just had a lot to talk about."

The three rejoined the family on the bench.

"Any news of Eli?" Nick asked awkwardly.

"No son." Said Dick, "They have given up any hope of finding him."

"Oh! Sorry to hear that."

"Mrs Cohan is better, though." Said Elsie brightly, "She seems to be eating again, and Mr Cohan says she's improving every day, thank gawd!"

The family left the hospital with expressions of hope for Nick's good recovery.

"Maybe you won't have to go back," said his mother, "that would be good!"

Cissie walked back with him to the ward. She took his face in her hands, "I love you, Nick Clayton, and I *will* wait for you."

Nick said nothing. With tears in her eyes, Cissie kissed him on the lips and said goodbye.

Return to Normandy

Nick was discharged at the end of August and boarded a ship for Normandy. No sooner had he settled down on the ship than Charlie Smith approached.

"Well, there's a coincidence, we meet again!" He said, smiling broadly. Your burns all okay then?"

"Yeh, an' you've got rid of your crutches too?"

"Yeh, and me 'eart's beatin' too." Charlie said, crossing his hands on his heart and rolling his eyes to the sky. "I met the girl of my dreams!"

"Good luck to you, mate!"

Charlie pulled a picture from his back pocket and proudly displayed a picture of a dark-haired beauty.

"That's her."

Taking a packet of cigarettes from his breast pocket, Nick offered one to Charlie and glanced at the photo.

"Charming!" he said.

The two joined a group of sappers and some Household Cavalry new recruits. They chatted and joked in a cloud of cigarette smoke for the sea crossing. Nick liked Charlie's cheerful countenance and infectious smile, and he was glad to be back in the company of the soldiers; he felt better than he had since the tragedy of Wilf's death. As they chatted, Nick's thoughts began to wander. He recalled how he had last sailed from England with the Regiment less than two months ago. So much has happened since then. It seemed like a distant memory. He thought about Cissie but dismissed her quickly from his mind. Soon, the ship docked at the end of the Mulberry Harbour.

Mulberry Harbour was a huge engineering structure that served as a portable harbour, with no ports available for ships to land that were not under enemy control. It was built in various sections around England's south coast, including Portsmouth. It was sailed across the Channel where, within hours of D-Day, it was put together off the Normandy coast.

The soldiers disembarked in pouring rain and were driven back along the length of the pier to the beach. Dozens of supply lorries jammed the beach and road with dozens more wet, black American soldiers waiting for orders to deliver to the front. Nick, Charlie, and the new recruits were met by an officer who introduced himself as Lieutenant Medlin. He directed them to a three-ton lorry, and with the windscreen wipers struggling against the driving rain, they drove past the waiting vehicles and headed south along the coast road.

"Regimental headquarters are based near the town of Beauvais, about a hundred miles distant." Said Medlin. Looking at his watch, he calculated that the journey would take about three hours if the road were clear. "It's not the quickest, but it's the safest."

Charlie relaxed in conversation with the Lieutenant and the new recruits. Nick was quiet, his thoughts occupied with what might lay ahead. Aware of Nick's mood, Charlie blurted out,

"Give us a song then, Nick, like you used to."

Nick screwed up his face, "Nah! I don't feel like it. Sorry, mate!"

Lowering his voice, Charlie said to the others, "He's had a bit of a rough time."

"So, I heard," said Medlin, "I don't think you'll be going back in the Daimler Trooper," he added.

Nick glanced up at the officer and nodded.

An hour later, the lorry was hailed to a halt by local people. They were told the town ahead was enemy-occupied with a battle between Polish and German armies. The driver was advised to detour across the country. The three-toner drove northeast until they entered a small village. Going in the opposite direction, German prisoners passed by wet through and with their hands on their heads, escorted by the dreaded French Machis who stopped the lorry to warn the newcomers. Gesturing and struggling with the French and English languages, Medlin understood that more Germans were in the woods nearby. They drove on, passing the village square where another eight German prisoners sat in the rain on the edge of a dysfunctional fountain facing a little French man holding a rifle.

Reaching the outskirts of the village, the lorry stopped at the side of the road next to a field enclosed by a hedge. While Lt Medlin and the driver studied a map, the lads jumped out of the back. Charlie was first through a gap in the hedge. Suddenly, they heard rapid gunfire, and a minute later, a young German soldier appeared in the gap. He dropped his Schmeiser on the ground with a clatter and surrendered. Another soldier could be seen dashing away toward the distant wood. Advancing cautiously towards the gap in the hedge, Medlin went into the field; there on the grass lay Charlie face down in relentless rain. The officer returned to the group of Troopers.

"Charlie's dead,"

Nick pulled out his revolver and fired the first shot, then the others opened fire, and the young German fell dead. Shocked and confused, Nick rushed into the field to see the officer bent over Charlie's body. He turned the body over, and they saw that he was riddled with bullet holes from his right shoulder across to his left hip.

Nick drew in a sob and turned away, "Fuckin' hell!" he exclaimed.

"He only wanted a fuckin' pee! He wasn't even armed!"

For a moment, he knelt beside the body, "You up to

removing his identity disks?" asked the officer.

Nick bent to remove the disk, then his papers and the photo of his girlfriend. He pushed them down into his breast pocket.

"I should take those," said Medlin.

"Let me have 'em, Sir," pleaded Nick, "I can give 'em to the right person."

"You can have his personal papers, but let me have his identity discs."

Handing the discs over, Nick looked down at the body, "We can't leave him here, sir." he pleaded.

The troopers climbed back into the lorry and, between them, helped to get Charlie's body on board. They drove back to the village square just as a squadron of infantry arrived in two Bren Gun carriers.

One of the drivers wound down the vehicle window, "Where the hell are you a lot from?" he yelled.

The lieutenant answered the question and directed them to the woods where the German soldiers hid. As the carriers sped away, Nick and Medlin carried Charlie's body into a churchyard. The officer stood momentarily at the spot where Charlie lay, then turning to Nick, he said, "Come on, Trooper, we've got to go."

Nick stood for a moment longer; as he did so, he noticed the upright gravestones positioned side by side bearing the names of Australian soldiers who died in the First World War. Turning to go, he heard gunfire in the distance.

He kicked the stone wall as he left the graveyard, "Bloody, fuckin' war," he yelled.

They left Charlie's body with a few of the local people who promised to bury him. Just as the Lorry was leaving, a young boy ran across the road, rain dripping from his cap; carrying a makeshift cross, he ran into the graveyard.

Late in the afternoon, after cutting across open fields in driving rain, crossing weak bridges spanning narrow streams, negotiating churned-up lanes and deep-rutted puddles, the three-ton lorry reached the Divisional Headquarters without further incident.

Nick and the new recruits were greeted by squadron leader Major Wignall, who ordered them to be directed to their squadrons the next day. Handing Charlie's personal papers to the Major, Nick asked that they be delivered to Charlie's brother, Trooper George Smith, in 'D' Squadron. The Major took them, promising to deliver them personally.

Nick slept badly. Rain thundered down on the tent that served as overnight accommodation for him and the recruits while the unrelenting distant sounds of war continued. Adding to the misery he felt over the death of Charlie Smith, recurring images of Wilf returned along with the hatred he was beginning to form for the Germans. He thought about the German he killed and the power and satisfaction he felt when he shot him. He remembered how he stepped over his dead body carrying Charlie. "I should've trodden him into the ground," he said aloud.

Battle for Albert

The next day was the first day of September, and by midday, Nick and the new recruits had re-joined the Squadron at Amiens.

Benny Osbourne was glad to have Nick with him in the A.E.C. Mark III Matador he named 'Blaze Away.' There was only enough time to introduce Jack White, who joined the troops before they were bound for the French town of Arras.

Nick had gotten to know the new recruits over the last 24 hours since leaving England. Jack White, whom he nicknamed Chalkie, was 20 years old, sandy-haired, and of medium build. His clear blue eyes and strong features gave him an air of confidence and dependability that Nick liked.

Rain continued overnight, but it had reduced to a miserable drizzle by the following day. Mist hung low over the surrounding fields as Nick climbed into the Matador, and, taking his seat, he took charge of the wireless controls. Chalkie sat on the side of the ammunition, and Benny slid into the driver's seat. Lt Medlin, who had travelled with them in the three-toner, took his place as the Troop Leader.

....

Back at HQ, there was some confusion about conditions in the town of Albert through which B Squadron was heading en route to Arras. Initially, they were told that the city was liberated, but Divisional Headquarters now heard differently. News came to say that it was seething with German soldiers guarding their store depot. Rather than send complicated messages by radio, attempts were made to send a dispatch rider to find B Squadron with maps and revised orders. However, the attempt failed when the dispatch rider came under fire, and his vehicle was put out of action. Meanwhile, the armoured cars of B squadron - with the dangers yet unknown to them, troops three, four, and five, head closer towards Albert.

Leaving the Boccage behind, the road ahead ran like a long winding ribbon between a neat patchwork of flat, wide-open agricultural fields. Along this open wet road, the Daimler armoured and scout cars travelled ahead of the Matadors of Heavy Troop. Not a tree or hedge was in sight—just miles of flat multi-coloured fields and a huge canopy of grey sky. The spire of a church poked its pinnacle over the distant horizon, as did the occasional Poplar treetop. Neat isolated farm buildings and clusters of red-roofed houses whose front doors opened onto the narrow street were temporarily woken to the noise of the armoured cars passing through. Even in these isolated, tranquil spots, the enemy appeared from their holes, after which a short exchange of gunfire quickly put them to route, killed, or rounded up for the local people to hold and guard until they could be taken to secure places.

Entering Albert from the southern end in drizzling rain, the leading armoured cars drove into the quiet, empty streets. Surprisingly, there were no joyful scenes of relief. Instead, there was a sense of unease about the emptiness; villagers and townspeople seemed cautious, slipping discreetly out of sight behind closed doors. Just one resident stepped into the street to warn the convoy. A shot rang out, and the man fell dead. Suddenly, an explosion sounded, and the leading car of three-troop blew to pieces, ending in a burning wreck. Another explosion followed, and a second car burst into flames. Wireless communications buzzed with instructions, and the sedate convoy of cars opened fire. Aware of the commotion, the two Matadors of Heavy Troop approached the rear to see the armoured cars firing into houses on all sides. Equally, they were met with German grenades and bren-gun fire.

"What's happening sir?" Nick asked.

Benny watched as the turret of another car was hit and put out of action; it continued bravely along the street, firing its Besa gun.

"Looks like we've been ambushed!" murmured Chalkie.

Seeing the village was already in a major battle, Lt. Medlin yelled, "Order to fire at will!"

Jack and Nick hurriedly loaded and fired the gun between them, joining the melee of vehicles and noise. In the smoke and chaos, bullets and grenades rained down on them from above.

"The bastards are firing from the top of the bloody buildings, sir." yelled Nick above the din and commotion, "And I can't elevate the gun any higher,"

"I don't care how you do it, driver Osbourne, yelled the Troop Leader, but find a bloody way out of here!"

Blocking the road ahead was a Scout Car burning fiercely, the crew cautiously making their way up the street on foot. The bombardment of bullets and grenades continued as the Matador inched its way around the obstacle and headed off in the direction of the church cemetery. Orders came from the Squadron's Second in Command, Captain Ward, for them to stay in the vicinity of the cemetery and wait for the infantry and scout cars of the Support Troop to join them in flushing out the German stragglers hiding there. On their arrival, commotion and chaos ensued as guns were directed into the cemetery, firing volley after volley. In the confines of the Matador, the crew sweated and worked to maintain momentum, firing their guns at anything that moved. One by one, the fleeing Germans fell; those that didn't escaped through the streets of Albert. Dripping with sweat and perspiration, the crew of the Matador continued to battle it out with the enemy. With another round of ammunition empty, Nick bent to pull open the lid of another canister. With the force usually taken to lever off the lid, Nick pulled; it shot up easier than expected, and the jagged foil edge cut open the soft underneath of his nose. Nick let out a yell, and blood dripped everywhere. It ran down Chalkie's neck, who suddenly let out a scream!

"Nick's been hit, he's been hit!"

"No, I haven't," Nick yelled back, "I've cut me bloody nose!"

The roaring, grinding sound of the Churchill tanks and

trucks and the clattering of infantry boots along the street brought welcome relief. On their arrival an order came over the radio from the Divisional Squadron Leader for the Squadron to withdraw to the area of Douai. The crew of the Matador breathed a sigh of relief. Benny slipped it into gear and drove off. The convoy was soon on the edge of the town and out on the open road. As they did so the sun appeared in a gap of blue sky.

"Well done, lads," said Medlin.

"Thank you, Sir," said Chalkie.

"Sir," mumbled Nick, still holding a cloth to his nose.

Benny turned and laughed at Nick, and Chalkie joined in. Laughter could be heard from the Matador as they travelled along the wet tree-lined avenue reflecting the late afternoon sun.

Albert to Douai
By-passing Bapaume, the convoy laboured on for another five miles before stopping to rest at the side of the road. The Troopers dismounted one by one, stretching their limbs. Relieved to be out of the confines of the armoured cars, they breathed deeply into the air. Gathered later in little groups with mugs of tea and a meal of tinned ham and dry biscuits, Basil, his horn dangling from his waist, saw Nick first.

"Hey Nick," he called, "Good to see you, how's the wound?"

"He's a bleeding mess," chuckled Chalkie,

"Shuddup Chalkie!" snapped Nick, adding, "Huh! You should've seen his face when he thought I'd bin hit!"

"Determined to get back to Blighty again, ain't yer," said Archie.

"What about you lot then?" asked Nick.

Basil slapped Archie hard on the shoulder, "We're 'ardened soldiers, ain't we mate?"

"Been to hell and back since you left! We lost two troops in another town, and back there, we lost another troop, and three troopers and the Troop Leader were taken prisoner,' he said.

"Bob didn't make it either," murmured Harry quietly.

Nick breathed in deeply and lit up another cigarette. He turned his back on the group of soldiers and kicked the earth. He sniffed, then swung back around with his head down, looking at the ground.

"Fuckin' war!" he spat.

Realising the extent of his friend's recent loss, Basil patted Nick gently on the side of his arm, "Sorry, mate! You've had a rough time." Then, to lighten the situation, he chuckled and walked away.

"What's funny?" Snapped Nick,

"It's your red and puffy nose, mate!"

It worked; Nick smiled. Chalkie stubbed out his cigarette and, putting a friendly arm around Nick's shoulder, he laughed, "Thought we'd been hit!" he chuckled, "Nearly shit meself!"

The convoy moved on towards the concentration area passing through small towns and villages on the way. At each one the Troopers were greeted with warm exuberance by the local people singing and dancing, cheering and crying in a sea of red, white and blue. Flags and handkerchiefs waved from top floor windows; people crowded in the streets temporarily blocking the way forward whereupon girls climbed on the cars and tanks hugging and kissing the troopers. The armoured cars inched their way forward, through the streets and out of each town only to be held up at more places with the same greeting. By early evening they had met up with the other Squadrons just south of Douai where, by now two or three hundred vehicles of the Guards Armoured Division were concentrated.

Douai to Brussels

The Troopers stood together the next day to hear the Squadron Leader give them details of the next objective.

"Brussels!" He announced.

A murmur of surprise rippled through the tent.

"Like it or lump it, all ninety-six miles by tomorrow night. The Squadrons will be split to run two different routes. Where possible, there will be no stopping for major battles with the enemy; go on your way, and the tanks following will deal with them. What may slow you down will be any bridges you find on the way, which you will hold until the arrival of tanks and infantry relieve you. If we do it in the time allotted, it will be recorded in history as the fastest military advance ever made!'

Nick blew out a breath of air; his eyes widened. "Better make the most of tonight then," he chuckled to Benny.

"There'll be no comfortable beds for you tonight," interjected the Lieutenant with a wry smile, adding, "Get stuck in to digging a trench for the night."

"But sir, we've been offered billets by the locals," grumbled Nick. "Not my decision trooper, orders are orders. There's a report that German 88s are guarding the aerodrome nearby and saturation allied bombing is likely before an airborne operation can take place. For your own safety you dig a trench, so get on with it!"

"Great!" Mumbled Nick.

"Come on, mate, don't be so bloody miserable," Benny added.

"Go and doss down in a comfortable bed if you want to but neither you nor the bed, nor whoever keeps you company will be there in the morning!"

After a wet, cold and uncomfortable night the troopers were roused at 4am bemoaning the fact that overnight rain had seeped into the slit trenches muddying their clothes. They stood on the damp grass in the early morning darkness to wash and shave in cold water and, with the best efforts, made themselves presentable.

"Huh!" sighed Nick, "The bombing attack was cancelled then!" No one responded. "Be glad to get a clean uniform," he added, sponging a remaining dry blood stain on his jacket. A lone blackbird began the introduction to the dawn chorus as Chalkie started to make the breakfast of porridge and black tea which the troop consumed in silence; all of them still half asleep.

All four sabre squadrons prepared to move off at 7am. C and D were first to leave Douai followed by the newly formed Grenadier Group. A and B Squadrons left soon after, followed by the 32nd Brigade made up of the Welsh and Irish Guards. The two groups separated in the direction of Tournai. The Grenadier Group went off in a northerly direction and 32nd Brigade taking a southerly route and the race began to see which Squadron would get to Brussels first.

Avoiding any skirmishes with the enemy that would allow the Matador sped on in the wake of the Daimlers and scout cars of B Squadron. Any enemy opposition they encountered was quickly dealt with and, finding the nearest diversion, they went bumping across open fields leaving the job to the impending tank divisions to finish off.

Their first major obstacle came when they were just ten Kilometres from the first Belgian town. Finding the main access over a river on the Belgian border destroyed, the Squadron

Leader sent a message to all cars to divide up and search for another way across.

It took an hour of reconnaissance driving armoured cars up and down the river bank criss-crossing each other through cultivated agricultural fields before an isolated small bridge over the river dividing the fields was found intact, unguarded and strong enough for the tanks to follow safely. The squadron cars met up and together they crossed the river to continue their journey to the next town. A message was relayed to the Matador Troop Leader to remain and hold the bridge until reinforcements arrived.

While the Daimlers and scout cars prepared to leave, Nick and the crew of the Matador dismounted and waited on the edge of the river surrounded by cultivated fields that stretched to the horizon on all sides. The sound of the armoured cars gradually grew distant, and silence descended. Glad of freedom from the confines of the Matador, the troopers smoked and rested in the late morning sunshine. Apart from birdsong, the silence seemed tangible, and no one wanted to disturb it. They waited a long time until a crackled voice rudely interrupting the peace, came over the wireless, and Medlin looked at his watch and spoke.

"They'll be here very soon,"

"They can take their time!" mused Chalkie, half asleep.

"I agree!" added Nick.

"This is too good to leave, sir!" murmured Benny

Before long, the first tanks came into view, skirting the river between the fields. Reluctantly, the lads got to their feet and brushed the grass off their uniforms. The leading tank shuddered to a halt, and then the tank commander exchanged words with the squadron leader from the turret.

Leaving the tanks to do their job the armoured car crossed the bridge and continued along the route towards the next town. Along the lonely narrow and empty grey lanes overshadowed by a tunnel of leafy, overhanging trees they travelled for miles and, later that day, entered the town of Lesdian to a resounding roar of cheers and singing where they found the rest of the squadron cars parked up, along the road. There was no sign of the occupants. A sea of red, white and blue flags and overwhelming cheers and singing hailed the arrival of the squadron.

"Huh!" grunted Lt Medlin, "The Squadron leader didn't mention people blocking the way when he spoke about the obstacles we might meet!"

"Takes the monotony and boredom away, sir," Chalkie said.

"Yeh! It almost makes the journey worthwhile," remarked a smiling Nick as he gaped through a vision slit at a group of cheering girls looking fresh and bright in the sunshine.

Benny turned off the engine, and the crew climbed out of the Matador to see the excitement.

Nick stretched, "My bones feel like they are all jumbled up!"

"Mine too," said Benny and Chalkie in unison

Breathing in the sunshine and fresh air, a group of young girls came running towards them, squealing with delight. They flung themselves into the arms of the boys, kissing them and crying with relief at their presence in the town. Carrying a huge amount of flowers in her arms, a woman pushed her way between the crowds and threw them onto the armoured cars. Two men were distributing bottles of wine, and, from others, food of all kinds was being handed out; in the crowd, Nick, holding a girl in his arms sporting his beret very cheekily on one side of her head, reached past her to take a proffered bottle of wine.

Above the noise, a horn sounded, "Basil!" Yelled Nick to his pals. They looked to see where the sound came from.

"Hey Nick, Chalkie, where 'ave you been?" Basil called.

More troopers came into view and spent a precious hour together before any further advance could be made. By this time, a different girl was in Nick's arms. He gave her a final embrace, kissed her passionately, and climbed back into the Matador.

"That was alright, Chalkie," he chuckled as he settled into his seat. You looked as if you were enjoying yourself!"

"Had no choice, really, she hung on to me!" replied Chalkie, "I got a girl back home."

"Huh!" Nick puffed, "More fool you!"

Benny eyed Nick from his seat, "Thought you got a girl back home, haven't ya, Nick?"

"Not me! Nah, live for today; I might be dead tomorra!"

"What about Cissie then?"

"That's over!"

Benny expressed surprise, "Thought you and she were never to be parted!"

Nick changed the subject. 'Where to now sir?'

Tournai

Confident that the Americans had already liberated the Belgian town of Tournai, the convoy moved into the broken, ruined streets from the east. Standing amongst the rubble of bricks and concrete that were once their homes, the people cheered and waved. Nick strained to look through the vision slit.

Subdued and thoughtful, he murmured, "It amazes me how they can cheer and greet us so wildly when it was our bombs that wrecked their homes."

"I guess so," said Chalkie, equally thoughtful.

Negotiating the narrow streets crowded with army vehicles, the cars stopped at the town centre square, where the convoy met with the armoured vehicles of C and D squadrons and the tanks of the Grenadier Group. Packed in the spacious centre square beneath the shadow of the tall shells of once-grand buildings, jubilant rioters amassed in a sea of orange.

The Troopers walked in the street where, above the clamour and noise of euphoric singing echoing through the air, one trooper from 'C' Squadron welcomed them and shouted, "We arrived nearly an hour ago."

Heady with alcohol, his face covered with red lipstick, he was snatched away by friends and disappeared into the crowd.

On seeing the new arrivals, the people's enthusiasm re-ignited, and the repetition of everything from fruit, flowers and cognac bottles were distributed along with hugs and kisses from both male and female, adult and child.

The rejoicing was short-lived for the squadrons; there was a deadline to meet in Brussels. Through the traffic bottleneck, C and D had the advantage of leaving the town first. Still in a party mood, Nick, Benny and Chalkie climbed noisily into the Matador laden with food and bottles of alcohol.

Storing a couple of cognac bottles under his seat, the Lieutenant said, "Settle down, lads. Set down. You've had your fun. Now, keep your mind on the road. We're still not clear of the enemy."

As soon as they could, A and B squadrons moved sporadically along the packed, noisy streets and onto the road.

Taking their allotted route, the first two troops of B squadrons were well out of sight when the Matador and others left the town. They had not gone far when they met up with an American troop.

Running parallel with them, they were found at a standstill on the side of the road, looking fed up and miserable. "Got any gas to spare, Limeys?" They yelled from the top of their Greyhound tanks.

"Nope!" Came the reply. "Come on, you owe us. We just battled it out with Gerry in that town so you could get through safely."

"We'll send some back from the next Kraut tank we get! Krauts an' all!" Yelled one trooper as they drove on by.

Leuze, Ath, Enghien - Brussel's

Apart from the odd obstruction in the narrow lanes, negotiating local farm carts and horses going about their business, and army vehicles going in the opposite direction, the slow journey from Tournai to the next town was surprisingly clear of the enemy. Frustrated by the convoy's slow speed, the order from the leading car was to plough on through. People continued to turn out in every town and village to greet them in the way the troopers were becoming familiar, but there was no stopping. Instead, the people ran alongside them, throwing their gifts of food and flowers into the armoured cars. The atmosphere was electric! Standing next to the Troop Leader in the turret of the Matador, Nick soaked it up. Suddenly, he let out a moan as something hit him hard in the face.

"You okay?" Medlin enquired,

"Not sure sir. What the hell hit me? It nearly knocked me out."

Nick lowered himself onto the seat below and groped around for the offending object.

"A bloody rock-hard apple!" He exclaimed

The convoy passed safely through the towns of Ath and Enghien. Soon after leaving Enghien, with the new addition of flowers draped over the gun barrels, making them look like carnival floats, they met a company of more than fifty German infantry and a self-propelled gun threatening to cause trouble. Still, the squadrons passed by without either side firing a shot.

"That was weird!" murmured Nick.

"Probably waiting for the tank division following us," said Benny. About a mile further on they heard the distant sound of gunfire. "The Welsh Guards have found them," said Lt Medlin, "I guessed that. Ha!" said Nick with satisfaction. But the peace of the afternoon was not to last. "A Squadron has hit trouble," said the Troop Leader listening into the radio message. "There's a company of infantry and another SP ahead; we're going off road to pass them."

From where he was seated, Nick glanced to look out of the vision slit. He watched as they turned into a farm lane. From there, they bumped across a field where, by now, the familiar sight of a small herd of bloated cows lay dead and crawling with maggots. "Funny how they lie there with their legs in the air," mused Nick; "they look like they're movin'."

Benny grimaced, "I told yer. It's the maggots that are moving!" he said.

Now, without the support of the Welsh guards whose delay with the SP gun held them back, the little armoured cars of A Squadron were engaged in a battle. On the road ahead, two troops of B Squadron and the Matador came up behind the enemy. Rising in the air, black smoke billowed up from a burning scout car, the occupants of which lay injured on the side of the road. At once, all the reconnaissance vehicles of B Squadron discharged their ammunition. In the enclosure of the Matador, Nick loaded the 75 mm, and Chalkie fired with ferocity and speed while from the driver's seat, Benny let rip with a rapid burst of machine-gun fire.

"Let the bastards have it, Chalkie!" yelled Nick.

Between them, the armoured cars demolished the enemy guns, after which Nick picked up a Bren gun and fired it from the turret at the German infantry escaping across the field.

"Run rabbit, run rabbit, run, run, run!" sang Nick.

With the enemy on the run, the guns ceased their noisy barrage and only the sound of voices and the wind in the trees could be heard. The injured trooper's wounds were treated, and the convoy moved on. Medlin glanced at Nick.

He sniggered. "That's some black eye you've got there!

And what with that scab on your nose? What are you going to get next?"

"Would you like to see the scar on me leg then, sir?"

Chalkie laughed, "You're a walking disaster, mate!

The race to Brussels picked up again. Passing through Halle on the last leg of the journey, a radio message came through at 17.32 to say that the leading car of A Squadron had just entered Brussels to receive an overwhelming welcome. The squadron's vehicles vibrated with cheering.

The race over, the squadron settled down to a steady drive on the road into Brussels, passing an armed group of French Resistance loitering at the end of a road junction. Further on, dozens of German prisoners were coming towards them, herded along the road by infantrymen. Defeated, tired and dirty, the miserable rabble trudged by, some holding up injured fellow soldiers and helping them along. Suddenly, a few young soldiers broke from the line and ran alongside the convoy. With a look of fear and desperation, they begged to be taken on board. You'll be lucky, Nick thought. The sound of gunfire brought the prisoners back in line.

"I reckon they're taking them back to that group of Resistance workers," said Benny.

"Good!" snarled Nick, "Hope they burn them alive like they did Wilf."

While A Squadron enjoyed the hospitality of the people in

Brussels, the squadron vehicles of B, C and D Squadrons were drawn into the harbour on the city's outskirts. A mass of armoured cars, tanks, and soldiers were gathered in a large field. To the Troopers' disappointment, their orders were to guard Divisional Headquarters.

That night, Nick and Chalkie were on duty. Standing around on a chilly September evening, Nick yawned. He looked up at the multitude of stars in the cloudless sky. The breeze filtered through the trees, but no sound could be heard above the endless drone of traffic going back and forth along the Halle to Brussels road. He breathed in the air and thought how good it was to be out of the stifling, smelly confines of the Matador.

He longed for a bath and a change of clothing, "Hey, Chalkie, do I smell?" He said.

Chalkie bent his head closer to Nick, "Yeugh, to high heaven!" chuckled his friend.

Nick gave him a friendly shove, "You ain't particularly smellin' o' roses neither!" he retorted

The rhythmic sound of boots coming along the road alerted the pair. Chalkie frowned in Nick's direction, "What do you think Nick?"

Chalkie moved forward with the intent of challenging the intruders. Nick held up a hand to stop him, "Let them get a little closer," he whispered.

They made ready their guns when two other guards, alerted

by the noise, came over to watch with them. Suddenly, someone came through the hedge and into the confines of the tanks and armoured cars; one, then another and another. All four guns were aimed when one of the intruders cried out in German, 'Surrender, surrender!'

More than forty German soldiers came through the gap in the hedge. Awoken by the noise of raised voices, Captain Ward appeared with Lt Medlin. "What should we do with them at this time of night?" said Captain Ward, scratching his head and looking at his watch.

The sorry group of weary young soldiers were herded into a corner of the field, where they sat on the grass. They said nothing and were soon spread out, sleeping, guarded by the four troopers until they were relieved by the next watch.

At first light, Nick awoke and went over to see the captives. It was then that he realised just how young they were. He eyed them with contempt, recalling once again how his friends died. Slowly, the prisoners began to move and sit up.

They were surveying their guards with fear and uncertainty, wondering what would happen next when a thin voice was heard to say, 'Wir können jetzt nach Hause gehen?'

Another spoke in broken English, 'Can we go to our homes now, please?'

Nick was still angry, but hearing the pathetic question, he felt a twinge of pity. He could see that underneath the dirt and grime on their tired faces were pale, youthful complexions - not unlike his sisters, he recalled. Turning away, he looked up at the sky. He clenched his fists and breathed deeply, "I don't want to feel sorry for them; I hate them all," he thought.

The prisoners ate every scrap of food they were given and were sent off under guard to an empty barn, where they were promised protection from the Belgian Resistance.

"Double those prisoners!" bellowed Captain Ward.

Nick chuckled as he, Basil and Archie broke into a trot, "Sneller, you Krauts", urged Archie digging the butt of his rifle into the leading prisoner.

Nick smirked, "Where did you learn that word?" he jeered.

Entering Brussels

The move towards the next objective was imperative. Still, the local authorities deemed the plans for a ceremonial entry into Brussels to be of utmost importance for the newly liberated citizens. The crew of the Matador spent the next few hours polishing every nut and bolt, button and boot until they glistened in the sunshine; every speck of mud and dirt was cleaned from the car chassis and tyres. Troopers had been busy all morning preparing to enter the city. They smartened their uniforms before joining their fellow troopers gathered on the grass in the shadow of the armoured cars, smoking and chatting together.

The tune of *'Two Lovely Black Eyes,'* got louder as the

three troopers came near the group, reminding Nick of the black eye he received in Tournai. Nick groaned, "Shuddup!"

Archie laughed, "You look like a panda."

"Yeh, and you'll look like one if you don't shuddup! I'll 'ave you know I got runner-up in the regiment boxing championship back home!!"

"Ooo, I'm scared!" mocked Archie.

"Get lost!" snapped Nick

The people of Brussels gave the convoy the welcome of a lifetime. General Adair led the parade of tanks and armoured cars in a Cromwell tank. Just one troop from B and C Squadron and the Matador driven by Benny were chosen to join the parade. The Belgian Infantry brought up the rear, proudly marching through the cheering crowds. Mesmerised by the attention, Nick stood in the turret of the Matador next to the Troop Leader Lieutenant Medlin. Moving slowly through the narrow roads past the seething mass of jubilant people, Nick soaked up the adulation. When he thought it couldn't get any more exciting, he noticed some girls begin to surge through the thin police cordon. They climbed onto the armoured cars, and some could be seen writing messages with chalk on the sides. Two young girls in pretty cotton frocks ran alongside the vehicles, and, climbing aboard, they kissed the troopers and draped orange ribbons around each neck before moving on to the next one. Nick responded to the girls with enthusiasm and lingering kisses. Overwhelmed, he looked around open-mouthed at the bomb-damaged buildings where bricks and rubble lay in piles on the pavement against their broken walls. In other undamaged buildings, he observed people high up in open windows cheering and waving anything coloured orange. He was thrilled by the haunting drone of chanting and singing vibrating through the air and held out his hands to receive flowers, fruit, and more bottles of cognac as the convoy - now carrying extra passengers passed slowly through the streets. Amid all the rejoicing, he was surprised by a different sound.

He turned this way, and that before settling his eyes on a group of screaming, dishevelled girls being dragged away by their hair, "Collaborators!" spat the girl in his arms.

She turned his face towards her and kissed him passionately; she leaned across to kiss the Troop Leader, who was happy to oblige. Climbing off the matador, she moved on. The flow of joyful girls boarding the car continued, but Nick was still distracted by the screaming girls. Looking back at the ugly sight, he saw the victims now surrounded by a mob of jeering people.

"War is war," the Troop Leader commented, "you can't blame them for wanting revenge."

"I hate the Germans, but I don't think those girls deserve that," said Nick.

"They're not German girls," said Amstrong. "Their sin was to befriend German soldiers. Some may have had babies by them."

Unable to loosen the grip of the crowd, the convoy jolted

slowly by the Palais de Justice, still burning, its German archives set on fire the night before by the fleeing enemy. They slowed almost to a stop when suddenly the cheering swelled to a crescendo that Nick thought would burst their lungs and his ears. Lt. Medlin informed the troopers that the General had just returned the city to the Burgomaster.

The troopers were allowed free time to roam the city for the next three hours. A gang, including Nick, swaggered down the street intent on finding a beer and a bit of fun; they didn't have to look far; girls clamoured to entertain their liberators generously. The loud soldiers and girls filled a corner cafe where a musician played the accordion. Soon, the place was filled with smoke and laughter.

Vic grimaced and put his fingers in his ears, "What is that man playin'?" he asked, irritated.

The others moaned in agreement.

Nick looked bewildered, "What's wrong with it? It's nice, and I like that sort of music. It's romantic!"

The girls agreed with him and said as much. They requested an English song, and soon the raucous sound of vocal voices singing *It's a long way to Tipperary, it's a long way to go...* resonated into the street drowning out the musician.

"Hey look at this," exclaimed Nick suddenly.

He had been picking at the corner of the label on a bottle of wine. As he did so, the label came off, revealing another one,

"'Réservé pour le Wehrmacht'," he read.

"It's what you do when you are under enemy occupation," said Benny casually.

"Yeh, but how did they manage to paste another label with 'Réservé aux libérateurs' so quickly?"

"They've had all night," laughed Chalkie.

The girls looked embarrassed. Leaning close to one of them, Nick began humming a tune.

'Tu Chantes,' she said.

Nick didn't understand her, but she signalled for him to sing. "I think she wants you to give us a song, Nick," Chalkie said.

Nick didn't wait to be asked twice. Standing up, he flicked the last of his cigarette into an ashtray and pushed back his chair.

"Go on then!" The lads chorused.

Taking a swig of beer and wiping his mouth. Nick boldly walked over to the musician while his friends jeer and hoot. The musician was only too pleased to accommodate Nick and gestured for him to sing. The cafe fell silent for a moment as Nick's tenor voice filled the place with the strains of *Begin the Beguine*. Sporadic hoots and jeers interrupted as he sang. Benny put an arm around Basil and sang along with the final words, *'Till you whisper to me once more "darling I love you," and we suddenly know what heaven we're in......'*

"Get off, you silly bugger," said Basil, pushing Benny away.

Nick struggled to sleep that night. So much had happened in the last few days since he arrived in France four days ago. He recalled the battle in Albert, the mixture of emotions he felt, from the real fear of his vulnerability to the extraordinary strength and resolve he acquired to protect himself and his comrades. He was staggered to think that the Squadron had succeeded in gaining nearly one hundred miles in a day. His thoughts drifted to the sad bunch of German boy soldiers whose uniforms were too big for them, then to the women collaborators - had they deserved the punishment they received? He recalled again the unbelievable reception the Regiment received when entering Brussels. He thought how lucky he was to have been there at that specific time - a day that filled him with pride and one he would never forget. He thought of Wilf and Charlie, "you'd 'ave loved it," he murmured.

4th Sept Leaving Brussels - Beringe

Back in the harbour, Nick sat at the open door of the Matador, nestled between the crowd of tanks and armoured cars. He wiped his mouth and gulped back the dregs of his tea.

He kicked Benny's foot, "I'm gonna get another mug. Do you want one?"

Benny shook his head, "Nah!"

"You can get me one," said Chalkie, handing Nick his tin mug. Nick wandered down the row of vehicles to the supply wagon. "Hey, Basil," he called. "Did you have bacon and eggs?"

"Yep!" said Basil, his chin covered with shaving foam. "Who had your butter this morning?"

"Chalkie! He gave me his sugar."

"I'll swap you next time for my sugar!"

"Hey Nick!" called Chalkie, "We ain't got time for another cuppa, you gotta come back, we're off in a minute."

Nick soon found himself again in the Matador's stale, dark, and cramped confines. Benny was already seated at the wheel, tucked away in the front of the armoured car. Easing himself into his seat behind Benny, he slammed the side door shut. Chalkie and Medlin, complete with goggles and headphones, were standing in the open turret, ready to go. The Matador moved in behind the second Daimler scout car and roared into action.

Passing through the city of Brussels, the convoy of vehicles moved along a tree-lined avenue where enemy armoured vehicles lay abandoned, broken and twisted beyond which lay flat open fields, the scars of war ever visible. Various lorries, half-tracks and motorbikes passed noisily by, going in the opposite direction, and a squadron of Typhoons blazed overhead. Roadblocks of cheering people slowed the convoy as it passed safely through the towns of Leuven and Diest, and the morning passed without incident.

Late in the afternoon, the squadron stopped to rest. The troopers dismounted at the side of the open road on the edge of a field, and stretching their limbs, they breathed in the clear, warm air. Benny and Chalkie wandered forward along the line of armoured cars to meet up with Basil, Harry Archie and other Troopers while Nick lit the stove at the side of the Matador to boil water for tea. He sniffed and frowned at the acrid air. As he waited for the water to boil, he spotted something just a few feet away from him in the ditch that ran the length of the roadside. As he drew closer, he saw that a number of Germans and two girls lay dead in the ditch. He gasped. Amongst the dead bodies that were crawling with flies and maggots, a decapitated body was propped up against the bank. He turned away and heaved.

"What's up mate?" called Benny.

Nick didn't respond.

Benny walked back toward Nick, "Hey mate what's up?" he asked anxiously. Curious, the others followed Benny.

"Can't you smell 'em?" said Nick, pointing, "In that ditch."

Other troopers joined them. The gruesome sight silenced them.

Then Archie spoke, "Looks like they were havin' a party."

"I reckon they were by the look of those empty wine bottles and the brandy," said Basil.

"Must've been a stray bomb," added Archie.

Medlin came between the Troopers and, seeing the spectacle, said, "Okay, you've seen enough. There's nothing we can do. I'll call the Support Troop, and the medics can clear them."

"And good luck with that job!" muttered Benny.

Nick stood on the other side of the armoured car, away from the scene, gazing out over the peaceful field with his teacup in his hands. It seemed like another world detached from what he felt was beginning to overwhelm him. Cissy's pretty face flashed briefly before him, and he wanted to take off and run across the space.

The convoy moved off again, arriving at the mining town of Beringen, where it drew to a halt in the road behind the armoured cars of D Squadron two hundred yards short of the Albert Canal, where they could hear the sound of battle. To the right was a wooded area where the tanks of the Welsh Guards were engaged in a fierce battle with the enemy firing from slag heaps on the opposite side of the bridge.

A Cromwell tank burned fiercely at the side of the road, having driven over mines laid at the entrance of the bridge. Nick and Chalkie walked over to join other troopers, loitering at a safe distance. He learned that the bridge had been blown, but the ramparts remained intact. It didn't take long for Nick to realise that no one could go anywhere until the bridge was secured and safe enough for the tanks to cross. Determined to hold the bridge, the Germans battled it out. Equally, the guns of the Welsh guards pounded the north bank. As Nick and the crew of the Matador watched the battle, first Panther went up in a cloud of thick black smoke and then another, until finally, the German armour began to withdraw.

With the guns silenced, guardsmen spilled out of the tanks. Like so many exhausted athletes, they sunk onto the nearest grassy area of ground, each one silently reaching into pockets for cigarettes and matches. Officers stood together discussing the way forward while wireless operators passed messages back to Divisional HQ.

Three or four civilians arrived at the scene and were heard to say that some men were willing to form some kind of bridge with their barges. An hour later, the barge owners, civilians, and soldiers alike were busy helping to move the barges together to meet on the opposite bank. But just as the civilians were bringing up large planks of timber to strengthen the bridge construction, they were fired on, after which the terrified civilians dropped the planks and fled! Without the help of the civilians, the repair of the bridge ceased.

With nothing more to do, the troopers of B Squadron hung around in small groups, chatting and smoking with guardsmen while others lay on the bank sleeping under gathering dark clouds. Unheaded by warnings to stay away for their own safety, local people filtered back, laden with the gifts for which the soldiers were becoming used but were always grateful. Some of the residents responded to the warnings and left quickly. Others hung around until the first drops of rain began to fall. It wasn't until dusk that the sappers arrived to finish the job of rebuilding the bridge.

That night, the troopers slept shallowly under bivouacs in pouring rain. Nick and Benny awoke as rainwater seeped under the makeshift covering. The echoing sound of metal against metal and shouting commands from the Sappers kept them awake. They worked until two in the morning to repair the makeshift bridge.

Damp and miserable, Nick and the crew arose in the early morning by the sound of the tanks and armoured cars preparing to move out over the Albert Canal. The sound of battle somewhere rumbled on while birds sang in joyous oblivion from their perches concealed in the foliage of the dripping trees.

Officers and troopers milled silently around. Some stood with mugs of hot tea, watching the bulldozer move the burned-out tanks away from the entrance to the bridge. Someone snapped an order at the other end of the line of armoured cars. Nick crouched to set up the stove to boil water while Benny took the spade and disappeared into the undergrowth. Between the armoured vehicles, little groups of troopers were standing over their pans of water bubbling away on primus stoves when the tanks of the Welsh Guards began to rev up. Five minutes later, they started their journey. Troopers stood to watch as their bulky frames shunted around the bend of the road before going forward, clanking noisily over the unsteady makeshift bridge and along the road toward Helchteren. A lone enemy SP gun expelled its ammunition, but after a couple of bursts of gunfire in retaliation, the tanks moved safely on.

All was quiet when, later in the day, B Squadron moved out and over the bridge, leaving the Matador behind to guard it. The Troopers watched the armoured cars leave when suddenly an explosion rented the air.

"Shit," exclaimed Benny, "that's Lt Everard's car gone up!"

In an instant, the crew were back on board the Matador. Medlin scrutinised the area for a moment before rotating the gun turret vigorously to face the offending SP gun concealed in hedges that encircled the base of the slag heap. He yelled an order: "On the left, take it out!"

Chalkie and Nick swiftly brought the loaded 75mm gun into action and fired toward the enemy gun. The familiar cloud of thick, black smoke curled upwards, after which, from out of the undergrowth, came three German soldiers ready to surrender.

Running across the bridge, the lads hurried to help the injured Troopers. They pulled Vic Jenkins and Lt Everard out of the damaged armoured car and set them down on the roadside where half a dozen Infantrymen lay injured and broken. Benny stood guard over the demoralised German soldiers sitting on the grass on the edge of the slag heap, bedraggled and miserable.

Curious, Nick said, "They just gave up."

The Troop Leader looked in the direction of the prisoners and said. "They've had enough, I reckon."

"Not without a final killing," Nick spat.

Flames flickered up in the damp hedge where the SP gun lay bent and broken; around it, in the undergrowth, lay some of the bodies of the crew that manned it.

"Guess we should remove the dog tags while we're here," remarked Lt Medlin thoughtfully.

"Yes," he snapped. "Remove their dog tags."

The lads made their way up the slope of the slag heap to find three bodies, and then they began removing the tags.

"Look here," cried Nick, "This one's got a camera on him!"

"Leave it!" snapped Medlin.

The road fell silent as the last vehicle sped off, passing one tank that remained on the side of the road. Still, the muffled sounds of gunfire boomed in the far distance. Otherwise, the only sounds were the moans of the wounded and the wind in the trees.

With the German prisoners safely secured and guarded, Lt. Medlin and the crew helped the injured men.

"Taffy Jones is dead. Get a blanket to cover him," Medlin ordered.

While Chalkie covered the body of Taffy, Benny offered Vic a cigarette beside whom Lt Everard lay unconscious, his leg maimed and twisted awkwardly. One or two injured infantrymen recovered enough to sit up and smoke; the others lay still. Puffing away on a cigarette, Nick stood leaning on the side of the Matador when he heard the clatter of people crossing the Bailey bridge, bringing bandages and water with them. Out of the houses nearby came more people offering help. Nick bent to say hello to a small group of children who giggled shyly and ran away to the safety of the adults. One little boy looked up at Nick and took hold of his hand. As Nick wondered what to do next, the child pulled him between the people and across the road. He stopped alongside a pretty young girl carrying a baby in her arms.

"Ma soeur," said the child. Nick was embarrassed, and the girl laughed.

In broken English, she told him that the child was her brother Hugo. Women watched curiously.

"Je vous remercie," said the child.

The girl crouched to hear her brother whisper something in her ear. Her lip trembled as she explained to Nick that Hugo asked if the British soldiers would bring back their fifteen-year-old brother. He was taken by the Germans to work in a German factory. Tugging at Nick's arm and in his language, the child cried, "You must, you must."

Two or three of the onlookers spoke in French and gestured for him to help, but before he could respond, Chalkie's voice rent the air, "Nick, Nick Clayton, c'mon, we're off!"

Bending down on one knee, Nick handed Hugo a bar of

chocolate and said he would try to find his brother and bring him home. Resisting the temptation to kiss the girl, he smiled gently and moved his head to give her a reassuring wink; she blushed and lowered her eyes.

He shook his hand loose from the boy, saying, "I gotta go."

Two lorries arrived at the scene, and a squadron of infantry spilled out and clattered past him in preparation to hold the bridge.

The road was still full of people as the Matador followed the Cromwell tank in the direction of Helchteren and the rest of 'B' Squadron.

Beringen - Helchteren X roads

A few hours later, B Squadron stopped on the road at the end of a convoy of dozens of tanks and armoured vehicles. In the driving seat, Benny removed his goggles and pushed back his hat.

He stretched, "What now, sir?" he said.

"The Welsh Guards have relieved the Paddy's, and they're guarding the Helchteren crossroads just ahead," said Medlin.

"I need a bloody pee!" exclaimed Nick.

"Just don't make a worse ruddy smell than there

already is in this tin can!" sneered Chalkie.

Nick sniggered, "You can talk! The Lt nearly passed out the last time you…"

'Yeah, yeah, all right!' Chalkie laughed.

Standing on the grass verge, Nick stretched and soaked up the warm sunshine. Close by, the noise of battle raged; too close for comfort, Nick thought.

"Get your arse off and do what you have to do," yelled Medlin from the turret.

Nick returned and climbed back into the Matador; Benny revved up, and the convoy shunted forward past several tanks lining the road. He stopped where D Squadron waited for them and where yet another row of demoralised prisoners sat, under guard, with their hands clasped on their heads and their boots removed. The crew of the Matador exited the armoured car and stood by to observe the situation. Ahead, two destroyed tanks were burning fiercely near the remains of two Daimlers. Hit by an SP gun, they were scattered over the cross-road junction. Nearby, a row of guardsmen and two troopers lay dead on a patch of grass. Nick and Chalkie walked over to them. Overwhelmed, Nick looked at the row of dead soldiers. Only their highly polished boots could be seen at the end of the blankets that covered them.

He moaned with horror. "Poor bastards, every one a mother's son," he muttered.

An injured soldier came alongside them, "There's been a terrible battle here, mate!" said the newcomer, "I'm lucky to be alive!"

Deep in thought, Nick did not comment.

"We're nearly out of ammunition," added the soldier, "so we're waiting for reinforcements."

A gentle breeze rustled mournfully through the leaves on the trees when, suddenly, the tarmac road began to vibrate. In the distance, Nick noticed the first tank of a column coming into view. The Troopers stood on the side of the road, watching in awe as half a dozen great bulky tanks crunched and rattled noisily past, halting at the junction of the crossroads.

"Ain't they reassuring!" purred Nick. They continued to watch in silence until Nick, squashing a fag end under his foot, asked.

"What's the time Chalkie?" Finishing a sentence with Benny, Chalkie spun round, "I reckon it's about time for summat to eat!"

"Yeh, that's what I was thinkin', mate!"

"Sounds like a good idea," said Benny, "Is there any chance of that cheese and ham that we got in Brussels?"

"Nope!"

Hearing the conversation, Chalkie walked past Nick and flicked his hand across the back of Nick's head, "You finished it up, I know," he said accusingly.

Nick instantly reacted with a friendly punch aimed at Chalkie's belly.

The two continued sparring when the Troop Leader loudly interrupted the proceedings, saying, "And you'll be lucky to get anything this time tomorrow because provisions are low and the echelons are not getting through," his words followed up with an audible groan from the troopers.

....

Two days later, with the additional help of a heavy bombardment of ammunition, the tank battle was over. The Allied dead were buried, and the injured were sent back to the safety of a medical unit while the prisoners were taken off to a safe building nearby. Moving out of the area, the Welsh and Irish guards, followed by A and D squadrons, went over the crossroads littered with debris and towards the Escaut Canal at Lommel. B and C Squadron were ordered to stay in harbour at Helchteren to guard the guns of the 55th Field Regiment.

"At ease, Trooper. Two letters arrived for you," said his Troop Leader, handing them to Nick.

"Thank you sir."

Finishing his guard duty, Nick returned to the armoured car with his letters. A galvanised can was boiling on the primus stove on the grass. He smacked the side of the armoured vehicle with the letters. "Hey, Chalkie, you get any mail?" he called.

Chalkie appeared from inside the vehicle, "Yep! Dya want a cuppa?"

"Could do with one, yeh!"

Dropping his rifle at his side, Nick slumped to the ground. Leaning against the wheel of the armoured car, he removed his helmet, shaking loose that lock of dark hair that fell across his forehead. Closing his eyes, he lifted his youthful face towards the warm sun and breathed deeply into the air.

"Here you go then," said Chalkie, handing him a tin cup of steaming hot brew.

Nick sipped from the cup, "It's quiet round here. Where's Benny and the lads then?"

"Gone into Brussels on the wagon."

"Lucky bastards. There ain't much time left to go now."

"Who says? The night is young," Chalkie sang, imitating a dancing couple, "There's another lorry going in soon," he added, emptying the dregs of his tea onto the ground. "I'm going whatever."

Nick wasn't listening. Deep in thought, he absorbed the words he had read in one of the letters.

"These are well out of date!" he groaned. The news, he realised, contained information related to him when he was in Basingstoke Hospital. His mum and dad were well and hoped Nick was too. Eli's parents had given up all hope of any good news. Other news was related to the good crop of tomatoes and other vegetables that his parents hoped to yield later in the year.

Nick sighed, "Wish that was all I had to think about," he murmured.

With his elbows on his knees, he thoughtfully massaged his chin with his forefinger and thumb for a moment before opening Cissie's letter. As he expected, it was full of love and anticipation for his safe and speedy return. Repressing his heartbeat, he pushed the letters roughly into his breast pocket, drew in a deep breath, and clambered to his feet.

Brushing the dust from his trousers, he said, "Okay, Chalkie. Did you say we're going into Brussels then?"

Dusk had fallen by the time Chalkie and Nick caught up with Basil, Benny, and Archie in Brussels.

"Where's Harry?" asked Nick.

"Left him reading 'War and Peace,'" Basil chuckled.

It wasn't long before they noticed a crowd of noisy soldiers gathered outside a building. A red light came on, and a roar of approval sounded. With a rush to enter the building, the young soldiers jammed the doorway.

"What the heck?" questioned Nick!

"It's a brothel, mate, you don't wanna know!" slurred an American GI. "unless you got your French Letters!"

"And make sure you use 'em," said another, adding, "You don't know what you're gonna get from them!"

Two girls outside the building approached the lads seductively, "Vous voulez jolie fille pour vous rendre heureux," said one, moving close to Basil, who frowned and moved away.

Nick pushed Basil closer to the girl, "You know what she wants. Go on, Basil," He laughed, "I dare ya!"

"Get lost, Clayton," Basil spat, "I'm not interested."

Nick raised his hands in defence, "Okay, mate!"

'Et toi?' the other girl asked, sidling up to Nick.

The friends laughed and moved up the road, leaving Nick to wriggle out of the offer. The evening was spent partying at the bars in the city, constantly being stopped by grateful local people offering them drinks and entertainment.

That night, as he lay under the bivouac canvas, Nick thought about the evening and the two young women who approached them in the street. He found himself shamelessly wishing he had taken up the offer.

From Helchteren to Joe's Bridge

The arrival of tanks to guard the 55th Field Regiment the following day allowed B Squadron to move out from Helchteren. Followed by the Welsh Guards, they moved along the road leading into the next town, only to be greeted again by the sound of battle. The tank division fighting to regain a small bridge over a canal was relieved and pleased to see the Welsh Guards' arrival go straight into battle. B Squadron passed by the area and escaped across the fields where more cows lay upside down with their legs in the air and crawling with maggots.

The troop was now heading towards yet another bridge over the Escaut Canal. The Squadron moved on with little opposition other than a German soldier they came across who pleaded to be taken prisoner. Ignoring him, the Squadron went on its way, arriving at dusk in time to see a green Verey light light up the sky. There followed immediately a barrage of gunfire. A red Verey light lit up the sky within a few minutes, and the gunfire ceased.

Having spent the last few hours battling to capture the bridge, the enemy was quiet. The Irish guards' next move was to dash across the bridge to secure it. The green Verey light signaled all guns to fire at the bridge. The red Verey light was the signal to stop firing to allow the tanks and infantry to make their dash, which they bravely did in the face of enemy gunfire. Sappers and infantry scrambled around to make the bridge safe, cutting wires and dismantling fuses made ready to blow the bridge. Once across the bridge, the tanks of the Irish guards finished off the enemy with a barrage of gunfire.

With the bridge held intact and leaving a company of tanks to hold it, the entire Regiment retired to an open stretch of heathland near the village of Vlasmer, where they were to refit. The order that came from the Squadron Leader was to "Top up, tidy up, tails up. And no move for several days!'

Their journey to Vlasmer took them into a village where they met with the Welsh Guards in the closing stages of another battle. The Troopers were ordered to guard the prisoners on the side of the road.

"They're a horrible-looking lot," muttered Benny. "Especially that great big one over there with the skull and crossbones on his shirt,"

"Surly looking bastard!" Nick commented, pointing toward one of the prisoners.

"That's the one you're going to search, Clayton!" called Medlin

"Sir," sang Nick.

"Get on with it, and the rest of you can search the others. Move!"

Suddenly, the green traces of two 88mm guns zipped over the Troop Leader's head.

"Watchit, sir!" yelled Benny.

"Jeez! That was close!" said the relieved Lieutenant.

Nick chuckled under his breath; serves yer right! He thought! Cautiously, he set about the task of searching the big German prisoner who stared threateningly down at Nick's five foot eight height.

"Handy hock!" snapped Nick.

With stony-faced insolence, the soldier put up his hands. While Nick searched for the big German prisoner, who fortunately gave him no trouble, the exchange of ammunition between the Welsh Guards and the German battery fell silent.

A couple of hours later, B Squadron drew into the harbour on the heath along with the entire Guards Armoured Division.

There were several reasons why the advance came to a halt. As long as the German army occupied Antwerp's port, the only supply port was from Normandy.

Having captured Paris, the Free French and American forces were advancing further into Europe. In doing so, they, as did the Guards Division, outran their supplies. The good but rather narrow roads caused traffic congestion and held up supply lorries. Then came the brainwave of creating a road system called the 'Red Ball Express,' which eased the system to a degree. It made a one-way system that travelled the supply lorries and prohibited local and military traffic. The lorries were driven mainly by black Americans. Still, nearly 6,000 vehicles carrying 12,500 tons of supplies per day were backed up nose to tail on these roads, slowing down the delivery of supplies to the front.

....

Amongst the conglomerate of vehicles that filled the Heath, Benny, and Nick met up with other troopers, including Basil, Archie, and Harry, who were socialising in the evening light. The indistinct, carefree sound of birdsong, crickets, and bees could be heard above the constant drone of traffic along the main road.

"At least it's peaceful," said Benny.

"Too peaceful if you ask me," replied Nick.

"Make the most of it. We've got to get over the next bridge yet!" said Chalkie.

"Who's leading that recce then? Do you know?" asked Benny.

"D Squadron, I think." Lt Medlin came alongside the group, "Nice evening," he said, adding, "There's a beer in the tent over there if you want one, compliments of Brussels."

The lads were amazed at the quantity of alcohol they found in the tent.

Nick gave a whoop, "Sir, where did that lot come from?"

"There was a stash of the stuff in a warehouse in Brussels

just waiting to be taken, a lot more than that, too. It belonged to the German officers, who didn't want it anymore! The British officers didn't want to waste it, so they had a great time consuming it at their leisure!"

With a guffaw of laughter, they passed the evening with more amusing exchanges of stories over a beer or two.

"How long do you think the war will last then, sir?" mused Nick.

"We're not likely to be going anywhere at the moment, trooper, because we're running out of supplies," answered the Troop Leader.

"But," chipped in Nick, "there were hundreds of supply lorries waiting on the beach when we came through there a few days ago, wasn't there?"

"There was, but you have to consider that they have to supply the whole army, including Patten's army."

Another soldier, the lads recognised as Corporal of Horse Mackey, came over to the group and joined the conversation, "You've also got to understand that they are driving under difficult conditions, and some of the drivers are inexperienced. Once we win the port of Antwerp, supplies will get through much quicker. But the Germans are holding on to it like grim death. They know how useful the port is to us."

"So we won't be home by Christmas then," moaned Nick,

"Doubtful!" said Mackey, adding, "I think the war will drag on for a few more months. Arnhem is about another sixty kilometres away, and more bridges to battle for before we get there!"

"Taking that last Bridge at Lommel isn't the end of the battle," said Medlin. "The next breakthrough will be the road ahead of it," Medlin continued, adding, "I heard that two cars from D squadron were sent to recce it. They returned in a shower of bullets with the news of a small bridge further along the road."

A lot of alcohol was consumed that night, and the troopers returned to their beds the worse for wear. Staggering together under a new crescent moon piercing a starry night sky, Nick hummed a tune. Screwing up his face, Charlie said, "Whassat tune you're hummin? You bin hummin' it all ruddy day!"

"Funny how songs get stuck in your 'ead," slurred Nick.

He burst into song! *"My funny Valentine, sweet, funny Valentine...."* He stopped. His eyes filled with tears. "Bloody 'ell, I miss her!" he spluttered.

An awkward silence followed before Chalkie blurted out, "I know it. It's from the film 'Babes in Arms' with Mickey Rooney."

Nick sniffed, "Yeh, I took my girlfriend to see it. That's where the song comes from. My funny Valentine."

Nick began to sing again, *"Sweet comic valentine, you make me smile with my 'eart."* With renewed gusto, he sang aloud, and the lads joined in with raucous singing, *"Your looks are laughable, unphotographable, yet you're my favourite work of art....."* Nick's voice faded into the background, his eyes filled up again, and he began to laugh!

'Stupid, stupid, stupid,' he murmured.

***

The next few days were spent maintaining vehicles and making good the damage of the last hundred miles. Guard duty and route marches were also compulsory requisites. Returning from a route march early one morning, the lads were able to take showers in a mobile bath unit that had arrived and were given a change of clothing. With no modesty, the troopers stripped off and washed down their bodies with great satisfaction.

Benny sighed, "This is luxury," he said.

"I 'ated bathing in a tin bath," said Nick, adding, "Did you ever use a slipper bath, Chalkie?"

"Nah!"

"I did," mumbled Benny through the towel he was drying his face with,

"Did yer?" Nick remarked, adding, "Yeh, you lived in Hackney not far from me, so did you use the Walt'mstow Baths then?"

"Did, often!"

"Huh! It's a small world!"

Wrapping a towel around his waist, Nick stood in front of a small mirror to comb his hair, "Home," he said thoughtfully. "Did you ever go to 'ackney Empire?" he enquired of Benny,

"Yeah! Great place! Went there often. Saw Marie Lloyd and Tommy Trinder and an amazing magician….and loads of other acts,"

"I used to go to the Walt'amstow Palace, yeh, and I went with me dad to the dog stadium,"

"And them lovely double seats in the Palace cinema. I cuddled up with a girl many times there," Benny remembered. "Hmmm, me too," said Nick.

The lads dressed and, before long, were joined by other troopers to relax for the evening.

"So what football team did you support then?" Nick asked Benny.

"The Arsenal."

"What!" Nick spat, "I 'ate the Arsenal! Them and Spurs are arch enemies!"

"Ahh, you wanna support a decent team like Reading FC," chipped in Chalkie.

The lads laughed; Chalkie frowned, "What yer laughing at? They're a great side!"

"You gotta give 'em credit," chirped Nick, "They beat Arsenal in the London War League and Cup competition."

"How do you know that?" queried Benny.

"I read the papers. I like to follow the teams. I've got a huge collection of fag cards too, and I've got one of Tommy Tait, the top scorer for the Reading club in his first four seasons. Ain't they called The Biscuitmen Chalkie?"

Surprised, Chalkie said, "Cripes, you know your football,"

"Love the game! I played for Walthamstow boys, and I'm Gonna play professional when I get back home."

....

Relieved from further maintenance one morning, Nick lay on the grass with his arms under his head, looking up at a clear blue sky. A little further away, Benny sat busy writing when more troopers joined them, "Our peace is over," murmured Nick. He lifted his head and rested on one elbow, "Who're you writing to anyway?"

"Who says I'm writing to anyone?"

"What you writing then, your memoirs?"

Interrupting the conversation, Chalkie approached, and with a sideways jerk of his head, he said, "Just seen that Mackey talking to Lt Medlin; he's arranging a lorry to take them into Brussels tomorrow,"

"Lucky him!" sneered Nick

"You know 'e's bent, don't yer?"

"Who?"

"Mackey!"

Nick laughed, "You gotta be jokin'. 'E aint bent!"

Chalkie shrugged, "They don't all look feminine!"

"Heard the supply lorries will be here soon," Nick sighed, "I guess that means we'll be off again then."

Chalkie grunted in reply while lighting up a cigarette.

Nick stood up and brushed his trousers, "Might see if I can get a lift into Brussels with the Lieutenant and Mackey before we leave." he thought for a moment, "wonder if there's a cinema in Brussels?"

"There probably is, but it won't be in English mate," said Chalkie.

"Hadn't thought of that; I'm so missing John Wayne,' Nick sighed, shoving his hands in his pockets. The lads spent the morning lazily kicking a football around and generally relaxing before strolling over to the supply lorry for lunch.

"There ain't much left worth 'avin," called out Basil, holding a mug of tea and crunching on a dry biscuit.

Later in the day, half a dozen lads joined the two officers in a three-ton lorry on a trip into Brussels. Benny thought for a moment, "I'm gonna get me coat," he said, trotting off. "Reckon, it'll be chilly later on."

"Bring mine, mate?" called Nick.

"Get it yourself."

"O, come on, be a mate!" Nick sighed, "catch yer in a minute," he called to the others and dashed after Benny. Catching up with him, he put out his leg and tripped Benny. Benny staggered, cursing his mate while Nick ran on laughing, "That'll teach yer!"

The bumpy and uncomfortable journey was relieved by jokes and songs that the lads shared on the way. Mackay sat uncomfortably close to Nick. Chalkie looked across at Nick. He winked and gave him a wry smile. Nick grimaced.

Arriving in the City Market Square the young troopers clattered to the ground and looked around for some amusement. Digging his elbow into Nick, Chalkie sniggered, "'He likes you, Nick!"

"Yeah, well, he'd better not try anythin' on me!" spat Nick. "One o' them tried it on with me once at Waterloo Station. He was leanin' on a walking stick, so I kicked it away from him, and he nearly fell over. I walked off laughin'. Served 'im right to an' all!"

Finding a cafe, the lads poured noisily in. Sitting down, they waited to be served. Smiling warmly, beers for the Troopers were put on the table by the unassuming, thick-set proprietor wearing a white pinny tied around his waist. Amongst the troopers on the trip, sitting at another table, was Bill Bradshaw from D Squadron, "Hey Bill," called Nick, "Do you know anything about the reconnaissance trip out of the bridgehead at Lommel?"

"I do. I was one of the drivers." came the reply.

"What?" exclaimed Nick. "You've got a tale to tell, mate!" Shuffling back his chair, Nick went to sit at Bill's table. "What happened then?" Silence ensued as Bill related his story.

He was the driver of one of two scout cars deployed to recce the road beyond the bridge that the Irish Guards had taken at Lommel. Having surveyed the long straight road that led into the next town and, with the help of binoculars, found it clear the decision was made to see what lay ahead. The two cars drove for a mile until they stopped at a lone cafe on the right of the road. From there, a small bridge over a river could be seen. The Troop Leader reported that the bridge was intact but wasn't sure it looked safe enough for tanks to cross. But as he was still surveying the scene, an enemy tank crawled over the brow of the road and sat on the bridge like a huge toad. Undisturbed by the enemy tank, the company went into the cafe to a welcoming group of locals, all chattering excitedly to see their first liberators. After some time, the Troop leader managed to get some understandable information about the enemy. He was warned about an ambush that lay in the undergrowth along the road they had just travelled, where a whole army of German soldiers was waiting.

Boarding their little Daimler scout cars, they said their goodbyes to their new acquaintances, and both of the little vehicles sped in full throttle, nose to tail back to the bridgehead.

"I had my foot to the ground praying we wouldn't be hit, and the Troop leader was blasting me with orders to go fucking faster!" declared Bill. "We were lucky in a way because we were going faster than the bastards could aim their guns at us. But still, they got some shots. The cars were covered in bullet holes."

"Crickey!" exclaimed Nick. More questions were asked over more pints of beer, and conversations turned to other things until they left the cafe in high spirits.

They turned down a narrow street where, to Nick's delight, they came across a cinema showing the film Casablanca. "Casablanca's a good film," Nick persuaded.

"Don't care," said Benny, "I'm not going in," adding, "You won't understand it mate!"

"Yeh, well, I've seen it before, so I know the story. Go on!" he pleaded.

Nick went into the cinema alone, arranging to meet up with the others outside the cinema later.

No one was outside when Nick exited the cinema later. Waiting for his friends, he lit a cigarette in the quaint, narrow street, where tall, grey buildings stood untouched by the bombing. Wrought-iron framed balconies hung from the first floor. As he waited, some local people passing by stopped to talk to him in their own language and shook his hand in gratitude. Nick acknowledged them politely. Two girls passing by giggled and planted kisses on his lips. Nick noticed a woman hanging around on the street's other side. He tried not to look at her but couldn't help noticing how good-looking she was for her thirty years - he guessed. She wore high heels and a pretty blue cotton, short-sleeved dress with white collar and cuffs. Her auburn curly hair hung loose to her shoulders, and Nick noticed she kept looking at him. When the street emptied, her presence made him uncomfortable, and just as he wished his friends would hurry up, the woman walked over to him. She smiled warmly.

"I'm waiting for my friends," Nick spluttered.

"Voulez-vous me prendre pour un verre?"

Bewildered, Nick shrugged his shoulders in acknowledgement, "I don't understand; I'm waiting for my friends." Nick insisted.

The woman signalled a gesture to explain she wanted Nick to join her for a drink, and taking his hand in hers, she gently pulled him along the street.

"No, non!" he spluttered, "I'm waiting for someone."

"Come," said the woman.

Nick couldn't sleep that night recalling the steamy couple of hours he spent with Ellen and the new experiences she had taught him. He could still smell her perfume. He thought of her voluptuous body and silky white flesh against his and the sensual way she opened her mouth when he kissed her. He felt grateful and satisfied.

"Where'd you get to?" asked Benny the following day.

"I was led astray. Bloody hell, she was good," exclaimed Nick.

Chalkie raised his eyebrows with interest, "Who was?"

"Ellen,"

"Who's she?"

"Someone I met last night outside the cinema while I was waiting for you lot to turn up!"

"How d'yer get back then?" asked Benny

"A Belgian Resistance Worker gave me a lift on the back of his motorbike, got back about 2 am."

"You tellin' me you got to bed a girl?" Chalkie interjected.

"That's nothin' new," muttered Benny. "She ain't no girl Chalkie, she's a woman!"

"And there's a difference?"

"There sure is!"

***

Standing together back at Vlasmer Heath, the Household Cavalry Troopers listened again to orders from the Squadron Leader. They learned about a military operation code-named "Market Garden." The plan was to capture strategic bridges, including Eindhoven, Grave, Nijmegen, and Arnhem, in order to clear the way swiftly into Northern Germany. Forty thousand airborne troops were to be dropped at the various bridges to capture and hold them.

The Squadron Leader concluded, "Our job is," he impressed them, "Should any of the bridges be destroyed, it will be up to us, the reconnaissance group, to urgently find another bridge."

The lads heard that if all goes according to plan the war may end before Christmas.

With the arrival of the supply lorries earlier in the day, the lads could enjoy a good meal together over jovial conversations.

"By gum!" exclaimed Basil as the troopers discussed the Colonel's instructions.

"It's some exercise!" By gum! Thought Archie smirking. He grinned and snorted. Benny glared at him and shook his head with disapproval. "You're right, Basil," he said, "It is some exercise!"

"Market Garden," mused Nick, "Wonder where they dug that name up from?"

"Well, he doesn't want us vegetating here!" chuckled Benny, lightening the atmosphere.

"It's the fork that counts!" joked Chalkie, waving his fork in the air.

"That's a good one, Chalkie!" Nick chuckled.

"And if we stay here too long, we may take root!" Archie quipped.

Harry looked up from his book, rolled his eyes, and shook his head with disdain.

"Seriously, you idiots," he said, "it's a major operation!"

Archie looked at Harry, "Aw, stop worrying. You 'eard the Colonel; he's got everything under control, and it's gonna be a joint Anglo-American operation, so the Yanks are coming to our rescue,"

"Yeh," Benny commented, "But they've got to drop yet and take the bridges before we can go any further."

The next day, there was a hum of conversation among the young Troopers speculating the time and where the airborne operation would be. Dozens of them converged at a vantage point where they would have the best view of the planes. Lt. Medlin strolled over to the lads to inform them that the planes had left Britain and France and were on their way. They didn't have to wait long before the first tiny dots appeared in the distance, growing rapidly until they were overhead and the markings on the planes became visible. They roared over the trees and disappeared northwards.

"Did you notice something?" Nick asked Benny. "There was no opposition. No enemy planes and no ack-ack!"

"You're right! Well, that's gotta be a good sign."

Leaving the Heath on 17th September

With all the necessary petrol, food, and equipment on board, the regiment prepared to move on to their next objective: the bridge that the Irish guards were holding over the Escaut Canal at Lommel.

The night before the Regiment moved out, the troopers were having a few drinks in the tent with the Troop Leader when news arrived that the Troopers who were captured in Albert were back in England recovering from their injuries.

"How did that happen?" Asked Basil.

"I heard that some chaps from the Belgian Underground Movement rescued them after a battle with the Krauts," said

CoH Mackay.

"That was a bit of luck!" commented Nick.

"Yeh, they ambushed the Krauts soon after the battle at Albert, taken by complete surprise, I was told."

The conversation was interrupted by Lt Medlin, who stood up a little unsteadily and bellowed, "Get yourselves back to your billets, you lot. Reveille is at 4.30 am."

Before the dawn chorus began the next day, the heath lay empty of vehicles. Moving off the Heath towards the Escaut Canal, the first Daimler armoured cars arrived at their destination with a tail-back of tanks and vehicles still a mile or two behind. Apart from the usual evidence of battles that left vehicles broken and buckled on the side of the roads, it was an uneventful journey.

TWO BRIDGES

By the middle of the afternoon, the tanks of the Irish Guards lined up, ready to cross the bridge that they had taken a week ago, but the Germans, still bent on recapturing the bridge, continued their bombardment. Ahead of the convoy was a heavy artillery vehicle. B Squadron was close behind the Irish Guards. All was quiet in the confines of the Matador, with a distinct feeling of suspense. Nick sat with the Number 19 wireless, awaiting the following orders, glad his vehicle was not in the lead.

Suddenly, it seemed that all hell was let loose as a barrage of gunfire opened up from the Heavy Artillery vehicles. Then, without warning, the roaring sound of Typhoons rents the air, adding to the chaos. The crew of the Matador strained to watch the scene through the vision slits as they swooped low, firing rockets into the woods lining the road where the enemy lay hidden. Thick black smoke engulfed the trees, and the typhoons disappeared into the distance, bringing the bombardment to a halt and allowing the first tanks to move over the bridge. Once again, creeping up the main road towards the next town, enemy guns opened fire from the woods abounding the left-hand side of the road. Lt Medlin sat in the Matador, watching through the periscope with his mouth open in astonishment.

"Good grief," he exclaimed, "you'd never believe it! There's still some left, and by golly, they're having a go!"

The rest of the crew were silently listening to the chaos around them. "You'd think the Typhoons would have cleared the area!" exclaimed Chalkie.

Several tanks and lorries were knocked out as they passed along the road, the crew of which were killed as they made their exit from the burning tanks. One of the cars of B Squadron was hit, killing the crew. The road ahead was now jammed with burning tanks and lorries. Enemy guns continued their relentless barrage of gunfire as the convoy manoeuvred their way slowly around the debris and continued bravely along the road with all guns blazing. Gunfire erupted from the armoured cars, joining the melee of utter disruption and chaos. The crew of the Matador feared for their lives as one then another explosion resounded close by. There was no escape or respite along the fourteen-kilometer road known as 'Hell's Highway.'

The first tanks reached the small concrete bridge ahead in front of the convoy of more tanks and armoured cars. The Matador followed them along the endless road, with the crew firing in all directions. Not until they were out of range and crossed the small concrete bridge that led into the town of Valkenswaard could the troopers breathe a sigh of relief and still their beating hearts! The Matador came to a halt behind the tanks and armoured cars.

Chalkie strained to see through the narrow vision slit, "Hey! They're coming out of the woods in droves." He moved to get a better view, "They're just standing on the edge of the woods. They look terrible!" He paused. "I can see 'em crying too; some carry their injured mates. Tough, dirty-looking lot!"

"Well," interrupted Medlin, somewhat relieved, "We've made it to Holland. We've just gone over the border!"

Benny drew the Matador to a halt ahead of a long line of vehicles that extended back into Belgium. Thoroughly exhausted physically and mentally, the crew of the Matador slumped in their seats.

They emerged slowly to the familiar sound of townspeople turning out of their damaged and obliterated homes to welcome their liberators with flowers, food, and drink while singing and dancing. Some found space to scribble welcome notes with chalk on the sides of every vehicle. Soldiers milled around with the locals, eating and drinking, smoking, and making light of the day that did not relate to anything like the emotions of fear and excitement, nor the anxieties they felt so recently at the time of the battle.

Later that evening, the squadron troops of the Household Cavalry gathered together to hear the somber tones of the squadron leader's report on the six soldiers from B Squadron who had been lost in the battle. They bowed their heads as the Padre led them in prayer before hearing from the Squadron leader about the next objective.

Clearing his throat, he began, "Congratulations on your efforts to get up that road. It wasn't easy battling against the 9th Panzer Division! Well done!" He added, "By now, the American Airborne forces will have dropped at their strategic bridges, which they will take and hold until forces arrive to support them."

"The ninth Panzer Division!" Nick hissed. "Struth, they're Hitler's elite!"

"Shuddup!" snapped Benny and Basil in unison.

The Squadron Leader continued: "Our job is to plough over the bridges towards Grave and Eindhoven, to recce a safe route for the Guards Armoured division, to meet up with the American forces, and get to the final bridge at Arnhem. I wish you all a safe expedition."

The last conversations drew to a close, and the soldiers slept as best they could under their bivouacs in the rain on the side of the road. "Sleep well, you lot," called Medlin. 'It's an early start tomorrow to meet up with our American friends, the 101st US Airborne Division.

Sleep was hard to come by that night. So much had

happened in the last twenty-four hours. Unable to sleep, the crew of the Matador sat around with a couple of bottles of wine, going over the events of the day. It wasn't until the early hours of the morning that they retired to their beds. "Can still hear the blasts of that battle ringin' in me ears?"

"I'll sing you a song," chuckled Nick, "Goodnight, sweetheart….." he began to hum.

"Shuddup," hissed Benny.

Leaving Valkenswaard on 20th September

The town was jolted awake early the next morning to the sound of dozens of engines revving up and the commotion of varying voices of hundreds of soldiers preparing to leave the town. As the ground vibrated, The church, in danger of falling, dominated the town square. Its spire seemed to pierce the cloudy sky. People spilled out of their homes to cheer them off, some still in their nightwear. The final distribution of food and drink was quickly dispersed to the ranks of soldiers, and soon after, the squadrons and tanks moved noisily through the streets and out of Valkenswaard.

Once on the road, the squadrons split up to reconnoitre different routes towards the first two main bridges at Grave and Eindhoven. With B and C Squadron now under the command of the Welsh Guards, Lt. Medlin's Matador followed the Daimler armoured cars toward Eindhoven to complete their first Market Garden mission at Grave.

Passing through the suburbs of Eindhoven, the Troop

bypassed the city where the Squadrons of A and D were heading and detoured across the country. Frustrated by the many streams spanning small bridges unsuitable for tanks to cross, the squadrons separated, each taking a different route. The Matador travelled with five troops in search of a safe bridge, nervously negotiating each corner or blind spot. Suddenly, shots were fired from a lone barn at the side of a damaged farmhouse. Ahead of the armoured car, more shots were fired. Chalkie fired back, and as he did so, a German soldier appeared in the road ahead and made to escape on a bicycle. Charlie fired again, and the man fell to the ground with the bicycle clattering on top of him.

"Good job!" shouted Nick, patting Charlie on the back. Shots were still firing from the barn. "Put your foot down, Trooper, and let's get out of here," yelled the Troop Leader. Benny needed no encouragement. He revved the car and drove quickly along the road.

Lagging some distance behind the rest of the troop, the Matador carried on across a large field when Benny finally drove it through a gap in the hedge and continued the journey to catch up. The dappled sun glinted through the tree-lined road creating a dance of sun and shadow over the front of the Matador. After a short distance, Benny slowed the armoured car.

"What's the matter?" called Medlin.

"Not sure sir," replied Benny, "But I think I see something in the lane at the next junction."

The silence and tension that followed was tangible; no one said anything while Benny slowly approached the junction. Stopping at a safe distance he said, almost inaudibly, "There's a Panther tank on that side turning, can you see it?"

Medlin donned his binoculars and searched the area. He agreed there was not only an enemy tank, but the occupants could be seen resting on top, unaware of the approaching Matador.

"How did the Daimlers miss it?" he hissed as he began to report the incident to HQ.

"We have orders to remain quietly until a tank division turns up," he said.

It wasn't long before a lorry carrying a company of infantry arrived. They dismounted and scuttled out of sight in the vicinity of the Panther tank. The occupants of the Matador watched as best they could through the narrow vision slits and heard the first explosion from a grenade. But before any other exchange of gunfire the Panther revved up noisily and disappeared along the road at speed. Medlin had an exchange of words with the officer in charge indicating that he was moving on and soon the armoured car resumed its journey.

Woensel 20th September

With the way clear the armoured car travelled on arriving in the town of Woensel, north of Eindhoven where they caught up with the rest of B Squadron resting in a side street with the usual gathering of local people keen to welcome them.

Archie approached with a girl clinging to his neck, followed by Harry and Basil, "Where've you been?" asked Archie.

"We were struggling in the muddy fields you lot chose to drive across," Benny replied.

Wiping his brow with his sleeve. Basil chuckled, "I was just about to blow my horn to let you know where we were!"

"Yeah, well we had to deal with a Panther!" yelled Nick from a short distance away.

The lads turned to listen. Nick was in his glory, he had their attention. Curious, Harry asked in his quiet way, "What do you mean you had to deal with it?"

Nick drew nearer, "It was resting in a side lane and we crept up on it and blew it to pieces!" acting it out Nick added, "They came out through the turret like rats abandoning a sinking ship and we shot 'em down like skittles!"

Benny sniggered, "Yeah, then Winston Churchill arrived with the cavalry and gave us all a medal!"

Basil rolled his eyes, "It's all bloody lies! God knows how you're going to get through the rest of this war!"

Nick slapped him on his back, "With you and your horn by my side Basil how can anything more go wrong?" He lit up a cigarette, "Come on," he added, "it's me birthday, let's see what the crumpet's like round here!"

"Since when have you needed an excuse to let your hair down, mate!" laughed Basil.

"Seriously, I'm twen'y one today," retorted Nick. "Free to do as I please!"

"Not 'till you get out of the army Trooper Clayton!" growled Lt Medlin standing nearby.

"Sir!" Responded Nick, saluting casually.

"Happy birthday," added Medlin, "Just make sure you're back, sober, before midnight."

The young troopers walked away and Nick grabbed Basil's horn, "Let's 'ave another go on that 'orn of yours Basil." He gave it a blow but nothing came out. "I'll do it before I'm another day older!" he said, handing it back to its owner.

As he hoped, the girls gathered in the town to greet them, dragging them into the milling crowd and plying them with wine and Calvados, which they readily accepted. With a few glorious hours of freedom to spare, they disappeared into the multitude of soldiers and civilians bent on having a good time. They went from cafe to cafe, drinking, smoking, laughing, joking and flirting.

The sultry sounds of Edith Piaf's voice filtering into the street enticed Nick into yet another cafe. "I love French music," he mused.

The troopers followed with a string of giggling girls. "I feel like Cinderella with no time after bloody midnight," Nick slurred.

"Okay, Cindy, let's make the most of the time we 'ave left," chirped Benny.

Passing by the cafe the Squadron Leader and another officer overheard the disjointed sound of Basil's horn emanating into the street. "They're well oiled," The Squadron Leader said to his companion.

The door opened, "O Gawd look who's just come in," slurred Benny pushing back his chair to stand.

Scraping chairs resounded as the lads struggled to join Benny standing to attention. "Come in to spoil our fun," groaned another trooper.

"At ease," sighed the Squadron Leader.

With a clatter, the lads sat down again. Nick's head was nestled into the bosom of a young woman who was holding it tenderly. Down by his side hung the horn in his hand; half-empty tankards of beer stood in a pool of beer on the table. Basil went to take the horn from Nick. The Squadron Leader looked at the officer, rolled his eyes, and sighed. To the troopers, he snapped, "Get that trooper sobered up and back to harbour before I put him on a charge!"

Nick grimaced with dissatisfaction.

The next day, 20th Sept, Still in Woensel

There was a distinct autumn chill in the air the next day as Chalkie and Nick, in a delicate state after his night of over-indulgence strolled across to an American Sergeant standing by the side of a Humber scout car smoking a cigarette.

"Didn't know you were with us," queried Chalkie.

Unmoved, the sergeant looked at the two soldiers, "Hi I'm Mac" he said, holding out a hand.

Chalkie took his hand and apologised, "O sorry, I, I'm Chalkie," he stuttered and, with a jerk of his head towards Nick he added, "But me proper name is Jack. I'm mostly called Chalkie because me surname is White.

Their new acquaintance gave a quizzical look.

"Oh and this is Nick." Nick nodded in response and shook the guy's hand. "We were wondering why you are with us," he said.

"I'm a wireless operator," said Mac, "hoping to make early contact with the Airborne divisions,"

Bewildered, Nick asked, "Are you all called Mac? Only I met another Mac on board a ship earlier this month."

"Nah!" drawled the Sergeant stubbing his cigarette into the ground. "It's a popular nickname for us Americans especially when you've been christened Cecil! Nick raised his eyebrows but resisted saying anything while Chalkie tried to conceal a smile and offered another cigarette to Mac.

Nick pulled out the camera he had found on the dead German, "Do you mind if I take your photograph?"

"Don't let Medlin see you with that," warned Chalkie.

Nick shrugged, "Aw shuddup Chalkie," said Nick. Giving Chalkie a gentle shove, he added, "Go and sit next to Mac!"

As he took the photo, Chalkie noticed a group of American soldiers approaching them with the Squadron Leader.

"We're damn pleased to see you!" drawled the Brigadier, who introduced himself to Mac as second-in-command of the 101st US Airborne Division.

Nick and his fellow Troopers stood by, within hearing distance, listening curiously into the conversation that followed. They heard that parts of Eindhoven were still in enemy hands and that just as the American paratroopers of the 101st were approaching the bridge at Son, north of Eindhoven it was blown to pieces. Measurements and dimensions of the damaged bridge had been passed back to Divisional HQ in the hope that the Royal Engineers could help repair it without too much delay.

The Squadron Leader was pleased to report news to the Troopers. "We are the first squadron to link up with our American allies! Back at HQ, they went mad with excitement when they heard the news," A cheer went up from the Troopers in response.

The rumble of tanks approaching interrupted the moment and soon after the Troop Leader was heard to bellow, "Get mounted! We're off again heading towards Grave. I heard the 82nd US Airborne have taken the bridge at Grave."

Heading toward Grave

The advance to find the bridges proved to be tricky. The terrain changed from open ground to narrow boggy roads enclosed by thick woods added to which was the ceaseless congestion of armoured traffic going both ways. The squadron progressed sporadically, jolting the crew inside the armoured cars. Yet another pencil dropped onto Nick's head from the turret. Frustrated, he looked up at the Lieutenant who was standing in the turret occupied with proceedings. Bending to pick it up he muttered, "Bloody butter-fingers! How many more times have I got to pick up 'is bloody pencil?"

Concentrating on the road ahead, Medlin absently reached to take the pencil from Nick and called to Benny, "You're doing well, Trooper. There's no time to waste if we are to get to Arnhem in the next two days."

They hadn't gone far when Benny slowed the car to a halt.

"What now!" yelled Medlin from the turret.

"We stoppin'?" Nick asked Benny.

"The leading car has stopped. Not sure why!" Benny

replied. He strained to see what the problem was. Chalkie peered curiously through the vision slit at the side of the armoured car.

"Something is going on ahead," Medlin said.

They soon discovered that American soldiers from the 101st Airborne were clustered around the leading car, gesticulating further up the road. Listening carefully to the radio, Medlin heard a message to say that the Son Bridge had been blown, but another bridge had been found west of the Son Bridge, still in enemy hands and heavily guarded. An American paratrooper nursing a head wound came alongside the Matador and yelled up to the Lieutenant in the turret, who lifted his earpiece to listen to what he had to say, "Bloody glad you've arrived. Some of our paratroopers are wounded, and we desperately need your help to take another bridge further downriver."

The Squadron Leader contacted the Divisional Headquarters to help the paratroopers. Permission was granted, and a small Troop of two Daimlers, two scout cars, and the Matador prepared to fight a battle alongside the Americans.

The Battle with the Americans at a Bridge near Son

In the seclusion of trees and shrubs the armoured cars joined in the melee of guns and ammunition to dispel the enemy on the opposite side of the river. Even the Bren guns of the two little scout cars effortlessly included their share of ammo. Nick grimaced at the heavy smell of cordite that was again beginning to fill the confines of the Matador. Wiping the sweat from his brow, he continued to feed the 75mm gun as fast as he could for

Chalkie to fire while Benny pounded away with the Besa Machine Gun. Above the noise, occasional thin shouts could just be heard as the guns of a dozen or more U.S. Paratroopers fired from their positions and were seen darting about in the undergrowth.

A couple of frustrating hours passed, and it seemed no further progress had been made. "These bastards are well dug in," Medlin said with exasperation.

"Yeh and the ammunition is getting low, sir!" cried Benny from his position in the armoured car. Hunching his shoulders with determination, he gave another blast from the gun. Smoke from every corner clouded the scene, and debris flew up and rained back down everywhere in the commotion. The fighting continued until dusk when no further progress was made, and the order was given to withdraw.

With the bridge still in enemy hands, worn-out Troopers helped the injured and exhausted American Paras board the armoured cars. Wearily, they drove them back to Son, where they met with their regiment.

The lads were invited to join their American hosts for a meal of Chicken stew and a bottle of Calvados gifted to them by a family nearby. Relaxed and merry, the Troopers retired for the night. Still, the intermittent banging, clattering, enemy potshots, and the shouting of orders from the Royal Engineers tirelessly working to repair the Son Bridge kept them awake.

"I was just drifting off," grumbled Nick when the order came to move out again.

"Me too!" said Chalkie. "Huh!" retorted Nick, fixing his beret in place, "You snored all night, Chalkie! You could sleep on a bloody clothesline, mate!"

A breakfast of American provisions was consumed in the dim light of early dawn. Nick sighed, "Wish we had this every day rather than that watery porridge you dish up, Chalkie.'

'Make it yourself then, be my guest!' Chalkie spat.

As the crew prepared to board the Matador, a thin red glow of sunrise appeared on the eastern horizon, signalling a warm, dry mid-September day.

By now, the unpleasant smells of body odour accumulated in the Matador over the last few weeks were becoming evil. Entering its confines, Lt Medlin winced. "Keep the bloody doors and windows open overnight; perhaps we can freshen up this tin can!" Revving up the Matador engine, the crew began the next lap of the journey toward Nijmegen and Arnhem.

By 6.30 in the morning, the squadron had crossed the bailey bridge over the Wilhelmina Canal and was travelling along a pleasant poplar tree-lined road. Under peaceful circumstances, the scene would have been a tranquil one. Still, now, with the constant flow of military traffic that ground both ways along the corridor from the front to the coast, creating a curious rhythm as it passed the Matador, it was far from tranquil.

Moving on, the Squadron met no opposition other than a few shots from enemy snipers, who, when fired on, fled the scene. The forty-kilometre drive from Son Bridge to Grave Bridge was clear thanks, partly due to the successful accomplishments of the 82nd and 101st American Paratroopers, who dealt rapidly with the enemy in securing the many and various water obstacles. Arriving at Grave Bridge, which the Americans had captured intact, the troopers greeted the soldiers who were here to stay. Tents had been erected, and soldiers milled casually around as though they had been there for ages. Injured men lay on camp beds or were seen sitting on the grass bandaged up and smoking outside a small hospital tent.

However, the Squadrons were held up because of the amount of bombs still tied to the Bridge. Nick and the crew of the Matador stood together on the bank of the river in awe, watching as Sappers crawled about, looking for anything that could destroy the bridge in the steel rafters of the 250-yard bridge that spanned the river. Its structure, which consisted of more than half a dozen great curved steel girder frames on both sides, stood out against the sky. An intricate web of girders formed a covered way the length of the bridge spanning the River Meuse.

"Struth!" Nick gasped when he heard how a small platoon of the 82nd Airborne led by Lt Thomson passed through deep waterlogged ditches to get close to the bridge.

"Caught the Germans by surprise they did," a soldier explained, "We littered the place with machine gun fire to stop them from blowin' the bridge and then overran the place." Taking a drag on his cigarette the soldier continued, "Jerry used the Dutch defence shelters as bunkers. You can see one there and one there," he said pointing to the left and far right distant stone structures on the banks at each end of the huge bridge. The lads were mesmerised as their spokesman went on, "You can still see the damage made by the Typhoons. It was carnage!"

"Bloody hell! It's a wonder the bridge is still intact!" exclaimed Chalkie.

At Grave - Petrol and other supplies and New recruits

Distracted by the sound of a convoy of RASC lorries that ground their way into view, Benny punched the air and yelled, "Petrol and ammunition, yesss!"

Four new Daimlers with an officer and recruits were accompanying the line of supply lorries. The lads wasted no time and busied themselves refuelling and restocking supplies. Medlin welcomed the officer and new recruits, "Glad to see you," he said, shaking the hand of the new Troop Leader Lt Charlton.

Distracted by the conversation, Chalkie looked up to see Vic Jenkins approaching him, "Hey Nick, Vic's back!" he said, giving Nick a shove in the back. Benny climbed out of the Matador, wiping his hands on a cloth. He shook Vic's hand, smiling warmly,

"Good to see you Vic!"

"You too!" replied Vic

"Is that a newspaper you've got there mate?" Asked Nick.

"Yeah! And there's some books and comics in the supply lorry and some letters too." Benny took the letters while Nick took the newspaper and opened the pages.

For a moment, he looked up and asked, "Don't suppose Palmer's with you?"

"He didn't make it. His wounds were too bad," Vic replied.

'That's too bad,' said Benny.

An awkward silence ensued, "Tough," said Nick, returning to his newspaper. The other new recruits wandered forward to introduce themselves. "What's it like back home?" Asked Chalkie.

"Oh, you know, everyone's waiting for the next air raid or news from the boys out here!" said one of the new recruits.

"Yeh, that, rationing, and loads of worried mothers and wives," said another.

Benny restocked the food while Nick rudely buried himself in the newspaper article. "Get yer head out of that newspaper," yelled Benny, "and give me a hand, yer lazy bastard!"

"Who are you callin' a lazy bastard?" Nick retorted, slapping his newspaper shut, "Someone's got to keep you up with what's goin' on at home!"

"O yeh? Well, hand us up that box of stuff over there,"

snapped Benny. A very boyish-looking man with a shock of dark, wavy, brylcreemed hair offered to help, and handing another box of supplies to Benny through the door of the Matador, he asked: "So what's been going on here then?"

"We're waiting for the bridge to be made safe to cross, then we'll be back on our way heading towards another bridge where the Americans have dropped at Nijmegen," Benny replied.

"Benny Osbourne," he said, holding out a friendly hand.

The young Trooper took Benny's hand in response, "Pete, Pete Brand." Pointing to another young soldier, he added, "There is Tommy Porter, Jim Taylor, and Vic, you know, oh, and the Lieutenant is Cavendish over there."

Pete nodded in the direction of the officer.

"He's a good guy, very easy going." Benny climbed out of the armoured car, and in turn, he and Nick shook hands with the lads as they were introduced.

Within an hour of the new arrivals, the lads returned to their vehicles, and, picking up the advance, they crossed the river safely.

***

Journey to Nijmegen

The journey from Grave Bridge to Nijmegen for the

Squadron was uneventful. At each point in the roads, the convoy of armoured cars of A and B Squadron sped swiftly past to the cheering and waving of their American counterparts. The squadron finally arrived on the outskirts of Nijmegen, where British tanks of the Guards Armoured Division, alongside the US 82nd Airborne, were engaged in a fierce battle for control of the bridge. The battle continued all afternoon, and by early evening, the Allies had gained ground to three hundred yards from the bridge. The tanks were withdrawn soon after while the enemy continued their bombardment all night, giving the Troop Leader a headache!

With dusk falling, the crew of the Matador were left with nothing more to do than settle down to spend their time smoking and trying to block out the noise of enemy guns with any conversation, amusement, or occupation they could find.

"Anything interesting in the newspaper, Nick?" asked Harry. "There's a lot about the Germans' withdrawal from Normandy only to be caught up in Falaise. Stuff you already know about. There's also something about Russia and Finland. Here, you can read it for yourself," Nick replied, handing the newspaper to Harry.

Remembering his recent letters, Nick moved away to read them in the light of his torch.

My dear Son

I hope you are well and staying safe in this awful war. We are okay but living in fear that one of those flying bombs will kill us all! The family got together to celebrate dad's birthday last week. It was sad to see so many of your cousins missing. I hear that your cousin Billy is somewhere near you. You might meet up with him. Gran is still going, although she is very thin and frail. The doctor told me not to take away her daily bath bun and Guinness. He said it would kill her. Joyce has had measles, which scared me. You have to watch; they don't go blind with measles, so I did my best and closed all the curtains. She seems to be okay now. The blackout has been relaxed, so we don't have to be so careful about blocking out all the windows, but Mrs Green and I are not taking any chances. Our blackout curtains go up every night. Dad is still going out on patrol with Mr Green. He likes to think he's doing something for the war. I hope Mr Churchill can find a way to stop it all. He's doing a good job, though, and someone said it should be all over by Christmas, and you will come home again. Cissie's leg is getting better, but she will not be back at work for another week or two. She always talks about you when she's here, but she told me not to tell you because you don't want to hear anything. Have you broken up? She seems to think so anyway. You should write to her because she misses you and she really needs you and her mum is worried about her too. Alan had gone off the scene at last, and he was really worrying Cissie and her family. We have had a nice lot of vegetables from the allotment and sell what we get left over to the neighbours for a small price cheaper than the shops anyway.

I think about you every day, son, and look forward to the day when you get home.

Dad sends his love

Write soon Mum

Nick pushed the letter back into the envelope and looked blankly at the other one. He knew it was from Cissie but pushed it into his jacket pocket with his mother's letter after some thought and rejoined his fellow troopers, discussing the news Harry had read out to them.

"Did you see that article about the V-1 flying bombs the bastards dropped on London in August?" Nick asked. "My mum's living on her nerves worrying about one dropping on her house."

A buzz of conversation ensued as more news reports were discussed, including the allied plane that was flying in a storm and crashed into a village school in Lancashire, killing the crew and many people.

It wasn't until the next morning that Nick opened Cissie's letter and read:

Dear Nick

I hope you are well and not in any dangerous places. I think of you often, and as I promised, I will wait for you. You will be coming home soon, I hope, and you will see that we can get on together. Remember how we loved being together and were both so sad when Kenny died? And remember how we laughed at every silly thing we did and how we touched and kissed. You know it makes sense, my dearest darling. I miss you so very much. Please come home safe and soon.

I love you and will always.

Cissie X

Nick pondered over the contents of the letter. He warmed to it as he recalled the times and moments Cissie reminded him of.

'Nosh is up!' called Benny, interrupting Nick's thoughts.

He pushed Cissie's letter into his jacket pocket and went to the call for breakfast. The three troopers, Benny, Chalkie, and Nick, sat in silence with their bowls of porridge as soldiers, carrying rifles and ammunition bent on their mission, moved cautiously about in every direction. The bombardment of guns continued their onslaught. Benny broke the silence. "Wonder what adventures are in store for us today," he said thoughtfully.

Severe fighting broke out again early that morning, continuing the onslaught that began a month earlier, costing hundreds of civilian lives and the destruction of homes and buildings in the once peaceful town. Nijmegen town was crawling with American and Polish Paratroopers intent on capturing both the railway and the road bridge. German troops deployed from Arnhem were heavily guarding the bridges from the opposite side of the river, ready to defend it at all costs.

After days and weeks of fighting, the bridges were still under the control of the German army. Now, it soon became apparent that the fighting could take even longer before an assault could be made to cross the bridge. But if the North Bank could be taken, it would reduce the time needed to do so. However, to do so would mean crossing the river, but with no available boats, the question was how? The order was "find boats!" At the earliest opportunity, canvas boats arrived from Belgium within a day, and the crossing was made under heavy fire. Only sixteen out of twenty-six boats with heavy losses made it across the river. A severe and bloody battle ensued, and by late afternoon, at the cost of many US soldiers, the north end of the railway bridge was won by the Allies. Ready and waiting for a German counterattack, the paratroopers were taken by surprise when a trickle of German soldiers approached them to surrender. Still, it took another day of fighting before both Nijmegen Bridge and the liberation of the city were won. Both allied and enemy bodies lay strewn all over the north bank.

With the possibility of the bridge at Nijmegen being blown, the Squadrons were ordered to reconnoitre the area for another river crossing. Leaving the battle for Nijmegen Bridge to the tanks and infantry, the four squadrons fanned out to explore the river bank. For many miles, the crew of the Matador followed in the wake of B Squadron's armoured cars, encountering nothing in the way of a suitable crossing. The boredom of the crew was alleviated as they passed through a small village. Once again, the few locals turned out to greet them. The cars stopped in a layby to enjoy the moment.

"Ten minutes!" bellowed the Troop Leader. As they savoured the time, a German soldier appeared from a barn with a bicycle. Hoping he hadn't been noticed, he mounted the bicycle and rode off along the road, but he was stopped in his tracks when a gun fired from one of the scout cars, killing the cyclist. The sound drew the attention of the troopers, and the people gathered there for just a moment when everybody turned to see what was happening but, ignoring the result, turned back to enjoy the celebrations as if nothing had happened, leaving the man lying on the road.

It seemed that no sooner had they stopped than they were on their way again with the added extra gifts of eggs, bacon, bread, wine and another German dog tag. The sun glinted on the rear of the scout car in front of the Matador as they went on their way, and the cool September air gently brushed over Benny's face as he drove, bumping over fields close to the river bank. Breathing deeply, he fought the desire to sleep.

Aware of his dilemma, Chalkie called to him: "You stayin' awake, mate?"

Benny fidgeted in his seat, "Yeah, yeah, I'm alright,"

The troop of armoured cars continued their exploration when the troop leader noticed a small ferry moored and operated by a chain on the opposite bank. Further downstream he was aware that small parties of German troops were crossing the river. After a radio conversation with the squadron leader, it was decided that it might be possible for an entire squadron to cross the river on the ferry so a decision was made to bring it across.

"Just keep your heads down. We don't want to draw attention to the Krauts upstream," said the Lieutenant.

With the help of the local people, the troop began the task, creating as little attention as possible. Upstream, the German troops seemed uninterested in their movements leaving the party to their task. However, all efforts to get the ferry moving failed. It was firmly stuck in the mud, and the plan was soon abandoned.

Further along the river, they came across another opportunity. A tugboat displaying a Nazi Swastika sailing upstream was towing a string of barges towards Nijmegen Bridge. In view of the situation, Medlin immediately contacted the squadron leader for advice.

After listening to the instructions, Medlin removed his headphones and said, "We've got orders to stop them without destroying the boat. It might come in useful."

The little troop of armoured cars positioned themselves where they could get a good view of the tug. Nick, Benny and Chalkie listened in quiet suspense. At the same time, Lt. Medlin, from his open turret, attempted to persuade the Nazi tug master to surrender and pull to the side of the river bank, but the tugboat, ignoring all orders to stop, chugged forward on its way. After more attempts to persuade the tug master to surrender, the troop leader gave orders to open fire, whereupon the battle for the tugboat from the banks of the river began. Soon, the tug was floundering noisily in the water, and with a loud hiss of steam, it disappeared below the water. Dutch civilians watched and cheered as the doomed tug sank, dragging the barges down with it, floundering and bubbling to the bottom of the river. A message of congratulations was sent from Divisional HQ when they heard about the event.

As dusk was falling, the Matador, along with the rest of the troop, drew in to rest at the side of a lane. One or two troopers stood around while others sat on the ground, finishing the food they had acquired recently. While Medlin was relating the day's work to HQ when Benny hissed, "Listen, I can hear something."

"Not another bloody skylark," moaned Nick before scraping a mouthful of beans off his fork.

The sound of twigs breaking in the undergrowth wiped the smile off Nick's face; he dropped the fork and reached for his handgun. Swiftly and quietly, the troop prepared for action. Suddenly, gunfire came at them from the undergrowth on the other side of the lane.

"Shit!" exclaimed Nick falling to the ground on his belly, "We're being fired on!"

A short exchange of fire followed when, without any warning, Archie fell to the ground close to Benny.

"Archie's been hit," yelled Benny.

The Troop Leader grabbed his first aid kit and crawled on his belly to where Archie lay seriously wounded. Digging his elbows into the ground, Nick crawled towards the casualty. The exchange of gunfire lasted for only a few minutes before the Germans scattered and fled. Immediately, the troopers gathered to see how Archie was. He was lying unconscious with a bullet wound in his cheekbone. It was an awkward wound to bandage, so with difficulty, Medlin was trying to stem the bleeding and dress the wound.

Frustrated, he looked up at the audience and cried, "Let me breathe, will you?" adding, "Move away and let me see what

I'm doing."

"We passed an aid station about a mile away, sir," declared Nick.

"Yes, thank you, I know that," snapped the troop leader, "We'll get back there as fast as we can."

Leaving the wounded trooper at the aid station, the troop rested for a while. The lads lit up cigarettes and shared only a few subdued words.

Handing two dog tags to Medlin, Basil said, "Sir, these are from two dead Germans who were firing on us."

"Well done, replied Medlin. Archie was still unconscious when they left to continue reconnaissance along the river.

***

In the meantime, well behind schedule, time was running out, and the next stage of the journey to Arnhem, just 30km away, was imperative. A troop from C Squadron was deployed to reconnoitre the road from Nijmegen to Arnhem, followed by more than one tank division. But the enemy appeared from every corner, and gun skirmishes held up the convoy along the way. At one point, the tanks were being followed by a column of Tiger tanks. Wireless communication was sent along the line of vehicles, and as the first Tiger tank rounded a bend in the road, an anti-tank gun ambushed it, knocking it out, at which point the second Tiger crashed into it, followed by the other German vehicles, leaving a great pile-up of German armour abandoned by the roadside. Efforts to reach the troops at Arnhem in time were slow, and the situation in Arnhem was becoming desperate.

When plans were drawn up for Operation Market Garden, it was thought that the bridge at Arnhem wouldn't be difficult to take, and the British and Polish airborne were given orders to land, capture and hold the bridge for only a couple of days until reinforcements arrived to relieve them. But things went badly wrong. The German army had regrouped, and the landing troops found the area fully armed with German Panzer Divisions. As a consequence, the airborne forces were now faced with a difficult task, much more than they bargained for. The enemy was putting up a massive fight to defend the bridge; faulty radio communications severely hampered the operation, and to gain control of the bridge, an attempt to cross the river by boat to the north bank failed with a huge loss of life. Supplies were running short, and planes carrying the supplies mistakenly dropped them in the enemy zone. After four days, there was no sign of reinforcements due to the fact that the battle for the bridge and the town of Nijmegen lasted too long, delaying any possibility of further progress to relieve the forces in Arnhem on time. After nine days of bitter fighting, what was left of the British and Polish divisions at Arnhem withdrew. The failure to capture Arnhem Bridge resulted in the end of Market Garden.

Back in Nijmegen the Troopers were woken from another night's sleep to the distinct sound of birdsong. The guns were silent and, but for the intermittent distant shouts that now and again pierced the air and the distant rumbling of tank movement there was a distinct sense of peace and silence. Local women appeared from their bombed and burning houses with pots of strong coffee and plates of bread, cold meats and cheese for which the lads were grateful.

Curious to take a look at the devastation around the bridgehead, Nick and the lads ventured closer. Damaged tanks and vehicles lay strewn in their path and around the entrance to the bridge. The length of the huge bridge against the sky hung alone and deserted over the width of the River Waal; potholes and bent and broken girders were the only signs of the great battle that took place. Still hanging by straps from the rafters were German soldiers shot and killed where they were positioned to fight the battle. The troopers watched as an army officer ascended the huge bridge and walked slowly along its emptiness, stopping after a few yards to survey the scene. Watching the scene, it was almost impossible to believe the deep peace that the Troopers felt among them; it was almost tangible. They turned to leave, bending their heads together in quiet discussion.

***

With the battle for Nijmegen Bridge over, the Household Cavalry Squadrons, minus the troop from 'C' Squadron who were on their way to Arnhem with the tanks of the Guards Armoured Division, were dispersed once more to reconnoitre the area. B Squadron was sent off to find suitable aerodrome sites for airborne supply drops. These drops had become necessary since the supply lorries were still having difficulty getting through the overloaded roads that were blocked with abandoned and broken vehicles and traffic congestion.

***

After the Market Garden operation ended in late September 1944, there was a period of rest and restoration for the whole regiment. Soon after, B Squadron withdrew to a small town which boasted a beautiful 13th century church within a grove of trees. While they were there, the troopers gathered together in a farm outbuilding, and the regimental Padre conducted a church service. Nick and his fellow troopers bowed their heads in reverence to hear the words spoken. There was a short pause in the service when the Padre gave the Troopers an opportunity to say something about their experiences while serving in the war. There was a moment of silence before a quiet voice spoke just a word or two, then another and another.

Nick listened intently to the voices, remembering Wilf and Benny but holding back tears, he just said, "The sight of the boots at the end of a blanket that covered a line of dead soldiers where a major battle had taken place at one of the bridges."

He took a breath, and with his head bowed he added inaudibly, "It was murder!"

The Padre concluded with prayer and the hymn 'The Lord My Shepherd.'

***

Throughout October, the weather was awful, but Nick and the crew of the Matador, along with all four squadrons of the Household Cavalry, continued to reconnoitre the area around Grave, splitting up into four separate squadrons to look for clear routes and signs of the enemy.

And so, the weeks went by on constant reconnaissance trips. Billets were found in random farm outhouses and barns for the Troops to rest and take cover from the weather. While on duty, if they couldn't find a farm outbuilding to spend the night, they slept where they stopped to rest for the night on the ground by the side of their vehicles under bivouacs out of the rain and damp.

For a while, at the end of October, Nick and 13 other troopers and Lt Medlin of 5 troops were billeted in a foul-smelling farmhouse in a small village. Nearby was an old brickworks yard where an old man kept watch. Nick and the lads often passed by him and noticed that he walked with an unusually thick stick. One day, as they passed the old man Nick made them laugh when he said, "Don't trust that man. I reckon he's a spy for the Germans and keeps a wireless antenna in his walking stick."

With the winter now beginning its annual cycle, the days became shorter and colder, and nights in trenches or under bivouacs were colder still. By November, the Squadrons had dispersed to various places for the winter. Nick's troops were permanently billeted on a farm in Nuth close to Achen and the border of Germany.

The Troopers became infantry for a while when patrols were made on foot without the security of the armoured cars. Nick hated it! The patrols continued throughout the day and night, and when they were not on duty compulsory exercise saw the troopers running through the highways and byways of Nuth and the surrounding area, once again collecting what they could in the way of provisions as they went. There were nights when a Trooper may not return to spend the night, preferring to take the opportunity to sleep in a comfortable bed next to a warm female body whom they had met on an exercise!

Arriving at the farm in the early hours one morning, Nick said, "I suppose it's not bad being infantry if you can share a comfortable bed at night with a soft-skinned female body."

However, the day came when a young woman arrived at the farm. Seeing her, Nick suddenly took cover in the Matador. Puzzled about Nick's behaviour, Benny asked Nick what he was doing.

"I don't want to see her," he hissed. "Tell her I'm not here."

Benny approached the woman and spoke to her. She soon left with a message to Nick. Benny passed on the message, "She was disappointed, man," he said.

"She likes me, but she ain't my type," replied Nick as he climbed out of the Matador.

The sounds of battles and enemy counterattacks continued to rage, reminding the troopers of the reason for their patrols. Most of their time, night and day was spent in a ditch somewhere, observing a river, road or railway with nothing more to do than smoke cigarettes. Likewise, the German infantry would be doing the same from their vantage points. The purpose of the patrols was to report back to Divisional HQ the whereabouts of the enemy in order to keep control of the area.

It was a boring, mundane time for them.

However, sometimes the boredom was broken with events that were meant to be useful in their entirety and could be reported back to their Squadron Leader. But there would also be the occasional skirmish, often to no advantage. At one such skirmish, there was an almighty battle with both sides firing at each other with no result.

Angrily Nick threw down his rifle with frustration saying, "Bugger this, we're wasting our time!"

One night, Medlin was ordered to do a patrol with half a dozen other troopers, including Nick and Benny. The patrol unit set off at dusk in pouring rain to ascertain whether a certain wood was held by the enemy. Finding a safe hideout in the woods, the patrol rested to watch and wait. Hearing a sound, Benny glanced back and saw a bush move.

He hissed, "Don't look now, but I think we're being watched!"

They were too close for comfort so Medlin signalled to the Troopers to position themselves where they could make a run for it and disperse. Crawling away, they went as far as they could before leaping to their feet and running in all directions as fast as they could. It seemed as though they had got away without any brush with the enemy until Nick tripped over a concealed trip wire that set off an enormous blast, alerting the enemy. Chalkie turned back to help Nick up, and they both ran with the enemy, taking potshots at them, hot on their tail. Rounding a bend in the road, Nick nipped behind a fence on the edge of a field and waited for the enemy to appear. Chalkie had run on, but aware that Nick wasn't with him, he turned and, seeing Nick, threw up his hands.

"What the fuck?" he gasped just as a couple of the enemy patrol came round the bend.

Nick quickly discharged his rifle and shot them dead. The sound of a scuffle and hissed words came from the direction of the rest of the enemy patrol, and no more was seen of them. The two troopers stood still for a few moments to ascertain what time it was and where they were.

"We're lost, I think," said Benny.

Nick looked at his watch, "Okay so it's 1.30 am. What do we do now?" retorted Nick.

"Not much we can do," replied Benny. For a moment, they stood together, thinking and looking around. They agreed to find somewhere safe to rest. Following the path they had taken in the murky darkness, they found a sheltered cornerand sat down to rest. They lit up cigarettes and chatted together for a while until they fell asleep. It was light when they awoke, surprised to find themselves on a tennis court.

"Huh," said Benny, "Look where we are!"

"Anyone for tennis?" Nick chirped. Somehow, the two mates found their way back to the farm. Nick was in good form, relating the story to his fellow Troopers.

"Yeh!" said Chalkie, "If you'd watched where you were going and not tripped over that bloody wire, you wouldn't 'ave a story to tell!"

"Well, you know me, Chalkie, me old mate," chuckled Nick, "It was well worth it!"

"And we wouldn't have had to spend the night in a bloody tennis court!"

There were many encounters with the enemy, and they always seemed to surface in the early morning after a long night of waiting and watching. One early morning in November, after another night of watch, the sun rose slowly, an orange orb between streaks of clouds pink and orange, revealing the dark shapes of the surrounding leafless trees clawing the sky. With the light of dawn came a renewed confidence from the tired and bored Troopers who shuffled about for comfort and entered into quiet conversation. The dawn chorus in the trees, insensible to the tensions held below them or the possibility of another day of fighting, opened their throats to welcome the day. On the other side of the river sounds of vehicle engines and a solitary raised voice confirmed the reality of the situation.

"I suppose they're doing what we're doing now," said Nick.

"With all the noise they're making, I doubt they are aware we're watching them," commented Medlin.

Couldn't we just lob a few grenades, sir?" chuckled Nick.

Medlin looked at Nick and, shaking his head in despair,

said, "You can if you want to, but I'm heading back to report to HQ."

On yet another watch, the patrol had positioned themselves behind a high hedge, discreetly observing a railway line with no sign of the enemy. However, dawn revealed the enemy patrol less than a hundred yards away on the other side of the hedge. Half a dozen grenades were lobbed from both sides before the enemy scuttled away into the undergrowth. No one was hurt from either side!

The Germans terrorised the local people into submitting knowledge of the patrols and the routes they were taking. Some people were even taken hostage. Creeping about in the night, the enemy laid mines and tripwires on the routes taken by the patrols, causing unsuspecting horrors to occur. A leading car ran over one of these terror traps, causing it to flip in the air and turn over before crashing back down on its side. Miraculously, two Troopers, Harry and Dave Brewer escaped with just a few cuts and bruises. Another similar incident left another two with acid in their eyes from the damaged car battery. Quick as a flash, Medlin grabbed his water bottle and emptied it into their eyes, which saved their eyesight. There were, however, occasions when the enemy simply surrendered, and the patrol would return with prisoners.

Chapter 17
Brussels

Brussels was the best place to be. Many trips were made when the opportunity arose. While the Household Cavalry Officers enjoyed the luxury of a hotel called the 'Eye Club', named after the divisional sign, the Troopers meanwhile enjoyed the cafes and the local dance hall. The local brothel was a favourite haunt for those who wanted it. It was at the Dance Hall that Nick met up with Ellen again. She surprised him when she approached him with a girlfriend.

"Bloody hell!" Nick exclaimed. "I mean, how did you get here?" he spluttered. "I never thought I would see you again."

Aware of Nick's confusion, though not understanding the vocabulary, Ellen chuckled and introduced her girlfriend, Marleen. Nick's fellow troopers looked on with interest. Gathering his wits Nick introduced Ellen to the lads who fell over themselves to be sociable. The women giggled. Benny rolled his eyes in frustration as Nick stood in a state of confusion. Nudging him with his elbow, he hissed, "Ask them if they would like a drink before you fall into a faint man."

"Yes," said Nick, "Um, er, can we get you a drink, ladies?" he spluttered.

Nick was pleased to meet up with Ellen again. After that, the couple met at every opportunity when Nick took Ellen to dances. Ellen took Nick to other places, including art galleries and the theatre, where they saw a production of Carmen, Nick's first introduction to Opera, and he loved it! They slept naked together in warm, clean sheets where they kissed and made passionate love. The days were all too short, and the longing was unbearable for them as Nick went about his nighttime watch.

***

Bad weather and exhausted soldiers during November and December grounded the American allies, halting major operations; planes were unable to take off the ground, and all Allied forces could do was rest. The German army took advantage of the opportunity to regroup and plan another offensive. The port of Antwerp was targeted to stop the Allied use of the Belgian port. A few days before Christmas 1944, they made an attack in the area around the Ardennes Forest, taking the Americans by surprise. The battle that ensued became known as the 'Battle of the Bulge.'

Nearing Christmas Day at the farm in Nuth, the family was listening to the wireless. They heard news that a massive attack had been made by the Germans on Allied forces in the Ardennes Forest. Two family members, great, strapping young men, ran from the room to report the news to their guests in one of the outbuildings that served as billets. Understanding what the two young men were saying, the lads wouldn't believe it.

"Nah!" said Nick, examining his hand of cards in a cloud of cigarette smoke, "You gotta be joking!"

The young men were adamant and pressed the news.

Chalkie listened more carefully. "Maybe they're right," he said thoughtfully.

The Troopers retired for the night but were rudely awoken in the early hours of the morning by Medlin with the words, "Get packed. We're on the move."

The armoured cars lay in bits, stripped down and with their sumps off for maintenance. Hastily, they were put together by grumbling Troopers before dawn. Not knowing what was going on, the Troopers could only guess.

"And just when I was thinking it would be all over soon." moaned Nick.

"I reckon the Americans just want our petrol," chuckled Chalkie.

"And our cars," interjected Benny.

"The Germans are up to something!" said Harry, stuffing his book into his holdall.

The convoy was soon on its way, under cover of darkness and thick fog, towards the town of Waterschei. Winding its way through the dark streets of Nuth, the convoy moved north along the road with no send-off from the unsuspecting community. It was a slow and weary drive in thick fog and along traffic-congested narrow roads. When the fog lifted, it gave way to fine rain.

Unaware of the German assault, the Americans were taken

by surprise at the convoy's appearance. They called out to the passing vehicles, "Hey Limeys, what're you doing here?" and cheerfully waved them on their way.

By some means, however, the Belgian people seemed to be aware of something happening as the convoys passed through their towns and villages. Flustered and anxious words were spoken of 'the Bosch', seen again in the area.

The Squadron finally arrived in Waterschei where they met up with the other three squadrons: A, C and D. Three of the Squadrons, including B Squadron, were later deployed to reconnoitre the fifty-mile stretch of the River Meus, while one stayed in Waterschei to manage wireless communications which had been unreliable. The squadrons split up, going miles apart and going in different directions towards the River Meus. Once again, the patrolling of the area began its monotonous drive up and down and criss-crossing, looking for the enemy and guarding bridges. It was a boring time that was alleviated only when off duty, by spending time in local cafes. Evenings and nights had their charm and comfort. Local people, in fear of the German's return, were only too pleased and relieved to open their homes for the Troopers, who in turn tried to quell rumours of the Germans returning to Belgium and convince them of their safety.

It's true that there were many rumours about spies circulating and that there were German soldiers in the area dressed as Americans and driving American vehicles in a ploy, it was believed, to alarm and confuse. The Troopers had never needed passwords before, but now, it has become necessary to use them. Guarding a small bridge on the outskirts of Huy, one day, Nick and his fellow Troopers are approached by an American soldier who says he wants to speak to their officer.

Nick jerked his head in the direction of a house nearby, "Over there in the big house," he said.

The soldier began to walk away in the direction of the house when, as an afterthought, Nick stood up to his full height, shook his rifle from his shoulder and, pointing it at the soldier, barked, "Wait! Who's Frank Sinatra?"

The soldier turned and smiled a big grin, "O yeh! He's the new singer that's putting the skids under the girls back home!" he drawled.

"Yeh, that's right," Nick replied, prepared to enter into further conversation, but the soldier turned and went on his way.

Nick turned back to face his companions, who were sniggering, "What?" he blurted out.

"Wait," said Benny, mimicking Nick. "You should've said 'Halt'!" chuckled Chalkie.

"Yeh, well, I wasn't prepared," he added brightly, slinging his rifle back on his shoulder. It was a good question, though."

The lads went back to the humdrum business of guarding the bridge, discussing other questions they could ask if a similar thing should arise. "Babe Ruth," said Nick, "that's a good one."

While on duty, Nick caught sight of a priest on a bicycle. Dismounting, he dropped it to the ground. Then, hitching up his cassock, he hastily approached a public noticeboard and angrily ripped off a poster advertising a dance at the local hall. Nick walked over to him and asked why he had removed the poster.

"Humph," replied the priest in the process of ripping up the poster. Then in broken English, he said, "I'm not having my young parishioners gallivanting with those sex-crazed Yanks, not that it's any of your business."

Mounting his bike, he flew off into the darkness of the night.

All hope of Christmas in the comfort of a family home was fading as the patrolling continued up and down the river bank. While the sound of battles could be heard nearby, they came into no conflict with the enemy.

Meanwhile, boring though it was for the Sabre Squadrons patrolling the River banks, there was relative comfort compared with the terrible battle the Allies were fighting.

Fifty miles away, under siege and in deep snow, the Americans were putting up a great fight against the German army, which had advanced as far as Bastogne. The arrival of the US 2nd Armoured Division on Christmas Eve finally ended the siege. However, the German offensive continued on for another month.

***

A few restful hours on Christmas Day were spent with a family in a large old farmhouse situated south of Andenne, not far from the river. Here, all 12 Troopers of B Squadron 5 Troop had been billeted for the past week and given the comfort of shared bedrooms and food. A couple of days before Christmas two or three lads had been wandering around the farm and spotted a little calf tethered to a fence. The ground was frozen solid, and the shadow of war was ongoing with the distinctive motorbike sound of intermittent Flying Bombs overhead and guns of war seeming ever closer. As they were petting the animal, a young girl came alongside them and spoke in her own language.

After some further conversation in sign language and odd words, Nick blurted out, "It's our dinner on Christmas Day!"

Not used to the idea of killing an animal to eat, the lads tried to say something meaningful to the girl about killing a sweet little animal before walking away and lighting up cigarettes. Turning around to face his friends, Nick danced backwards, saying, "I wonder if they've got mint sauce?"

The lads chuckled. Pulling up the collar of his great coat, Harry said, "I'm bloody freezing. Don't know about you lot, but I'm going to get comfortable with my book by that lovely log fire burning on the grate!"

"How are your eyes now since that stuff got into them," asked Benny.

"Better," replied Harry

"What yer reading now?" enquired Nick

"One of Ernest Hemingway's books,"

"My dad was reading one of his books," commented Benny. "Something about grapes."

"The Grapes of Wrath," Harry said, shaking his head impatiently. Continuing their conversation, they removed their boots in the farm outhouse. " I can't remember the last book I read!" Nick muttered.

"Let me guess," said Benny thoughtfully rubbing his chin and looking up, "I know!" he snapped, "Little Red Riding Hood."

Nick sniggered and gave Benny a shove while he was bending to undo his shoe whereupon Benny collapsed on the floor with laughter.

Christmas Day came with good food, for which the Troopers were grateful. There was no mint sauce! Later on, Nick couldn't lose the moment when the music was playing to ask one of the girls to dance in the space of the large room. Smiling, he held his hand out to the young girl in a most polite way. Shyly, she took it, and Nick waltzed her around the room to the delight of the family members and sniggers and knowing winks from his mates.

Christmas Day came and went. The next day, the Troops were back on duty, roaming the river banks with the distant, everlasting sounds of war. The Matador Troop was given the task of holding the small-town bridge over the river. Taking turns patrolling the area on foot, the boredom and freezing cold were the worst trials. Temperatures were at their lowest as the lads waited on the bridge for something to happen.

Nick entertained them with occasional news from the wireless he was in charge of. News about the other Troop's adventures in the depths of Belgium, where things were a bit more interesting. "C Squadron is right in the thick of the battle at Bastogne," he said, "They had no Christmas because they've been caught up in the fighting alongside the Americans, in the snow! And," impressed Nick, "Hundreds of enemy armour, including Tiger Tanks have been smashed up or abandoned on one road and they've taken hundreds of prisoners."

The German offensive ended on 4th February when the enemy was driven back and retreated with heavy losses of both men and equipment.

The departure from Belgium was greeted by so many grateful families who had housed the Household Cavalry troopers for the last few weeks. Their generosity was far-reaching, with gifts of food and drink to each crew. Then, as the first armoured cars began to leave their billets, the whole of the towns and villages turned out to wave them off, blocking the roads and byways while drivers struggled to negotiate their way forward.

The Battle for the Rhineland

The battle plan now was to cross the River Rhine into Germany. Both the Meus and the Rhine and the notorious

Siegfried Line were major obstacles. The Allies had won the battle for the

Meus but were now facing the Rhine. The next objective was the Reichswald Forest.

In the meantime, Nick and his fellow troopers continued their journey with the three other reconnaissance troops of the Household Cavalry. Like so many ants, the Sabre Squadrons separated into four different directions through towns and the countryside, winding their way north towards Nijmegen and the Rhine. Severe flooding from the thaw of snow and ice set them back. Bogged down in mud, they were forced to turn back more than once to find another route. Finally, after a journey of 147 km, they arrived back in Nijmegen with the rest of the Regiment. Here they rested. Tired out after a long journey, the crew of the Matador only had a desire to sleep.

Plans for the Regiment to move on were cancelled due to floods and impassable roads. Happily, the troopers heard the news that the regiment would be going nowhere for the time being. "You may as well go and find somewhere to lay your heads for a couple of nights," said Lt Medlin. Unfortunately, comfortable billets in the town were hard to come by. Most of them had been taken by those who arrived earlier. Once again, Nick and his friends resorted to cellars and outhouses. The next day, the troopers were given time off to go into the town, which was packed with soldiers. Shoulder to shoulder, they stood in a cafe with pints of beer in one hand and a cigarette in the other.

A soldier bumped into Chalkie on his way out, spilling his drink onto the floor. "Sod this," said Chalkie, "I'm off. Most of my beer is on the bloody floor."

With that, he squeezed through the crowd of soldiers and left. Soon after all the troopers went out and into the street, they found Chalkie sitting on a pile of rubble in a ruined park. The Allies had bombed it, leaving gaping holes in the ground where once pathways ran between lawns and bedding plots that held annual flowers and plants in the summer. Harry wandered off towards a brick and stone artefact. He stood for some time examining it.

"What yer looking at Harry," called Nick.

"Not sure," came the reply. "But I think it's Roman, some kind of temple to a god, maybe."

"Oh really? Roman!" mocked Nick, adding, "How do you know it's Roman?"

"I don't," replied Harry, "just guessing!" Turning to leave, Harry said, "Philistines. That's what you are"

"What d'yer mean, Philistines?" Nick retorted.

"He means we are ignorant of art and…. what's the other word I'm thinking of?" said Benny.

"Culture!" remarked Basil.

"That's it." said Benny, "Culture!"

Deep in thought, Nick muttered, "The only thing I've heard about Philistines is that story in the bible about a giant Philistine who was killed by a stone from a sling!" No one was listening. Then, rubbing his hands together, he said, "Come on, I'm getting cold standing about."

They left the park and headed out onto the road. Drawing alongside Harry, Nick slapped him on the back. "It's all that book reading that does it, Harry," he said, adding, "It can't be good for you!"

"Philistines!" spat Harry.

***

The Regiment remained in Nijmegen for the best part of a month. For the troopers, most of the time was spent in maintenance and compulsory training. Time off duty was spent in town, haunting the cafes and bars and finding any willing girl to walk out with. Nick could charm any girl into his arms; he was never short of a female partner to dance with and spend a steaming night.

Every now and again, there was an explosion that caused damage to the town and injured people caused by what was thought to be a self-propelled gun somewhere in the vicinity of the railway line. Although more than one patrol had been sent out to look for it, it couldn't be found. Back in the harbour where the Regiment was resting, Chalkie was one of three other troopers on guard duty. Nick learned that while on duty, the SP fired its illusive weapon, and Chalkie got a direct hit and was killed. The Squadron Leader himself decided to deliver the news to the troop, interrupting the conversation and laughter that emanated from their billet. Silence and a tangible sadness followed. Nick was devastated. He put his head in his hands, trying to conceal his tears.

11th March: The regiment moves out of Nijmegen

Soon after the Regiment made ready to leave, at dawn on an early March morning, Lt Medlin was standing in the turret of the armoured car, and Benny was in his seat revving up. Nick and Basil, who replaced Chalkie, climbed in and took their seats. Nick donned the Number 19 wireless set, and in silence, they drove off following the last scout car of B Squadron. The streets of Nijmegen were lined with joyful people as the convoy moved out, though one or two of the girls they had spent time with ran alongside in tears.

***

The Reichswald Forest.

The troopers were now used to the holdups, as, once again, mud, flooded roads, dead animals, and congested traffic slowed the journey to the Reichswald Forest. The landscape was apocalyptic. Receding floods revealed dead animals of all descriptions; demoralised people, young and old, stood by their ruined homes. Not a single house was left untouched by flooding or bombing, nor a tree remained standing.

Finally, all four squadrons settled into the Reichswald Forest, where they were to stay until they got orders to move forward.

***

The bridge at Rees spanned the Rhine into Germany. It had been destroyed by the enemy. There was a terrible battle to gain access to the bridge that lasted for four hours. British bombers added to the bombardment both day and night before US battalions began the process of building a pontoon bridge spanning the width of the river. The work began in the morning and was completed before 4 p.m. the next day.

***

The morning after arriving at the forest, a cold wind blew, but the weather changed for the better. Various log cabins were dotted about, built by the Canadians who had sheltered there before advancing to the Rhine and Germany. The neatly built cabins were perfectly comfortable for their new residents, and the change of scenery was a welcome treat to the weary troopers.

Stepping outside one of these log cabins, Nick lit up a cigarette, stretched and lifted his head to bright Spring sunshine filtering through the trees. He took in the scene around him where Many stockpiles of German accoutrements lay in huge piles, from 88-mm shells and hand grenades to belts of machine guns and gas masks. Taped pathways ran between the trees, a reminder of the danger of mines and tripwires. Even more welcome was the news that the lads were allowed forty-eight hours leave and that lorries were travelling back to various towns including Brussels. Taking the opportunity to go into Brussels once again, Nick enjoyed being in the company of his girlfriend Ellen. They walked and talked, danced and made love. As they were dancing together one day, Nick felt a tap on his shoulder and turned to see who needed his attention. He was surprised and delighted to come face to face with his cousin Bill. Keeping hold of Ellen's hand, he said, "Mum told me you were over here; it's good to see you. How are you?"

"I'm fine, Nick", replied Bill, who immediately introduced Fleur, the girl he was dancing with. "She's Dutch. We've been dating for a while now, and we want to get married."

"I'm Pleased to meet you," replied Nick. I hope you know what you're getting into."

Bill laughed, and, giving Fleur a loving squeeze, he said, "Slower Nick, she doesn't understand very much! "Though, he added with a grin, "Perhaps it's as well she didn't hear that last comment!"

Glancing at Ellen, Nick said, "Oh, and this is Ellen."

After a few more words Bill suggested that they sit and have a drink. Sitting comfortably, the conversation between Nick and Bill flowed with disjointed explanations to the girls. Bill related news about the family in England, adding, "Cissie's baby is due soon?"

There was a surprised silence before Nick spoke. His heart began to race, and he found he could hardly breathe.

"Is it?" he said almost inaudibly.

The look on Nick's face stopped Bill in his tracks. He fidgeted in his seat, "Oh, sorry! Guess you didn't know!"

Nick put his head in his hands to calm himself while the

girls looked on, bewildered at the uncomfortable atmosphere that had descended.

Suddenly, Nick pushed his chair back, "Who's?" he snapped. Bill was taken aback, "I was given to believe it's yours, mate!" Bill paused, "You really didn't know, did yer?"

Later that evening, with mixed emotions, Nick remembered the moment of passion he had with Cissie at the hospital. He hadn't forgotten her loveliness, even though he had thrown caution to the wind and enjoyed being in the arms of Ellen and other girls during his time in Europe. He sighed deeply. He recalled the moment he told Ellen the news and how well she had taken it, but he was not going to give up hope of more time with Nick and the hope that he would stay!

While Nick wrote a few letters to England, he received regular news from his mum and sister Joyce and a few from Cissie, but there was never anything about Cissie's condition; at the first opportunity, Nick pulled out his writing paper and pen and wrote to his mother. It was a few weeks before he got a reply from her saying that Cissie swore her to secrecy because they had split up, and she didn't want to make Nick feel obliged to her in any way. But his mother added that she thought it was a stupid idea and that he should face his responsibility. There was never another letter from Cissie.

In the next few days, Benny and the rest of the troop noticed a change in Nick. He was quiet and deep in thought. Cheerful remarks from his friends couldn't rouse him. It wasn't long before he needed to talk to someone, and finding Corporal of Horse Mackey alone in a bar one day, he joined him for a drink.

They exchanged a few mundane words before Nick asked him, "What would you do if you found out that the girl you left in England was pregnant with your baby?"

"Well," began Mackey, "For a start, it wouldn't happen to the likes of me, but seeing it from someone else's point of view, I suppose I would be pleased."

"Yes, but the person I'm talking about has split up with her and has got involved with a girl over here."

Mackey thought for a moment and, gently laying his hand on Nick's, said, "Tell you what, why don't you come home with me and meet Mother? That could solve all your problems!"

"Huh, me?" he said, removing his hand. Chuckling, he said, "Thank you, but I'm not sure it would."

"You got something on your mind, mate?" Benny asked as they sat alone together, smoking in the log cabin. Your miserable face is beginning to get on my nerves!"

Nick put his head in his hands and lowered it almost to his knees. "Do you remember me talking about Cissie?"

"Yes!" replied Benny.

Lifting his face to Benny, Nick said, "My old mate Wilf knew her. She's a girl I dated in England and the sister of my best friend who got shot down over the Channel in 1943." Nick then related the story of how he went back to England after he was wounded and the news he heard from his cousin just a few days ago. Benny gave a deep sigh, "Well, I ain't no Anna Raeburn but...."

"Who?"

"She's that agony aunt on the wireless who gives advice to people with problems. Yeh, maybe you should contact her!"

Nick hoped that another 24 hours of leave to Brussels would make him feel better, but he couldn't put Cissie out of his mind as he lay in Ellen's arms. Their interests and lovemaking, though passionate and satisfying, weren't the same. Cissie was back.

The order to move out couldn't come soon enough for Nick. He was glad to leave the Forest and the opportunity to leave Brussels behind.

For the last few days, the nearby road had been reverberating with hundreds of vehicles heading toward the German border in preparation to cross the pontoon bridge over the Rhine and into Germany. For three hours, hundreds of Dacota planes and gliders droned overhead, dropping fourteen thousand troops. Watching from a high vantage point stood Mr. Churchill himself to see the action.

At the end of March, the regiment moved out of the Reichswald Forest and headed toward the bridge crossing at Rees. The journey for B Squadron was not without incident. They were kept alert by enemy opposition that popped up as the Squadron drove through the villages and byways, but most of them scattered and fled when fired upon. Two were captured and willingly boarded a scout car. Irritatingly, the occasional pencil continued to drop from the turret for Nick to retrieve and return to its owner!

Two days later, in the early hours of the morning, the convoy of twenty armoured cars and the Matador arrived at last at the bridgehead that would take them into Germany. Peering through the slit holes, the troopers watched in silent awe as, in pouring rain, the cars in front started over the pontoon bridge that swayed gently in the water. When it came to the turn of the Matador to begin the journey across the bridge, its crew, feeling the sensation, held their breath as it lowered into position at the edge of the bridge. The armoured car rumbled and bumped its way across the wooden planks that were secured to the shallow draft boats floating in the water. It stalled more than once, holding up the cars behind, then, once safely ashore, Benny put his foot down and raced to catch up with the cars in front.

Once ashore at Rees, the squadrons separated in different directions and headed towards another major canal bridge. Along the road, B Squadron encountered tank troops worn out and resting beside their vehicles; damaged and burned out allied and enemy vehicles lay strewn for a hundred yards alongside the road. Hoards of German infantry who had been totally unprepared for an attack made rushed attempts to defend themselves but failed. In utter disarray, they achieved nothing worthwhile and even misdirected their guns to their own soldiers and vehicles. Many simply took to their heels and fled. The Matador had their share of the battles and dealt rapidly with everything they were confronted with. A bridge over a waterway was detonated and blew up just as the first armoured car approached it. Leaving the blown bridge, a truckload of

German infantry was spotted. The convoy opened all guns at the truck, blowing the tyres. It lurched sideways and dipped into a ditch at the side of the road. The troops fell out and those who survived the melee of shots from the armoured cars ran for cover. The convoy moved on to find an alternative route. Still, more enemy infantry were on the road in droves and were gunned down as the convoy passed by. Many were captured and seen marching under guard towards the resistance fighters.

After travelling all day, B Squadron pulled into a field to rest, not realising how wet and boggy it was. The Irish guards arrived later and pulled into a field on the other side of the road. The troopers were ordered to dig trenches for the night into which torrential rain fell overnight.

They were awoken in the early hours of the morning to a lot of swearing and shouting in German and loud bangs. Shaken out of their sleep, both Nick and Benny hissed, "What's happening?"

Medlin was still awake and fully dressed. He moved low to the trenches to tell them to stay put. The Irish guards were dealing with them. As it happened, the Irish guards decided that discretion was the better part of valour and did nothing. The guns and swearing soon stopped, and the troopers returned to their uncomfortable sleep. Soaked to the skin, they awoke to find the armoured cars had sunk into the sodden ground.

Standing around in wet clothes, a quick breakfast was had with a tepid cup of black tea before the lads attempted to dig the matador out of the ground. Troopers could be heard all around the field swearing and cursing, heaving and pushing their vehicles into action. "I think that's what was going on last night," said Medlin. "The Germans were trying to get their vehicles out of the mud to leave here."

Once the armoured cars were back on the road, there was no stopping until they realized that they were following the wrong maps. The convoy came to a grinding halt, and in pitch darkness and pouring rain, the Troop Leaders met together around one of the scout cars.

Tired out and sitting in damp clothes, the crew of the matador were in no good mood, "So we're lost!" remarked Nick.

"Oh shuddup!" exclaimed Basil.

Benny gave a deep sigh. Suddenly, gunshots rent the air, and Lt. Medlin yells directions to fire the gun. Springing from his seat Basil peeped through a vision slit.

"I see 'em," he yelled.

The gun was swung into action, and chaos ensued as they fired in unison with the other armoured cars. The enemy turned and fled, leaving three soldiers dead. The lads learned in the next few minutes that Lt Medlin, had been shot in the shoulder. The convoy of armoured cars moved on, and once the Medics had dealt with the Troop Leader's injury, the matador sped away to catch up with the rest of the convoy heading in the direction of Rotenburg.

Nick had been feeling unwell for a couple of days when

he started coughing and sneezing. When he began to run a temperature, Nick knew the warning signs.

"Bronchitis!" diagnosed the medical officer.

"That's what comes of sleeping in trenches full of water," complained Nick.

He was transferred to the medic's White Car, where he was given orders to rest and drink plenty of water. There was very little medication to help. All Nick could do was rest and wait for the bronchitis to clear.

"If me mum was here, she'd have me wrapped up in ipecacuanha and camphorated oil,"

The White Medical Car moved on behind the rest of the convoy, which continued on for many miles, travelling through towns and villages, dealing with the enemy whenever he reared his ugly head. They finally arrived at Zeven, a town in the district of Rottenburg, where they found billets. While Nick rested, there was no respite from the reconnaissance trips for the rest of the troop. A week later, the convoy was involved in an exchange of gunfire with some German half-tracks where they were resting on a small piece of open land. The next day, the troop came under fire again from somewhere in the village. Medlin decided to send out a foot patrol to search for the source of the gunfire. They crept out into the early morning mist but were ambushed by German infantry. Scattering to find safety, the troop entered into battle, street by street, with the enemy. For ten minutes in chaos and pandemonium, shots were exchanged. A voice yelled for the troop to retreat to the safety of the armoured cars; in doing so, Benny was injured. He lurched and staggered; Basil and other troopers moved to support him, but he fell to the ground.

After a short inspection, Basil yelled, "Leave him; let's get back to safety."

Hearing the news about Benny, Nick was shocked. "Is he dead?"

"I think so," replied Basil, "They got him in the chest, and there was a lot of blood. He was unconscious when we left him."

"You did the right thing by leaving him," said Medlin.

Anxious to get him back, Nick exclaimed, "Can we go and get him, sir?"

Medlin, with his arm in a sling as a result of the shoulder injury, said, "Absolutely not; it's too dangerous!"

Nick put his head in his hands and moaned.

The next day, as soon as it was safe enough to do so, Nick went to help recover Benny's body. As Basil said, he had just one bullet wound in his chest. Seeing Benny lying there on the cold earth, Nick was broken with sadness.

"Oh!" he said under his breath, "Poor Benny!" Bending to search for his papers, he noticed his clothing had been disturbed, "Someone's been and took his watch and his paybook as well as his boots," he cried.

The trooper gently removed Benny's dog tags, and between them, the troopers buried him in a shallow grave. They cut some turf and laid it on the grave. The Troop Leader joined the lads in finishing the job. Nick slipped away from the group of troopers. He began to hum a tune quietly, slowly forming the words, "What a difference a day makes, twenty-four little hours......" Choked with emotion, he couldn't finish the song.

While the last battle was going on, and to everyone's surprise, the mail came through. The link to home and family was as important to the troopers as food and water. The news Nick received was from his mother, who explained the reason why there was no news about the baby Cissie was carrying. This opened up the wound Nick felt about Cissie. Once again, his mind was in turmoil about his disloyalty to her.

A few days later, while resting on a farm on the outskirts of Zeven, three dishevelled and tired British escaped prisoners of war arrived. They informed the Squadron leader that the German concentration camp they escaped from was situated in Sandbostel.

The troopers were shocked when they heard about the camp and the things that went on there. On the whole, the inmates were treated decently, apart from one guard who seemed to get enjoyment out of randomly shooting and killing anyone without warning. But there was very little food to eat, and many inmates died of starvation.

Turning their sites toward the camp, the squadrons left their billets to fan out once again to find a clear route to the concentration camp. They drove on, meeting with the same obstacles as on previous reconnaissance trips, slowing down the progress: more damaged bridges and enemy snipers. at one point, the crew of the Matador were ambushed. Coming up in the rear of the convoy they had entered a field well behind the rest of the cars and got bogged down in mud. Suddenly, enemy guns fired on them, killing Medlin, who was standing in the turret. A troop of infantry came out from under cover, firing randomly. Pete Brand, who had replaced Benny as the driver of the Matador, fired the Besa machine gun, killing some of the infantry who had attempted to surround the armoured car. The rest fled in the wake of gunfire. Medlin was slumped down awkwardly in the turret. Pete moved on, struggling through the mud before stopping at a safe distance to see the Troop Leader.

Removing his body from the Matador, they laid the Lieutenant on the ground.

"He's dead," whispered Basil, "what should we do?"

"The rule is to leave him where he is and report back to the blood wagon with details. Then they come and find him. "I think we should take him with us," said Nick. Lifting Medlin back in the Matador, they took their seats and continued the journey to catch up with the rest of the convoy. Using the map that Medlin was following, now stained with blood, the crew eventually caught up with the convoy where they were resting on farmland. Medlin's dog tags were removed, and he was laid in a shallow grave. While the map reference was taken, the lads stood for a minute and looked at the grave.

Nick spoke quietly, "He was a good guy." His voice trembled, "I'm going to miss him."

"Yeh," murmured Basil.

All the Squadrons arrived back in harbour at Zeven by late evening, having tried and failed to reach Sandbostel, but they got close enough to the camp to catch the acrid smell that came downwind. It took a few more days of constant struggle to reach the camp, with obstacles, detours and the enemy who were dug in to defend the camp. It was the tanks of the Grenadier Guards who first reached the camp after a full-scale battle watched by the inmates who gathered to the wire fence cheering wildly. The camp was liberated.

The troopers were sent out on a mission to round up able-bodied civilians from the village to join captured German guards to clear the camp, see to the sick and bury the bodies found lying around the camp. Disbelieving civilians were adamant they knew nothing of the evil that took place at the camp. The troopers were then sent on another mission to look for German infantry who may be taking refuge in the houses. As they moved from house to house, doors were blocked to them with denials of harbouring the enemy.

"Good grief," said Basil as the lads shared their stories later on, "Those women were stronger than any man." "One of them spat in Pete's face, and he lost it. He kicked her in the shin real hard."

"We nearly had to break other doors down, and when we found the Krauts, all the women said they didn't know they were there!" said Pete.

"Yeh, a likely story!" remarked Nick.

"They were really ugly. We left with a load of abuse and spitting too," said Harry.

"I did enjoy marching them into the camp to see to them poor inmates!" added Pete.

"The women seemed genuinely shocked at the sight of some of 'em." said Vic.

After the fall of the camp, reconnaissance trips continued toward the naval port of Bremerhaven, with a distinct feeling that the war was nearing the end. They met with very few reprisals, and many tired and weary Germans surrendered.

Lt Cavendish replaced Lt Medlin as Troop Leader. The lads welcomed him, but all was not well within.

"For goodness' sake", barked Pete, "can't you stop that bloody coughing, mate? It's driving me mad!"

"It's driving me mad, too," exclaimed Nick.

"Drink some more water," suggested Cavendish, handing him his flask.

While in Bremerhaven, the troopers were billeted in requisitioned houses belonging to German families. Nick and the crew of the Matador moved into one such home, taking over the most comfortable rooms. The family was cold towards them and stayed out of their way in the basement of the dwelling.

One evening, the owner of the house appeared in the doorway of the room where Nick and the lads were playing cards, with news of the death of Hitler.

"He's dead!" Nick whispered.

"That's what I heard," said Basil.

"Goodness," remarked Harry, "We'll be going home soon!"

It seemed as though everyone was lost for words until Nick began to hum a tune. Before long, the room was bouncing with voices singing, 'We'll Meet Again—don't know where, don't know when!' Each one exchanged hugs and handshakes.

Eight days later, the family was gathered around the wireless in the same room as the troopers. Suddenly, the young men jumped up from their chairs in such excitement that they turned the table over. "Der Krieg ist beendet!" cried their hosts. Turning to their guests, one family member gesticulated madly and exclaimed, "War is finished!"

The lads were strangely quiet, glancing from one to another for just a moment before they leapt out of their seats, and, in so many words and joyous exchange of hugs and handshakes, they celebrated. Nick turned to greet the family, who in turn greeted him; after that, all the troopers shook hands with them, all except one who looked like the oldest member of the family.

Alone, he stood back with a look of resignation. Nick went toward him and offered him a cigarette. The man glared and smacked the whole packet out of Nick's hand before retreating to his room. No one saw what happened. Nick shrugged his shoulders. He picked up the cigarettes and rejoined the merriment. The celebrations went on into the night with food and alcohol, jokes, songs and stories of home.

Towns and villages in England were overjoyed with the news of the end of the war. London and many British cities were overwhelmed with joy, dancing and singing in the streets, pubs and homes. Back in Walthamstow, Nick's parents were beside themselves with relief. They joined their joyful neighbours in the street where bunting hung from doors and lamp posts.

There was to be no immediate homecoming for Nick for another two months. Soon after the announcement of the end of the war, the whole regiment travelled north to the naval port of Cuxhaven, where the regiment was to disband and return to its former glory.

The journey to Cuxhaven was interesting in terms of unusual peace. The squadrons drove in a relaxed mood through thousands of defeated, leaderless and demoralised German military. Arriving in Cuxhaven, the squadron rested. No billets were available until the German Navy left their barracks, so meals were made as usual in the street by the side of the armoured cars.

The next evening, Nick and other troopers were walking along the quayside in Cuxhaven. They surveyed the harbour, packed with sea-going vessels of all shapes and sizes; a lighthouse intermittently flashed its beam, and Raucous German songs emitted from the bowels of a ship. Little ship lights bobbed up and down in the water, and the lads felt an exhilarating sense of freedom. There was no creeping about wondering what was going to happen next, no fear of the unexpected. As they strolled in the cool of the evening, about forty or fifty people in dark brown uniforms carrying rifles came toward them. They approached the troopers and dropped their weapons on the ground.

"We're surrendering," said one in broken English who looked like their officer.

The troopers looked from one to the other, not knowing quite what to say. Then Basil spoke up, "You don't surrender to us! You need to find our commanding officer."

Between them, the lads pointed the men in the direction of a hotel where they knew some officers could be found.

Corporal of Horse Mackey came alongside them and, realising the problem, offered to take them to the hotel. "Well, that was weird!" remarked Nick.

"How about we find a beer somewhere," commented Basil.

Finding a pleasant little restaurant on the harbour, the lads were ordering their drinks when a young German sailor invited them to join him and his friends at their table. The lads were pleased to accept the invitation. Pulling out a chair, Nick was curious to learn about the men they met in brown uniforms. "We just met some of your lot in brown uniforms."

"Yeh, who were they?" questioned Basil.

"They are the SA stormtroopers. Their job is to keep control, security guards." Explained one of the sailors. As they spoke together, two or three German girls entered. They came over to the table and entered into rapid conversation with their countrymen. Nick and the Troopers could see there was a problem. The women left in a mood.

The sailors explained that the women disapproved of them associating with the English. "We told them to mind their own business. You, like us, have served four or five years of war, and now the killings have ended. We want to live in peace."

***

9th June Farewell to Armour

There was a buzz of anticipation about the reforming of the Guards Armoured Division. After some very difficult and complicated planning for a ceremonial 'Farewell to Arms', the date was decided for 9th June, and the place was a nearby airfield. German prisoners of war were rounded up and sent to clear the airfield of German armour and debris. Soldiers and troopers were employed to repair and make good their vehicles. Paint from the German ships was given to the regiment, and later on, the tanks looked very nicely painted battleship grey. Everything was in pristine condition in time for the big day. On a beautiful summer day, the Division formed up on the airfield. It comprised 250 vehicles, from the bulky Cromwell and Sherman tanks to the little scout cars of the Household Cavalry. Lieutenant-General Sir Miles Dempsey, the army commander, arrived and later came Field-Marshal Sir Bernard Montgomery. Nick and the crew of the Matador were part of the troop selected to escort the two great men to the saluting base situated in the centre of the arena. They then escorted the vehicle carrying the General and Field-Marshal as they inspected the armour. Returning to the dais, the dignitaries mounted again, and the massed bands played the 'Soldiers of the Queen' march. Each tank and the armoured vehicle drove past the dais; their guns traversed while every vehicle troop leader saluted with great dignity from the vehicle turret. The Household Cavalry troopers stood at attention to the side of their vehicle, watching the tanks and armoured cars pass the dais and then leave, disappearing over the horizon. Nick was just one of the troopers overcome with emotion. They were filled with a deep sense of sadness when the massed bands completed the parade with the strains of 'Auld Lang Syne'. Field-Marshal Montgomery ended the time by delivering a long address complimenting the Guards Armoured Division on their exemplary part in bringing the war to an end.

Nick lay on his bed alone that night, pondering the events of the 'Farewell to Arms'. It's like a dream, he thought. His heart swelled with pride. Turning over, he punched his pillow and said aloud, "How do I tell my mum that?"

Not only did the tank divisions return to their original roles of infantry, but the 2nd Household Cavalry Regiment also made changes. At the start of the war, it had become a composite regiment consisting of a mixture of Life Guards and Blues and Royals. Now that the war was over, it was time to disband, reverting to two separate cavalry regiments. Unsure of which regiment they were in, Nick and the other troopers were about to find out. On hearing their status, they discussed their future together. "Me and Nick are in the Blues and Royals," announced Dave Brewer. "Well!" said Basil. "That's a shame because I'm with Pete Brand and some of the others from B Squadron."

"Yeh." added Nick, "Vic and some of the others are with us too!"

"So, after all this time, we are going to be separated!" announced Basil. "I'll miss the safety of your horn, mate!" quipped Nick, adding, "But, think about it, we'll all be going to our separate homes soon anyway." Realising that emotions were beginning to rise, Harry closed his book and said, "Well, why waste time thinking about it? I'm going to get some shuteye." Leaving the room, Nick put a hand on Harry's shoulder, "So what regiment will you be then, old mate?"

"I'm with the Lifeguards."

In the weeks that followed, while they waited for news of their departure to other parts of Germany, the troopers spent their time on routine parades, long physical training exercises, and necessary guard duty at ammunition dumps where civilians were scavenging for ammunition and anything else they could find.

The day came when the troopers packed their belongings and prepared to leave Cuxhaven; all the emotions of the 'Farewell to Arms' returned as they said their goodbyes. Nick was grateful that he and Dave were the first to leave. Nick, Vic, Dave Brewer, and other troopers were posted to Bruhl. All the others were posted to Bonn.

***

In July, Nick was finally given leave to return home. He wrote to his mother to tell her the news. After receiving Nick's letter to say he would be returning home, his family was overjoyed and unable to contain their emotions. Elsie went door to door in her neighbourhood to tell the news. Families gathered together to organise a homecoming surprise for Nick.

After twenty-four hours of travelling, Nick gave a sigh of relief when the train pulled into Walthamstow Station. Stepping out of the train, he dropped his bag onto the platform to tidy himself. Retrieving his bag, he walked to the entrance and pushed open the door. Seeing him come through, a small group of young people, shrieking something incoherent, ran off toward Hoe Street. Nick saw them but dismissed them immediately. He hiked up the road into St Mary Road alone.

He could see the little group of young people running ahead of him, calling out, "He's coming! He's coming!"

Nick smiled to himself. People nodded to him as he passed them by. As he came closer to Church Path, he could see a crowd of people gathered, where bunting hung in Church Path. A large hanging that read 'Welcome Home Nick' was hung at the entrance to the Church Path. Joyce ran to meet him. Elsie and Dick were the first to greet Nick.

"Oh, my gawd," sighed Elsie with relief.

"Son," was all Dick could warmly say.

The crowd cheered. Danny Smith, Ginger Webb and Joe Packham, Kenny's brother, were all there to welcome Nick. Joe Burns was there also with a beaming smile. Nick looked around to find Cissie. He glimpsed her in the background with her mother but then he lost her again. It took a while for the neighbours to welcome Nick home with hugs and handshakes. It was Elsie who drew it all to a halt when she cried, "Okay, give him some space. I'm taking him indoors."

Nick enjoyed the welcome but was glad to be in and out of the commotion.

There was no one about when Nick stepped out into the garden of his home early the next morning. Walking toward the garden gate, he noticed his Dad's roses and marigolds planted randomly on the earth at the edge of the pathway. A train thundered by at the other side of the garden; smoke billowed up as it passed under the bridge. He gave a deep sigh and opened the gate. It clicked shut behind him as he walked the few steps to Cissie's door in Church Path. He stood for a moment, and thought of Kenny, and his heart began to race, wondering if Cissie was in. He turned back to his home and went in.

His mother was busy laying the table for breakfast. "Are you hungry, son?" she asked.

Nick took a deep breath, put his arms around his mother's waist and placed a kiss on the back of her head. "It's so good to be home and to think that I don't have to go back to war," he said. "What's for breakfast then?"

"Get off," said Elsie, shaking herself free of Nick. "Boiled eggs," she replied.

The family sat together over breakfast, catching up on all the news before Nick quietly asked about Cissie. "She's had her baby," Joyce blurted out. She's called Kitty, and she's so sweet!"

"Kitty," murmured Nick. A gentle smile crossed his face. "So, she had a little girl then?"

"Yes, two months ago," added Elsie. No one said anything for a few seconds then Dick asked, "Will you be seeing her? I…I mean, Cissie?"

"Yes, Dad," replied Nick.

Relieved, Elsie added, "Oh, that's good, Nick."

"Do you think she will want to see me?" Nick asked.

"Of course, she will," Joyce interjected. She loves you, Nick. I know she does."

"Okay, little miss know-all. Then I'll go see her as soon as I've drunk this tea!"

True to his word, Nick stood again for a moment on the doorstep of Cissie's home; not only did he want to see his baby girl, but more than that, he wanted to see Cissie. His heart was racing when he knocked on the door. Mrs. Packham opened it.

She gasped, put her finger to her lips and cried, "Cissie, someone's at the door for you", she called over her shoulder.

A few seconds later, Cissie was at the door, loosening the ties of her apron. Pulling it over her head, she patted her hair with her hands. She looked up and gasped! Everything drained from her body, and she felt suddenly weak.

"Nick! she whispered, adding, "You're here then. "W…Will you come in?"

Nick crossed the threshold and took Cissie in his arms.

"Oh, Nick," whispered Cissie, "Are you sure?"

Nick loosened his hold on her and looked into her pretty face. "More than sure, Cissie!" he replied. "I love you more than ever, and I'm sorry that I left you the way that I did."

"Oh, Nick!"

The two of them just held each other for a few seconds, warming to each other, their thoughts only for the moment. The room faded into oblivion, and it seemed as though they were in another world. A distant baby cry brought them out of the moment, and Nick swung Cissie around with joy.

"Can I see her?" Nick asked.

"Yes. We named her Kitty," replied Cissie.

Taking his hand, she led Nick up the stairs to see the baby. Nick wasn't quite sure what to make of the little bundle that lay in the crib, squirming and distressed. But, at Cissie's suggestion, he smiled and took the child in his arms.

"Kitty was the nearest I could think of to Kenny because we both loved him so much!"

"Perfect," said Nick. Then, looking at Cissie with a quizzical eye, he said, "Did we make this in that moment of passion?"

Cissie chuckled. "We did so."

"Amazing," whispered Nick. He stayed in the room while Cissie fed the little one.

"Marry me, Cissie," he said.

Cissie gasped! Then she gave him a haughty scowl, "Maybe!" she said.

Nick was taken aback, "Maybe? He questioned. "Only if you get down on one knee and ask me nicely."

It was another day or two later before Nick did as Cissie asked. Producing a beautiful diamond ring that he bought from Mr. Fish, the Jeweller in High Street, Nick repeated his request, "Will you marry me, my sweet girl?"

Cissie accepted Nick's proposal of marriage, and they were

married three days later in St Mary's Church by special licence. That night the two sweethearts melted into exquisite lovemaking

All too soon, Nick returned to Bruhl.

The next few weeks were very comfortable for Nick. He, Vic, and Dave had taken over a commandeered German house with all its comforts. When he wasn't on duty, he played cricket matches, and as the months went by, he played in goal for the Bruhl football team.

Nick took one last short trip into Brussels to see Ellen. They had a meal and a drink together. Ellen tried very hard to make Nick stay, promising him an easy life and everything he wanted. They parted at the train station with a very long hug and final kiss. Ellen didn't wait; she turned quickly and left the station.

There were many opportunities to return to Walthamstow over the next year, and in June 1946, Nick was demobbed.

On his return home, he announced, "One thing I never want to be again," he said, "and that is cold! I was cold most of the time while serving in Europe. I washed in cold water; I slept in the cold. I can only ever remember being cold.

Printed in Great Britain
by Amazon